12 STEPS
TO
FREEDOM

Also by Kathleen W.

Healing a Broken Heart: 12-Steps of Recovery for Adult Children
With Gentleness, Humor & Love: A 12-Step Guide
Adult Children Anonymous Group & Service Guide

12 STEPS
TO
FREEDOM

A RECOVERY
WORKBOOK

BY FRIENDS IN RECOVERY
EDITED BY KATHLEEN W.

The Crossing Press
Freedom, California 95019

Grateful acknowledgement and thanks to our anonymous friends who shared their experience, strength, and hope in creating this book. Special thanks to Jim W., whose technical wizardry transformed lumps of raw data into graphic gems. Thanks also to Charlie T., Joyce B. and Lisa B. for technical help and unfailing goodwill in supporting this project.

Cover art and design by AnneMarie Arnold
Printed in the U.S.A.

ISBN 0-89594-488-X paper
ISBN 0-89594-489-8 cloth

CONTENTS

Preface

Those of us who claim to have reaped the benefits of being restored to sanity speak only from the experience we've had, day by day, in gradually restructuring our lives. Will the 12-Steps work for you? Will the method work for your problem? There's only one sure way to find out. Try the method and see what happens. Those of us who have found joy and fellowship in the 12-Step programs are admittedly believers. We are grateful for the way the healing process works in our lives. But we don't promote our way of living; we simply offer to share it. Our goal is to provide information to others and then welcome those who choose to join us, as we trudge the road to happy destiny. If you decide you want what we have, we welcome you. In the 12-Step programs, you set your pace, establish your goals. And, if you keep coming back, we believe that you, too, will find love and peace and joy, as we have within ourselves.

I'd like to extend my heartfelt thanks to all of you who have supported me in completing this project. It is a blessing in my life to share in the gradual progress represented by this book. Please take what you find helpful. Yours in fellowship.

—Kathleen W., *Eureka, California. March 27, 1991.*

INTRODUCTION

Question: *Yes, I'm willing. But am I to be consigned to a life where I shall be stupid, boring and glum, like some righteous people I see?... Have you a sufficient substitute?*

Answer: *Yes, there is a substitute, and it is vastly more than that...you will find release from care, boredom, and worry. Your imagination will be fired. Life will mean something at last.*

— Alcoholics Anonymous

***

We are Kleenex-a-holics;
Kleenex tucked into our sox
Tuesday nite there'll be a meeting;
Everybody . . . bring a box.

—Carol Ann F., 7/28/89,
Vashon Island, WA

We come to the 12-Step programs for help and information. Personal pain brings us. Sometimes we are pressured to come by family problems, maybe even trouble with the boss, or with the law. We may expect to be lectured at 12-Step meetings. Perhaps we anticipate short-term therapy that will give us insight to take back to our regular way of life. The atmosphere at 12-Step meetings may have come as a surprise. The experience of being welcomed by a room full of strangers may have felt unreal, a bit hard to trust. If we persist, however, after a few meetings most of us begin to feel more at home. We begin to identify with others and to see where our problems are similar to theirs. As we become more relaxed, we begin to uncover feelings we may not have known we had. In sharing, we come to find ourselves accepted, perhaps even understood.

Some of us initially fear being cramped into spiritual pigeonholes (the 12-Steps). The Steps may seem, at first, more of a challenge than a help. Even the slogans and friendly invitations to keep coming back may prompt memories of empty platitudes spoken in the past which were used to dismiss legitimate needs and feelings. The emphasis on the Steps and the friendly encouragement that's common at meetings aren't intended to dismiss or minimize anyone's personal issues or feelings. 12-Step programs emphasize the Steps because they are a reliable framework for the healing process. By applying the Steps to our issues, we are able to give each other respectful, individual support. Without giving advice or caretaking each other, we simply share the ways we have been able to relate the Steps to our own lives and problems. In so doing, we share our experience, strength, and hope with each other, and we take what we find helpful from what is shared and leave the rest.

As members of a 12-Step program, most individuals go through several points of view over time. The chart below illustrates the stages of bonding that are commonly experienced.

The Cycle of Recovery
in 12-Step Programs

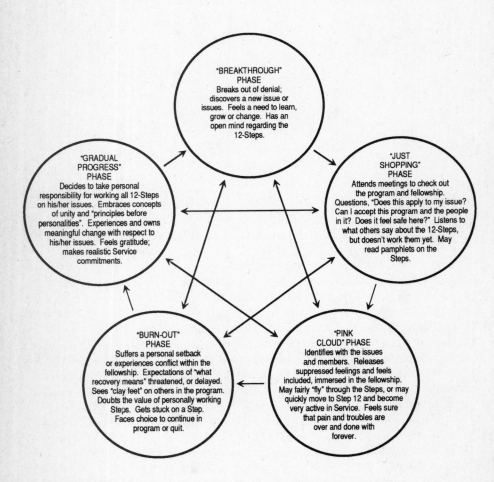

"BREAKTHROUGH" PHASE
Breaks out of denial; discovers a new issue or issues. Feels a need to learn, grow or change. Has an open mind regarding the 12-Steps.

"GRADUAL PROGRESS" PHASE
Decides to take personal responsibility for working all 12-Steps on his/her issues. Embraces concepts of unity and "principles before personalities". Experiences and owns meaningful change with respect to his/her issues. Feels gratitude; makes realistic Service commitments.

"JUST SHOPPING" PHASE
Attends meetings to check out the program and fellowship. Questions, "Does this apply to my issue? Can I accept this program and the people in it? Does it feel safe here?" Listens to what others say about the 12-Steps, but doesn't work them yet. May read pamphlets on the Steps.

"BURN-OUT" PHASE
Suffers a personal setback or experiences conflict within the fellowship. Expectations of "what recovery means" threatened, or delayed. Sees "clay feet" on others in the program. Doubts the value of personally working Steps. Gets stuck on a Step. Faces choice to continue in program or quit.

"PINK CLOUD" PHASE
Identifies with the issues and members. Releases suppressed feelings and feels included, immersed in the fellowship. May fairly "fly" through the Steps, or may quickly move to Step 12 and become very active in Service. Feels sure that pain and troubles are over and done with forever.

Often members move from point to point in the bonding cycle, encountering new forms of resistance followed by new breakthroughs and insights. The trust within a group usually influences how individuals relate to the program. A move to a new community or group can create a need to re-bond and re-evaluate our whole outlook on recovery. Changes within a group's membership may have a similar impact.

For some, the bonding cycle is gradual. For others, it is characterized by dramatic shifts in how they relate to the program and program members. Some leave the program entirely, either permanently or temporarily, to resume their old lifestyle or to attempt recovery by another approach. Experimenters who do this and then return are often free of the inner reservations that before may have made the 12-Steps seem unnecessary or outdated. Those who choose to leave, for whatever reason, are free to return. Program participation is always a matter of personal decision.

For those who make the commitment to the 12-Step method, joyful living is a central goal. We seek to discover and explore our real selves. As we are able to do this, we find that we can establish healthy boundaries and make realistic commitments. The work we do on ourselves is meant to be applied in our present lives. Recovery isn't theoretical. It's practical. We seek always to practice these principles in our daily lives, not just to study them.

Socializing and service work usually become more satisfying — and more balanced — as we integrate the 12-Step approach into our ways of relating to others. Often we become better able to accept praise and success. Authority issues may fall into more comfortable perspective. The Steps provide a path to free us gradually of insecurity in our relationships. We rarely become "boring and glum" when we make a commitment to the Steps.

Whatever issues bring us to a 12-Step fellowship, we are welcome in most groups if we say we are a member.[1] Whatever phase of membership we are in today, be it "Breakthrough," "Just Shopping," "Pink Cloud," "Burn Out," or "Gradual Progress," we have a right to our perspective. We see our position as valid, as an important part of our growth. We have a right to be who we are. We have a right to all of our feelings. We also have a right to heal and to belong.

✳✳✳

Some people move through the Steps in numerical order. Others find they prefer to jump around, surveying and getting a feeling for the Steps, answering their own questions about the way the program fits together before they actually work the Steps. If you are apprehensive about a Step, it is a good idea to risk investigating that Step first. If you find the wording of the Steps difficult to relate to, consider some alternative wording that you find more acceptable.[2] It's up to you; there is no wrong way to work the Steps.

When you feel ready to make a commitment to your recovery which includes working the Steps, consider asking someone to sponsor (or co-sponsor) you. A sponsor should inspire respect in you. Usually, prospective sponsors are people who have found some measure of (day-at-a-time) relief from their own compulsions as a result of integrating the Steps into their own lives.

If you wish to have someone sponsor you, you must ask the person if s/he is willing to take on that responsibility. Some groups may have a list of individuals who

3

are willing to be sponsors. Talk to the person before or after a meeting, or on the phone. If s/he is willing to sponsor you, establish some ground rules for working together: how often you will meet or speak on the phone, how much time you will spend on each Step, whether or not you will attend some meetings together, etc.

Co-sponsorship relationships are networks of individuals who are committed to working a 12-Step program together. There are many kinds of co-sponsorship arrangements. It may be two people who agree to support each other and share with each other, keeping the 12-Steps as a focus. Or co-sponsorship may include people with varying amounts of program experience, people of different ages, genders, ethnic backgrounds, or sexual orientations. Sometimes, co-sponsors may be members of a Step Study group which meets to read, discuss, and possibly journal through the 12-Steps. A suggested Step Study Meeting Format for use with this book is included in Appendix III.

Going it alone is an option, of course, at least to a point. Working Step 5 requires talking to someone you trust. It is possible to work Step 5 with a therapist or minister if s/he is familiar with the 12-Steps and feels the method is a valuable component in recovery from addictions and addiction-like problems.

✳✳✳

The exercises in this book are designed to alternate between engaging the mind and the creative spirit within which is often called the Inner Child. This is not done out of whimsy or to make it easy to work the Steps. Instead, the goal is to encourage and support the overall healing that takes place as we experience a re-opening of communication between the thinking and the feeling aspects of our personalities (and physical brains as well). Play can be very serious business to those who have lost touch with their inner sources of creativity and joy.

The reparenting exercises in this book involve drawing, acting, walking, or visualizing. These exercises are designed to help the mind achieve greater balance between their rational/verbal and their creative/imaginative aspects. By pulling creative images into the conscious side of our minds, these exercises tend to reestablish and strengthen internal communication between the various centers in our brains where different sorts of memories are stored. Memories from early childhood, feelings that we may have learned to repress, and other kinds of information about ourselves may come to the surface when we use these creative approaches to the inventory process. Dreams also may become a rich source of insight as we give our minds permission to become more unified. We can use our thinking minds to evaluate the feelings and images these creative activities bring up. By using our intellect to support and guide the creative Inner Child we find within ourselves, we may tap an unsuspected wellspring of new power in our lives. (Dr. Charles Whitfield, M.D., in his books, provides detailed information on the ways the child within is impacted by growing up in alcoholic, dysfunctional families.)

As we bond these powerful, creative techniques to the Steps, we are anchoring our self-discoveries. This is important because the insights we gain need to be given the benefit of time and practice in order to become integrated parts of our daily lives. When we work the Steps creatively and share our Inner Child's point of view at meetings, we gradually develop a new, healthy relationship with ourselves as whole beings. We may come to experience the fellowship as a healthier form of extended family life. Our families of origin may have lacked the commitment necessary to overcome the problems that existed in its members. Our new families of choice have the advantage in that each person makes a commitment to his/her own recovery which then becomes a source of security and strength for the whole group.

∗∗∗

All of the materials and techniques contained in this book are compatible with the principles and practices of the original 12-Step program, which credited innovative thinkers, including Dr. Carl Jung, for inspiration. Much concern has been given in this book to keeping alive the open-minded spirit which has made the 12-Step programs so vital and effective a force for healing. By crediting those who have added so much to our insight into the dynamics of chemical dependency and co-dependency, we have only continued a process of grateful acknowledgement that goes back to the earliest roots of the 12-Step programs.

Bill W., co-founder of Alcoholics Anonymous, advocated cooperation with professionals, ". . . we [in A.A.] regard all who labor in the total field of alcoholism as our companions on a march from darkness into light. We see that we can accomplish together what we could never accomplish in separation and rivalry."[3] Dr. Bob, A.A.'s other co-founder, was an active force in designing effective approaches to alcoholism treatment, and many concepts of modern chemical dependency and co-dependency treatment remain indebted to these pioneering efforts in the infancy of the 12-Step programs.

Religious and spiritual tolerance, too, is a central feature in all 12-Step programs. It is a vital ingredient for continued unity. In this book, care is taken to encourage universal toleration by refraining from gendering God (along with other sexist references). This is not intended as disrespect to those who are used to thinking of God as "The Father." Even for those who are committed to a male concept of God, it may be helpful to reexamine these beliefs, especially if their physical fathers happened to be alcoholics or addicts.

Experience has shown, too, that if sectarian religion is allowed to interfere with each member's right to the free exercise of conscience in building and maintaining a relationship with a Higher (or Inner) Power, 12-Step fellowships often lose their effectiveness. Religious study groups may choose to study the Steps, of course, but this does not make them 12-Step programs. Traditionally, all 12-Step programs are free of affiliation with religions or other organizations. By so doing, 12-Step programs support and cooperate with all forms of belief, organized or otherwise.

As a final note, please remember to give yourself permission to enjoy your progress through the Steps on your journey to sanity and serenity. Working the Steps needn't be drudgery. Even the pain and the grief we experience in the process are the pain and grief of healing, not the old pain of continued injury we have experienced in the past. Becoming a whole person is hard work, but it isn't wasted or doomed to failure. Old fears that our best isn't good enough are echoes from the cave of darkness where disease was in control. In recovery, willingness is enough, though it often requires taking risks. Give yourself permission to risk the Steps. Give yourself permission to experience your own freedom.

[1]Some fellowships have certain "screening" requirements to protect their members. For example, fellowships that focus on sexual abuse issues often exclude perpetrators.

[2]Several alternative wordings of the Steps have been offered for adult children and codependents. A metaphysical version is included in the Personal Sharing section of Step 3. Groups vary on whether or not they accept these alternative wordings for discussion at meetings.

[3]From the A.A. pamphlet, "Let's Be Friendly With Our Friends: Friends on the Alcoholism Front," by Bill W., (1958, A.A. Grapevine, Inc.) For further reading on "cooperation without affiliation," see Traditions 6 and 8, *12-Steps And 12-Traditions*, (1953, AA World Service, Inc.,) and AA pamphlets "The Co-Founders of Alcoholics Anonymous" and "A.A. Tradition: How It Developed," by Bill W.

Personal Sharing

Recovery means freedom
Just for Today
from obsessions and compulsions
which used to dominate us;

Recovery means freedom
Just for Today
from re-living "family patterns"
that once seemed hopeless or inevitable;

Recovery means freedom
Just for Today
to live outside the shadows
cast by others in our lives;

In my *personal Recovery*
Just for Today
I take the Steps
to accept these freedoms in myself,
within my heart
and in all of my affairs.

STEP ONE

We admitted we were powerless over (alcoholism) (other people) (a compulsive pattern), and our lives had become unmanageable.

> *With all the earnestness at our command, we beg of you to be fearless and thorough from the very start. Some of us have tried to hold on to our old ideas and the result was nil until we let go absolutely.*
> —Alcoholics Anonymous

It can be said that the pain of the Inner Child brings us to recovery, regardless of what program or addiction is involved. We come to recovery when our coping mechanisms and defenses fail. When this happens, we find ourselves face to face with our suffering, lost, frightened inner self.

It makes no difference whether this child screams because of the poisoning sustained by alcohol or drug abuse, or from the heartbreak and dread associated with unworkable relationships. The Inner Child calls out and makes us hear. Under the spur of grief, pain, and perhaps terror, we are forced, for at least a little while, out of the habitual denial that has become a mask we have worn to hide from ourselves.

Step 1 introduces us to practices of self-honesty that help us build from this flash of insight. It shows us a practical approach for nurturing and supporting our authentic self, free of compulsion and denial. The 12-Steps offer us a path to safety if we are willing to accept it.

Ultimately, we turn out to be the best experts on ourselves. As we learn to hear the voice of the self that has been buried within us, our real needs and goals, as well as our problems, gradually become clearer to us. We come to understand that this inner spiritual guidance brings the pain that brings us to recovery. We must be willing to hear the truth that lies within ourselves. As we build an honest bond with our inner selves, accepting first the child's pain and need, we are rewarded by the creativity and inspiration that are the child's gifts. If we resist, we may cut off the warning from the self within, and quickly find ourselves slipping back into confusion. Fortunately, self-honesty can be learned. It can also be practiced. All of the 12-Steps are designed to help us develop a comfortable familiarity with habits of self-honesty and to build a deep and lasting relationship with ourselves.

Step 1 poses two important challenges, both of which require self-honesty. The first challenge is stating what we see as the problem(s) we cannot solve for ourselves:

"We admitted we were powerless over . . . " Then, after we have admitted our defeat which caused our Inner Child to scream for help, we are then asked to follow up with a second admission. We are asked to acknowledge that, as a result of our powerlessness over this problem, *". . . our lives have become unmanageable."*

When we admit that we have a problem and have begun to attend meetings, it is often the case that we find honesty a little difficult to get used to. When we begin to open our inner selves, many of us find ourselves flooded with intense and sometimes unfamiliar feelings. Forgotten memories may return. Other people's stories may stir up deep feelings in us. We may feel overwhelmed.

It is wise to anticipate that at first we may need to give over some time to simply grieving. There is a store of sad memories we may find locked away inside ourselves. Several weeks or even months may be needed to give buried feelings a chance to rise to the surface. This is not wasted time. We are giving ourselves permission to feel what we feel. This is self-honesty in action. When we do this, we begin to see our life story in a new and clearer light. Then, when we are ready to move on, we have the tools we need to heal these old wounds.

The first great truth of Step 1 is that we cannot recover from problems that we don't own and acknowledge. The definition of a problem in Step 1 is whatever we find that we are powerless to eliminate or to change by our own unaided effort and will. Addictions, compulsions, and codependencies fall within this definition. Each involves behaviors we acknowledge as harmful or undesirable but cannot resist repeating. Uncovering our problems in Step 1 is the starting point of a personal program of recovery for every member of every 12-Step program.

Step 1 asks us to accept responsibility for our present situation, no matter what circumstances outside our control may have caused the problem in the first place. Real tragedy is often a fact in our past. We don't minimize the sadness or outrage we may feel, nor do we gloss over the facts. We acknowledge that we may have been wronged in the past but take responsibility for ourselves now. We needn't carry the burden of these old wrongs into our future. We are free to own the dysfunction that has taken root in us, acknowledge that we are powerless over these patterns, and then work the Steps of recovery for ourselves. Taking this initiative in healing our hearts and minds and twisted lives is the beginning of the reparenting that takes place in recovery.

✳✳✳

In the AA book *Twelve Steps & Twelve Traditions*, Bill W. noted that distortions of what begin as normal, healthy drives "cause practically all the trouble" in our lives and relationships. Out of balance drives for physical and emotional security (survival and commitment), for sex (gratification) and for social recognition (identity) can be seen as underlying a wide range of addictive and compulsive patterns.

Codependents mirror and react to these dysfunctions, developing coping mechanisms that become deeply ingrained, too. Codependents often can describe in detail the addiction or compulsion they are tied to by their reactions. They may also deeply dislike the problem and wish that it would go away. But until codependents detach themselves from their problem by changing their attitudes, the addiction remains. The reactions of codependents are attempts to satisfy their own deep needs for security, love and recognition.

The instinctive drives that motivate us, with the addictive patterns associated with each, are the basis for the wheel below. In this wheel, and in other wheel-diagrams throughout this book, addictive and codependent behaviors are arranged in pairs around the circles to remind us that we are bound to these disorders by our own denial. We are not bound to these disorders by the actions or behaviors of others.

Four common forms of addictive and compulsive patterns are arranged around the top of the wheel, directly across from the codependent behaviors that develop in reaction to them.

Addictive & Compulsive Disorders

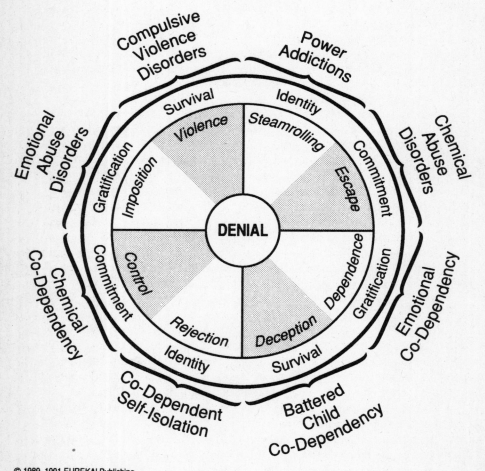

Chemical Abuse includes addiction to alcohol, drugs, food, and other related addictions to substance.[1] Escape is at the core of physical addictions, which is a perversion of our instinct to bond and form commitments.

Chemical Co-Dependency is characterized by an obsession with control, manipulation, or rescuing others. This sort of behavior is also a perversion of the instinct for commitment.

Power Addictions include a range of obsessive patterns designed to keep up some sort of public front and hold on to social standing. Lack of a real sense of identity underlies this addiction.

Co-Dependent Self-Isolation develops from living with those who compulsively keep up a front at all costs. Finding fault and looking for the lie becomes compulsive, too. This sort of behavior also underlies a lack of a clear personal identity.

Compulsive Violence Disorders include all the patterns where anger is used to dominate and survive. Feeling physically threatened is the instinctive motivator.

Battered Child Co-Dependency results from living in family or social systems which run on threats of anger or violence. Deep fears for physical survival result, which, untreated, can be so overwhelming under stress that most problem solving is impossible to carry out.

Emotional Abuse Disorders include all forms of compulsively using others to gain personal gratification. Shame-based feelings about the role of sex or about having sex needs result in dishonesty and acting-out behaviors.

Emotional Co-Dependency is also based in shame concerning sex and sexual boundaries. Loss of self in relationships, fantasies about being abandoned (or rescued), and obsessions with seeking approval indicate issues in this area. Sometimes these may be buried, with only vague or fragmentary memories surfacing, at least at first.

No matter what issue or issues we find within ourselves, acknowledging these limitations is the first step in overcoming them. Whether we see our problems as addictions or among the forms of codependency, Step 1 asks us to own up. It is by admitting what our problems are that we declare ourselves in the program. No one can make this admission for us. The diagnosis of experts, pronouncements by family, employers, even the judgments of a court of law do not count, when it comes to taking Step 1.

Just as no one can force us to take Step 1 or do it for us, no one can prevent us from taking Step 1. We take this Step for ourselves and only by our own choice. This is one of the great freedoms in recovery. When we accept this fact of self responsibility, we begin to set realistic personal limits and boundaries in what we expect from others. Such boundaries tend to free us from other people's actions or attitudes. For those who may have lived their lives in rebellion or in reaction to the impositions of others, working Step 1 may be one of the first self-directed experiences in memory.

∗∗∗

Honesty in admitting the truth about ourselves and our situation is called coming out of denial or "surrender." Surrender in a 12-Step program is very different from the personal despair or self-denigration we have experienced in the past. Instead of opening ourselves to injury, punishment or potential loss at the hands of other people, in coming out of denial in Step 1 we are opening ourselves to healthy change.

When we admit in Step 1 that we cannot solve or eliminate an addictive, compulsive, or codependent pattern by our own unaided efforts, we are merely ceasing to fight a battle which was already hopeless. We release ourselves from further vain attempts at control followed by heartbreaking disappointment when we give ourselves permission to admit the truth about our situation.

Of course, it may not be completely clear to us where self-control ends and addiction / compulsion / codependency takes over. We may not be certain how we have been impacted by family dysfunction. We may not know to what extent we are, ourselves, compulsive. These questions deserve serious consideration.

To clarify our own situation, we review the chart of Addictive / Compulsive Disorders in this chapter. If we suspect that a dysfunctional pattern may be a factor in our life, we can examine it in more detail by looking at the Victim Wheel (Appendix 1). This chart specifies characteristic behaviors in more detail. Are we addicted to behaviors that are a threat to ourselves and others? We can also consider the self-defeating ways in which we react. Do we have bad habits, compulsions and addictions acquired in living reactively? We catalogue all of our reactive and acting-out behaviors, whether or not we feel certain we are powerless over them.

Some issues seem more or less objective—food, drug or other substance abuses, for example. Other issues are more subjective—such as being stuck in painful attitudes or emotions. For those behaviors which we feel we may be able to master by willpower or self-knowledge, we resolve to commit ourselves to an honest experiment. We simply test ourselves, using willpower or intellect to regain control, and note what happens. If we are able to regain control, we congratulate ourselves. If we find that we cannot, we admit that we are, indeed, powerless. This sort of self-diagnosis is at the heart of recovery.

The Recovery Process Flow Chart taken from *Adult Children: The Secrets of Dysfunctional Families*[2], on the next page, tracks locating and evaluating issues and then moving into recovery.

$$***$$

The second challenge to self-honesty in Step 1 involves admitting how ". . . our lives had become unmanageable" as a result of our problems. We examine the ways our dysfunctions have damaged us. What have we lost (or never had) as a result of our addictions or compulsions? In what ways are we unable to take care of ourselves and those we love? What kind of trouble do we have with authority in our lives? This can be a painful experience. Not only is it saddening to confront the concrete results of our problems, it is also deflating. However, it's important that we not indulge ourselves in fantasies of self-deception. To deceive ourselves may cost us the very things we want most.

Those who grew up in homes where alcoholism or other dysfunctions were present may have learned to give in to pressures just to keep the peace. It may have been the way to survive — to avoid getting hurt or screamed at. For those who are the codependent children of dysfunctional families, it can sometimes be easier to identify the ways their lives are out of control than it is to identify specific problems. Coping behaviors rooted in dysfunctional families may be making our lives unmanageable. We may, for instance, still feel afraid to stand up for ourselves. We may dread being

Recovery Process Flow Chart

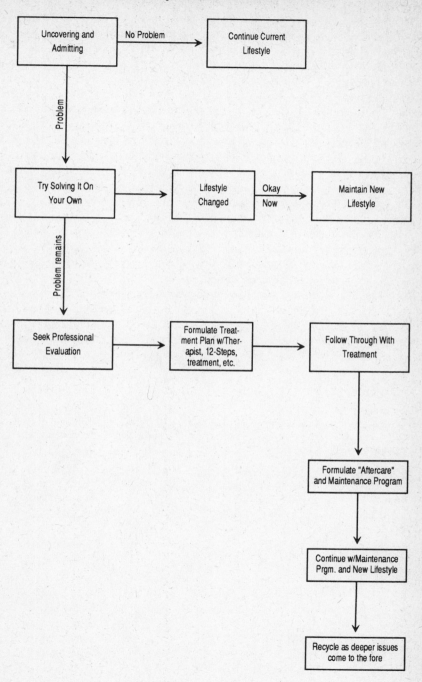

13

criticized or appearing foolish. To protect ourselves from the terror and risk of standing alone, we may have developed the habit of settling for what we can get, when it comes to friends or lovers. We may allow ourselves to get involved with people we don't respect. We may compulsively put up a front in order to be accepted by people, socially or sexually, and then lose respect for them when they are deceived. We may also feel most comfortable and attracted to people who continue to pressure and push us (like the members of our family). Much as we may dislike being pushed, it's what we're used to dealing with.

Whether or not we can spell out an addictive pattern in ourselves, we review the ways our lives continue to be unsatisfying due to our involvement with others, referring to the Victim Wheel (Appendix 1). We get as specific as possible about the patterns we act out and repeat. After we've located (or approximated) the patterns we seem stuck in from among the spokes on the Victim Wheel, we return to the Addictions / Compulsions chart and note the addictions and codependencies that are involved.

Backward as this approach to Step 1 may seem — going from admitting what is unmanageable to discovering what we are powerless to change — it can be helpful in uncovering unsuspected areas of addiction or of codependence within ourselves. This may be especially true in those cases where early childhood memories are repressed. If we feel an issue may apply to us, we can trust our feelings to guide us into an honest evaluation, even if we remember little or nothing.

Step 1 is often a starting point to be used again and again as our recovery carries us forward. Whether we first come to a 12-Step program as a substance abuser, as a codependent, or as the child of a dysfunctional family, the 12-Steps of recovery provide hope if we are willing to be honest. If additional, perhaps unsuspected, issues surface as we progress, we can always come back to Step 1 to expand our horizons for recovery as we go along.

[1]Some also include in this cluster internal forms of chemical abuse such as various "addictions to excitement." Compulsive stealing, gambling and other thrill-seeking behaviors stimulate production of adrenalin and other hormones within the body.

[2]From Chapter 18, page 183, *Adult Children: The Secrets of Dysfunctional Families*, by John and Linda Friel, (1988, Health Communications, Inc.)

Exercises

Exercise 1: Step 1 Worksheet

Look over the special focus inventories in Appendix II. Answer any of the questions that may apply to you or to your family. Give yourself permission to be completely honest about all of your feelings as you do this. Are you powerless over any of these special issues?

We admitted we were powerless over

_____

and our lives had become unmanageable.

Fill in the Step 1 blank for yourself with your issue(s).

Whatever you find that you are powerless to eliminate or to change by your unaided effort and will is an appropriate issue for this Step in recovery. Take the necessary time to do this in writing, so that you won't lose track of what your issue(s) are. If you don't make a note, you may forget why you need the Steps or the fellowship and you may revert to old ideas under stress or challenge.

Consider these basic needs to pin-point your specific issues as thoroughly as possible:

1. Survival issues

• Do you have any persistent problems with basics such as food, clothing, and shelter? Do you seem powerless to eliminate or change patterns which tend to threaten your survival (physical safety, food, clothing or shelter)?

• Do your problems stem from domestic violence or alcohol/drug abuse issues in your home (or do you have a family history of such problems) which cause you to move or to otherwise sacrifice these important needs?

• Do you personally have trouble getting or keeping a job (for any reason, including your reactions to other people's prejudices or power trips)?

• Do you lose control of your finances or other resources?

2. Emotional issues

• Are your feeling-needs for companionship, intimacy or recognition not being gratified?

• Do you become obsessed with other people, or with food, alcohol, drugs, work, sports, exercise, i.e., ways of running away from some or all of your feelings?

• Do you use flattery or do you play on others' guilt or sympathy to get strokes or attention?

• Are you hooked on depression, or excitement ?

3. Commitment issues

• Is there a lack of predictability in important relationships in your life, including, possibly, your relationship with yourself?

• Are your eating, sleeping, self-care, or recreational habits unstable?

• Are you able to set up projects so they stay manageable and then stick with them to a reasonable point of conclusion?

• Are you able to resolve conflicts and disagreements with intimates, family members, friends or co-workers?

4. Identity issues

• Are you out of touch with your feelings in some situations or under some circumstances? Are you not living the life you want most to lead?

• Do you have social or business fronts you consciously keep up that you wish you could discard?

• Do you automatically act out of fear, indifference or anger in some situations or under some circumstances?

• Do you reject criticism?

You may find it helpful to go over this Worksheet periodically. Use it to re-examine any specific issues you have such as alcoholism, incest-survivor, food addiction, etc. Consider how each of your issues interferes with satisfying your basic needs.

Assertive Styles

	Passive	Assertive	Aggressive
Characteristics:	Allow others to choose for you. Emotionally dishonest. Indirect. Self-denying, inhibited. In win/lose situations, loses.	Choose for self. Appropriately honest. Direct. Self-respecting, self-expressing, straight-forward. Converts win/lose to win/win.	Choose for others. Inappropriately blunt (tactless). Direct, self-expressive, derogatory. In win/lose situations, must win.
Your own feelings on the exchange:	Anxious, ignored, helpless, manipulated. Angry at self and/or others.	Confident, self-respecting, goal-oriented, valued. Later, accomplished.	Righteous, superior, depreciatory, controlling. Later, possibly guilty.
Others' feelings in the exchange:	Guilty or superior. Frustrated.	Valued, respected.	Humiliated, defensive, resentful, hurt.
Others' view of you in the exchange:	Lack of respect. Distrust. Can be considered a pushover. Do not know where you stand.	Respect, trust. Know where you stand.	Vengeful, angry, distrustful, fearful, hurt.
Outcome:	Others achieve their goals at your expense. Your rights are violated.	Outcome determined by above-board negotiation. Your and others' rights respected.	You achieve your goal at others' expense. Your rights upheld; others' violated.
Underlying belief system:	I should never make anyone uncomfortable or displeased... except myself.	I have a responsibility to protect my own rights. I respect others, but not necessarily their behavior.	I have to put others down to protect myself.

Exercise 2: What's Your Style?

Addictive / compulsive disorders may have a powerful impact on the communication habits and styles of those who are afflicted. Whole families may adopt a style of communication that is non-functional — either indirect and passive, or aggressive and abusive. What's your style?

Exercise 3: Assertiveness

The next time someone offers you something you don't want, or wants you to do something you don't want to do, notice what happens and how you handle the situation. Are you able to be assertive, or are you passive? Do you become aggressive when you try to say no clearly? Notice how you handle (or fall apart) in different kinds of situations — at work, in the family, in a social situation.

• When a friend wants you to do something, do you say no if you want to?
• Can you say no and give your honest reasons?
• Do your friends hear you when you say no, or do they push?
• Do you trust your own judgment, when you feel you're being pressured?

• Do you end up giving in and being pushed to do whatever it is, anyway?

• Are you a pushover for one of your parents? Friends? Other relatives?

• Do you push your friends to do rebellious things that may hurt them?

• What acts of rebellion that you can't resist cause you (or those you care about) trouble?

• What uncomfortable or painful feelings come up for you when you think about the way you push or are pushed? (Or do you try not to think about these sorts of questions, to avoid feeling your feelings?)

• Do you feel angry? Are you afraid you'll be judged or ridiculed?

When you answer these questions, be honest. Decide for yourself if you have a problem. Are you powerless over some of these behaviors? Do you feel that your life is unmanageable, out of control, as a result?

Put whatever you admit may be your problems on your Worksheet. You don't have to share your answers with anyone unless you so choose.

Exercise 4: Visualization

Visualizations are work that takes place within the temple of your own inner consciousness. Imagine there are no limitations placed upon you in a visualization except those you choose to place upon yourself. Don't let yourself be hindered by obstacles that may come up for you. If your Inner Child wants to offer you something very large such as an 80' world-class cruising yacht, you can sprinkle it with "shrink dust" which is in your pocket, so it will be easy to handle and not too much work to polish. (Later, in another visualization, you can use your "restorer ring" to beam it back into full size, and sail away.) Remember, you always have a spiritual right to complete success, serenity and joy within the temple of your inner self. (For step-by-step instructions for creating your own "inner sanctuary", see Step 11 Exercises, "Guided Visualization," in Chapter 11.)

1. What are your impossible dreams? Note one or two attractive goals that you would like to achieve, but feel are beyond your grasp (for any reason).

2. If you have difficulty thinking of anything, try taking a walk or doing some other kind of exercise. While you are walking, ask your Inner Child (your creative imagination) to show you his/her secret wish, however dusty or forgotten it may be. Try breathing deeply and moving in a smooth, rhythmic fashion. If tears or feelings of anger well up, welcome them and let them out. Keep looking into yourself all the while to see the goals you'd like but feel you cannot hope to achieve.

3. Imagine that your memory is an old house. Visualize walking

through the rooms. Look on the walls for plaques or pictures of your secret or forgotten goals. Notice any half-finished projects. What are they? Look into the closets. Go up into the attic, down to the basement. Is there a shed or garage where you may have stored your impossible dream? Just walk through, not allowing yourself to get too bogged down in detail. Give yourself permission not to become anxious or self-critical. There will be another time to complete projects.

4. Any goal or wish that appeals to you is ok. Maybe it will be a simple thing — a special car, a house, or a stylish wardrobe? Maybe it will be a relationship that seems hopelessly twisted, ruined by bitterness or events? Maybe you will have a secret wish to do something important in the world that you're afraid you may be laughed at for if you were to let others know?

5. You may see your secret goal as dusty, covered with cobwebs, faded. Imagine that you bring it back into the present and incorporate it into your present-day reality. Dust it off and polish it up. Imagine yourself in your here-and-now reality. Visualize your child within bringing this goal to you, holding it out to you, as a gift you can accept. Give yourself permission to accept it and allow yourself to pick it up. Release your visualization and return to regular consciousness.

6. Now draw a picture representing yourself toward one edge of a piece of paper, with the goal you have near the other edge. Then draw what you see as in the way, between you and your secret wish. If what is in the way is a feeling, make up a shape for it, and color it whatever feels right to you. If it is another person that stands in the way of your dream, be sure to put an expression on that person's face, or show what s/he is doing. If the lack of something is in the way, show what is missing, or what you didn't get when you needed it. Are there things you do which are in the way — compulsive behaviors or fears which block you? Be fearless! No one will see this picture unless you choose to share it with them.

7. When you've finished, take a good look at what you've drawn. Ask yourself: "Am I powerless over (whatever is in the way)? Is my life unmanageable in the sense that I'm not living the life I'd like to be living today?"

8. Put any newly discovered issues on your Step 1 Worksheet and give yourself a hug for coming out of denial! Welcome! You are on the path to personal freedom!

Questions to Ponder

1. Are there circumstances or people which you have been struggling with and not getting anywhere?

2. Are there behaviors you feel powerless over, whether or not you see them as effects of alcoholism?

3. Is your life unmanageable, because you can't seem to stay out of

certain patterns, ruts, fear-or-rage reactions?

    4. Describe these, including how you feel about yourself as the result of these patterns.

Personal Sharing

Prison

I spent a long, dark time
in this Prison
living someone else's life;
not mine.
A lifetime of fears and depression.
She laughed at me and taunted me;
her days were filled with gloom.
She asked me to call her Mom.
The sun shined thru my Prison
the first six years.
Days of play and fun and song.
My Hero was tall, played a guitar.
He asked me to call him Dad.
Never good enough; Honor Roll.
Never pretty enough; someone else's clothes.
Never clean enough or neat enough;
She'd pout in her room for days.
My Brother came to my Prison life;
would he be treated like me—by her?
No..his Family's a different one;
we both called her Mom.
Years of yearning and crying...
not understood rage.
More tears in my own Prison.
Would this life ever subside?
How long?
So dark;
So painful this Prison.
Why? I asked her why she did these things?
This person I called Mom.
She'd ask for pills or shock treatments.
I'd stay in my Prison...to serve...so long.
I tried to climb out of my Prison
so many times before.
I couldn't make any sense of this;
I had a singing, dancing soul.

"It would go to my Head", she said,
so I went back again
into my Prison...so dark...so long.
I bolted out, once and for all
not very long ago; two years.
My Hero's dead, she said it was my fault
He worried about me...you see.
She tries so hard now, to put me back
into my Prison...so dark...so long.
I'm out for good.
The Prison is gone; ashes left behind.
The Prison Matron is dead, too, you see.
She asked me to call her Mom.
My Hero lives his life inside my song
and dance and poetry.
I'm my own Hero now.
Carried me off on a shimmery white horse.
Depression...long, dark...gone;
Living and loving my life...for me
and freedom's liberating price...sharing.

—Carol Ann F., 8/5/89, Vashon Island, WA

STEP TWO

Came to believe that a Power greater than ourselves could restore us to sanity.

> *Well, at first, 'I came.' Then, after I stayed "dry" a while, 'I came to.'*
> *Finally, 'I came to believe. . .' after I had gotten willing to give the Steps a*
> *try and really tried to work them.*
> > —Les, an A.A. "oldtimer," Santa Cruz, CA.

We may have perceived a sudden recognition of our personal dilemma in Step 1. Perhaps we experienced feeling overwhelmed by our powerlessness? We may even have experienced a terrifying feeling of panic, sensing that we have truly lost control of our life and our fate. We may have wished that denial would wash over us again and wrap us in a sleepy forgetfulness. At the same time, we realize that the old game just won't work for us today. If we find ourselves in such a moment of vulnerability, we have come to Step 2.

✳✳✳

What can we believe in? Is there help? In Step 2, we are asked to open up our hearts and minds and to explore the options available to us in search of "a power greater than ourselves"[1] who is willing and able to "restore us to sanity." Thus, we acknowledge that having "a life [which] has become unmanageable" is not a sane state of affairs.

We may not feel very confident that there is such a power, or that we can be restored to sanity by it. If we have doubt and suspicion about spiritual reality, or if we doubt that we are worthy of being helped, it can be a good practice to start gradually in Step 2. In "a power greater than ourselves," remember, we are just seeking a resource which is not powerless over whatever we admit we are helpless to overcome without help.

We are free to conceive of this power as the God or Spirit of our understanding, or as something more tangible. The 12-Step group, for instance, or the 12-Steps themselves, may be seen as "a power greater than ourselves." In the sense that the group and the Steps help people who admit having problems, this is true.

In Step 2, we are asked to try to conceive of a power, however vaguely, that could help us overcome the problems we have acknowledged in Step 1. We entertain the possibility that something can actually help us. We can do this experimentally, by the "try it and see what happens" approach. It's important only that we make a beginning and offer ourselves new options beyond denial and rationalization.

22

It's a good idea to itemize the "powers greater than ourselves" which may have let us down in the past. This is a practice which helps us to overcome resistances to Step 2 that are centered in unexpressed grief. Often, we feel anger, shame or sadness as we admit the ways we have looked for help — for understanding, relief, security — and failed to find it in the past. These attempts may have lowered our self-esteem and contributed to the loss of our inner sense of identity.

Failed or inadequate "powers greater than ourselves" come in many forms. We may have been super responsible for a time, hoping to please the God of our understanding. We may have tried to earn God's help or tried to make deals with God. Either way, we may have felt abandoned, rejected or even tricked. Now, we may be deeply angry at God or at our church, or at those people who represented religion to us in the past. We may feel we have already taken Step 2 and been let down. Perhaps we abused substances as "a power greater than ourselves." Alcohol, drugs or food may have given us a way to turn off painful emotions, or gain feelings of courage, confidence or happiness. Work, sex or exercise can also be used to drown uncomfortable feelings. We may have made gods out of other people — parents, lovers, therapists — to try to find emotional relief from our inner turmoil.

When we think of the ways we have felt betrayed, do we remember any bitter promises we made to ourselves? Have we, for instance, sworn not to be fooled again? Have we resolved to keep up defenses, to not trust, not risk opening up to the possibility of disappointment? Perhaps we may find we are grimly committed to going it alone, unwilling to try Step 2.

If we had family members who abused or neglected us, we may feel even more suspicious. To children, parents are, in a real sense, powers greater than themselves. If we could not trust them, it is possible that we internalized feelings of unworthiness or a sense of being helpless pawns of fate. We may suspect any possible Higher Power as being a likely source of genuine abuse. We may feel compelled to test or defy authority when we encounter it. Suspicions rooted in the fears associated with experiences in violent families or communities can be powerful and persistent.

***

Fortunately, Step 2 does not ask us to *already believe* in a Higher Power that will somehow restore our lives to manageability. Instead, Step 2 starts out by saying, "We came to believe. . ." Remember that we are asked only to explore possible resources that we feel may work for us and then note the results. We do this just as if we were engaged in a scientific experiment. We will gradually discover what works for us. Those of us who started out as skeptics, rebels, or appeasers are not asked to deny our feelings or our opinions. We are asked only to experiment with concepts of a "power greater than ourselves" that we are willing to give an honest chance to help us, and to see for ourselves whether or not we are restored to sanity.

***

Some individuals find it difficult to accept the idea that some of their behaviors or attitudes have been truly not sane. Guilt, shame, and grief often make it difficult to admit our own share of a family pattern, especially those reactive behaviors that are easy to rationalize. If this is a sticking point, we can go back to Step 1 and look over the ways our own behaviors have contributed to making our lives unmanageable. Have we acted out of panic, for example? Aren't these acts, as well as any decisions made in anger, usually overreactions that serve to stir the muddy water in our lives? Do we risk blindsiding ourselves if we stubbornly justify our part in such an unbalanced drama?

When we run into resistance to a Step, we can remind ourselves that recovery isn't a footrace. Thoroughness counts for more than speed. In Step 2, we start by focusing on becoming willing to open up to a "power greater than ourself." Then, we try to be honest about whether this power actually does, in practice, help restore balance to our way of life. For many of us, doing even this much may prove a big order.

We may fear that a manageable life may not really be possible, at least not for us. Will Step 2 really work for us? The only answer is to risk it and see. What we seek is a power so strong and true that it can restore joy and meaning to our lives, no matter how twisted our lives may be. We can find a power that unconditionally embraces us no matter how unworthy we may feel. We can find it within our own hearts if we work to clear away the distortions of belief that block us from this power source within.

***

One of the common barriers to tapping this power source comes from unexamined personal values and old family rules we take for granted. Values are the ideas that we accept and use to define reality for ourselves. They are the bedrock we stand on when we express our point of view. Internalized values are, in effect, "powers within ourselves" because we automatically judge ourselves and others by these ideas. We live by our values, whether we are aware of them or not.

When we have values that are in conflict with a concept of a loving, unifying power within ourselves, these distortions block us from experiencing this power, even if we admit we need it. Inner conflict of this sort often shows up in daily living. We feel confused, we have a hard time making decisions, or we feel torn between the beliefs and opinions of others. Unresolved, such conflicts can produce a sense of hopelessness or depression. Feeling cut off from a source of inner well-being also produces trouble in relationships with others, as we try to get the validation from others that we need to find within ourselves.

Some of our oldest, most internalized values may be the spoken or unspoken family rules that we grew up with. Dysfunctional family rules, such as not being angry or not letting feelings of disappointment, sadness or other "unacceptable" feelings show, may be impossible to live by with honesty. We may have been taught to value keeping up a front, sacrificing truth in the interest of protecting family secrets. We may have learned to value lying to appease someone or avoid their rage. This sort of dishonesty creates disunifying inner conflict which generates a barrier to Step 2.

If we had come to believe we had to live a lie, we may find it hard to trust others. We lose touch with our intuitive sense of judgment — another indication of being out of touch with our inner spiritual sense. We may not be able to feel the warmth and love in the relationships we have, because we may not be able to reach those feelings in ourselves. Keeping up false appearances takes a lot of energy.

Because we tend to gravitate toward others who have internalized values similar to our own, dysfunctional family rules tend to endure and be passed along from one generation to the next. If we are trying to live by family rules that are painful, we are especially inclined to seek encouragement to keep up the effort from others who have similar beliefs. This makes us susceptible to peer pressure that tends to reproduce the same, or similar, dysfunctional patterns in our adult lives. As long as we try to hang on to family rules that cut off feelings or make us lie to protect each other, we can make little progress in seeing our lives restored to sanity.

Dysfunctional family rules are like the walls of a prison that keep us locked up. Denial keeps us from seeing these walls; we just kept running into them! When it comes to working Step 2, it's important to see where our values need to change so that we can find "a power greater than [or within] ourselves . . ." to guide us to a sane lifestyle. Healthy values are a "higher power" without which we simply cannot recover. If we are to be restored to sanity, we will need to contact those values we have internalized that are incompatible with sane living, and replace them with new values. When we finally realize that we are free to choose values of our own, we gain a new sense of independence. Fear or rebellion against authority tends to be replaced by healthy curiosity and interest in hearing different viewpoints.

We don't lose our personal independence by seeking a "power greater than ourselves" in Step 2. Instead, we begin to develop a healthy sense of self-identity as we begin the practice of really thinking for ourselves. True independence can be seen as the personal freedom to make choices in life, combined with the necessary information and the spiritual health we need to make these choices wisely.

[1]The language used in Step 2, "...a power greater than ourselves...," may seem in conflict with some concepts of spirituality. Those who prefer using different language, such as an "inner power," "a power within," or some other phrase more in line with a personal concept are free to make a substitution for themselves.

Exercises

Exercise 1: Authority

Here is an exercise to get on friendlier terms with authority and to get more open-minded about other's views and values. Several important thinkers from different centuries are quoted. Notice how their values are reflected through their beliefs about taking action, or through their expectations about life. Read over the quotes and see whether you agree or disagree. In this exercise, only your opinion counts!

It's a funny thing about life, if you refuse to accept anything but the best, you often get it.
—William Somerset Maugham

✳✳✳

...It matters not how strait the gate,
How charged with punishment the scroll,
I am the master of my fate:
I am the captain of my soul.
—William Henley

✳✳✳

We must undergo a revolution of values. We must move past indecision to action. If we do not act, we shall surely be dragged down the shameful corridors of time reserved for those who possess power without compassion, might without morality, and strength without sight.
—Rev. Martin Luther King, Jr.

✳✳✳

No man is a warmer advocate of proper restraints and wholesome checks in every department of government than I am; but I have never yet been able to discover the propriety of placing it absolutely out of the power of people to render essential services, because a possibility remains of their doing ill.
—George Washington

If there is sincerity in the heart,
There will be beauty in the character.
If there is beauty in the character.
There will be harmony in the home.
If there is harmony in the home.
There will be order in the nation.
When there is order in the nation.
There will be peace in the world.

—Chinese, anonymous

***

It is not a man's duty, as a matter of course, to devote himself to the eradication of any, even the most enormous wrong; he may still properly have other concerns to engage him; but it is his duty, at least, to wash his hands of it.

—Henry David Thoreau

***

The ultimate result of shielding people from the effects of folly is to fill the world with fools.

—Herbert Spencer

***

No great thing is created suddenly, any more than a bunch of grapes or a fig. If you tell me that you desire a fig, I answer you that there must be time. Let it first blossom, then bear fruit, then ripen.

—Epictetus

***

Of the second-rate rulers, people speak respectfully saying, 'They have done this, they have done that.' Of the first-rate rulers they do not say this. They say: 'We have done it all ourselves.'

—Lao-Tsu

***

What is a minority? The chosen heroes of this earth have been in a minority. There is not a social, political, or religious privilege that you enjoy today that was not bought for you by the blood and tears and patient suffering of the minority. It is the minority that has stood in the van of every moral conflict, and achieved all that is noble in the history of the world.

—John Gough

A full stomach is heaven; the rest is luxury.
—Chinese Proverb.

1. Do you have a reaction to the sort of authority you sense in any of these people? Allow yourself to see yourself on an equal footing with these writers. Imagine they are members of a 12-Step group or as members of your family. How do they fit in?

2. Imagine you are the same age and also a well-known figure. Does it make it easier to be honest? You do not have to go along with what these authorities say unless you agree with them. It's o.k. to have a different opinion or no opinion. Do you have trouble accepting yourself as worth listening to?

3. Do you agree that values can be, in a sense, "powers greater than ourselves"? What are some values you rely upon today? Write some of them down, as your own "quotes." Are they funny? Sad? Are there some basic values from your childhood you still cherish? Write them on balloons and tape these up to celebrate them.

Remember, you are free to change internalized values if you feel they are wrong for you in recovery. You are also free to affirm the values you feel in your heart are true and right for you. It's up to you.

Exercise 2: Draw Your Higher (Inner) Power

1. Using colored markers or pencils, draw a picture of a "higher power" that you believe may help you to live a sane life.

2. If you are uncomfortable with the idea of drawing "God," try just doing a circle filled with colors, as many colors as you like. Or draw some power that is in this world that you feel may be helpful to you. (Maybe a spaceship to take you away?) Don't be too serious!

3. Put yourself in the picture.

4. Draw yourself living a "sane" life. What does that look like? If you prefer to just use colors to represent a "sane feeling," do that, instead. (Or do two pictures?)

5. Put your pictures up somewhere where you can see them every day for at least a week or two.

6. Talk to these pictures (out loud, if possible) and ask this higher power to become real in your life. Ask for a clearer picture of "sane" living and "sane" feeling.

7. Replace your pictures when you feel it is time for you to do so. Save your old ones for a year or two at least.

Questions to Ponder

1. What Power (if any) do you trust?
2. Is there a hopeless feeling or an empty, confused feeling when you ask yourself this question?
3. What resources or authorities have proved to be unreliable or inadequate sources of help in your past?
4. Does the idea of calling yourself insane frighten you or make you angry?

Personal Sharing

Simply stated, Step 2 says that we need to believe in something that will help us to restore ourselves and our lives to health and well-being. Many of us have had major problems in dealing with authority figures or with a God whom we could believe in. It is a very scary thing to put faith or trust in something. We weren't able to trust or rely on our parents to bring us security, love, direction or happiness. Instead we relied on ourselves for survival.

We may resist thinking of ourselves in any way insane because we think insane people are in psychiatric hospitals or insane asylums. Simply defined, insanity is unsoundness of mind and emotions. When we acknowledge that we need to be restored to sanity, we are simply admitting the need to develop new, healthy attitudes and behaviors. Many people liken this process of restoration to sanity with bringing ourselves to a state of integration, wholeness and serenity.

One unique dimension and goal of the 12-Steps is the process of discovering, awakening, and evoking our child spirit so that the child within us is gradually integrated with the other parts of ourselves. The child within is that part of us that experienced what happened in our family system; it has incurred the deepest wounds and hence is in the most need of healing and restoration. This child spirit has been maligned, ridiculed, rejected and/or abandoned. It has been afflicted with guilt, hurt, fear and shame. Because of the disease that victimizes us, our child spirit was stifled and repressed, thereby never having the opportunity to be, to play, or to grow.

If we will welcome the child spirit within in Step 2, we will begin to discover the power of this child spirit for healing. It is the child within who has the capacity to feel and to give new life to us. It is the child within who enables us to be spontaneous, creative, playful, curious, loving, hopeful, and joyous.

By beginning to trust a higher power in the recovery process, we will begin to create a healthy connection between our adult and our child within. This connection will begin to fill the giant void we previously tried to fill unknowingly with destructive addictions, relationships, and other obsessions and compulsions. This connection strengthens us so we can let go of these addictions and move into the healing process.

—Mark L., Hartford, CT

Compulsive gamblers are different from their non-addicted fellows, only by virtue of the fact that non-addicts do not have a gambling problem. If non-addicts gamble, they know when to quit and can. Compulsive gamblers also know when to quit and they can, but they don't! The only place they feel they really belong is at the poker, dice or blackjack table, or wherever their favorite form of "action" is taking place.

There they are accepted and welcome as long as their money holds out. In reality, it is only their money that is welcome and accepted. They are only tolerated as incidental bearers of same. When their money is gone, their welcome's gone, too!

While their money lasts, they feel secure and comfortable. No great demands are made upon them, for they have succeeded in slamming the door on the cold, outside world of reality. They bask (temporarily) in the warm glitter, snug in the womb of their dream world of gambling, until the losing "rush" outlasts their chips and their dream world shatters, shards crashing down around them.

—Gus H., Gamblers Anonymous, Mountain View, CA

Look Within

Legs that can't run
Heavy with fear
Will someone help me?
There's no one there. Is there?
Dream life, all locked inside
your child-heart
Is there love? Is there hope?
There's no one there. Is there?

Aloneness leads to oneness.
Emptiness leads to wholeness.
Grief leads to joy.
Risk leads to fulfillment.
But I'm afraid
what if I fall?

You cannot fall, my love surrounds you.
You cannot fail, my voice will guide you.
Where were you while I slept,
and dreamed my life away?
Right here — within your child-heart.
Waiting for you to look within.

—Joyce B., Tsimpsian Tribe (Alaska)

STEP THREE

Made a decision to turn our will and our life over to the care of God as we understand God.

> . . . *in ancient times material progress was painfully slow. The spirit of modern scientific inquiry, research and invention was almost unknown. In the realm of the material, [people's] minds were fettered by superstition, tradition, and all sorts of fixed ideas. . . . We asked ourselves this: Are not some of us just as biased and unreasonable about the realm of the spirit as were the ancients about the realm of the material?*
>
> — Alcoholics Anonymous

Step 3 offers us the opportunity to recognize whatever form of spiritual guidance and support we are willing to accept. We have the right to define this power in any way we find acceptable. By acknowledging our relationship to an inner source of power and direction, we own that resource for ourselves. The practice of owning our choices is a way we build a clearer sense of identity.

We can call our spiritual resource by any name or no name. We are free to worship and create ceremonies of appreciation and respect in ways we find effective and satisfying. If the word "God" runs against our grain, we can modify the way we conceive of "God" to make it more comfortable and easier to embrace. We may think of this power as Spirit, nature, the Life Force, the collective unconscious — whatever we find within our own hearts. No one dictates to us or sits in judgment over our choice! It's entirely up to us. This is one of the great freedoms of the 12-Step programs.

In working Step 1, we already admitted that we have at least one problem that we can't solve or escape from by our own unaided willpower. Then, in Step 2, we explored some options for "a power greater than ourselves" that might help us, experimenting until we found a higher or inner power that we could accept and that was effective in showing us a path toward sane living. In Step 3, we are simply asked to drop our defenses and let this power help us. Much as taking Step 3 may make perfect sense, most 12-Step members find that it isn't easy to accomplish. Many 12-Step program members will admit to having trouble taking Step 3 or in sticking with the decision.

For a lot of us, Step 3 can present a mix of spiritual hurdles to be crossed, along with mental and emotional puzzles to be solved. We may need to reparent ourselves with patience, persistence, and a little humor to become comfortable with this Step.

***

If it's so much trouble, some will ask, why not skip over Step 3 and go on with the rest of the program? Or, why not use the group as a power greater than ourselves and leave it at that? Why make such a fuss over whether or not we have a personal spiritual connection?

The simple answer is that most of us have found that we need a personal spiritual connection in order to work the rest of the Steps effectively. Buried pain, rage, and fear we may uncover within ourselves can be overwhelming, and reliance upon exclusively human forms of support may not be adequate, or sufficiently dependable to see us through. (People have an uncanny way of going on vacation or being preoccupied with their own issues when we depend upon them instead of on our own internal resources.)

When we need an energy boost — encouragement, peace of mind, hope, and strength to see us through a challenge — we may be offered a lot of support from outside sources (meetings, books and tapes, or people in the fellowship.) But this support still has to connect with a receptive place within ourselves or we simply can't be helped. In taking Step 3, we are mainly acknowledging the existence of this inner personal connection that hears truth when it is offered to us, that feels goodwill, and that is ours alone. We must take responsibility for ourselves in all aspects of our recovery, and that includes nurturing the receptive place within us, the connection that can receive healing and that will begin to respond joyously to life. Without this personal contact, most of us flounder and make little progress.

***

To begin jumping the hurdles and unravelling the puzzles of Step 3, it may be helpful to examine Step 3 concept by concept, noticing where we are resisting the Step or where we are confused about how to do the action involved in the Step. The first of these concepts involves decision making. It turns out that many of us seem to fear (or are reluctant to make) decisions. Resistance to decision making may be justified in several ways. After all, there's always the possibility of making a mistake. Or, whenever we decide to stand up for something, we run a risk of conflicting with people who disagree with us, or else feeling our own conflicted feelings.

Perhaps in the past we may have felt that we became targets when we tried to define ourselves by setting goals or limits. We may find that we never learned how to make and stick with decisions. We never learned to reap the benefits to be gained in terms of self-identity and self-respect. We may come from backgrounds where nobody made decisions, but, instead, just drifted along from crisis to crisis. Maybe we were the responsible child who was imposed upon and made to hold up under responsibilities that we were tricked or pressured into "deciding" to take on? As a result, we may now face all decisions with anxiety. We may still be in the habit of "letting others have their way," even if this means recruiting someone to make our decisions for us, even when we have the opportunity to act freely and are under no pressure to do otherwise. It's possible that the whole question of decision making may need to be reworked to reduce this hurdle to a manageable leap.

***

The next concept to be considered in Step 3 is releasing personal control. This release is a necessary stage in becoming receptive to guidance or direction. Many of us are more than a little reluctant to lose control. We may not welcome the prospect of turning our will and our life over to anything or anyone. Those of us who lack a clearly defined sense of self-identity can be especially troubled by such fears. We may see ourselves only in terms of what we do, our position in the community, or in our peer group. We may be so used to controlling situations or other people that we don't know who we'd be if we were to stop.

Loss of control may bring back memories and feelings of being helpless victims in families where violence threatened everyone. We may have learned to go to extremes of self control in such families. We may be master acrobats of control, used to doing an elaborate interpersonal balancing act in order to protect ourselves or others whom we loved.

Violence or harsh competition in our communities may have been the source of training that taught us never to give up control, or to grab it back again, as quickly as we can, when we sense it's been snatched away. Many of us find that, even if we've mastered decision making, we may still be inclined to revert to old habits of snatching back control under stressful circumstances that bring up painful reminders from the past. We may find that we simply do not know how to turn it over, even when we decide we want to do so.

We need not remain passive when it comes to working this portion of Step 3. We have resources at our disposal we can use in order to become more receptive while, at the same time, strengthening our sense of integrity. Giving ourselves permission to re-contact and to grieve the painful incidents which made us so addicted to self-reliance is a positive choice open to us. We can reparent the battered inner child we find in these memories. Using visualization and other creative techniques, we can bond with and rescue that child. These are the forms of nurturing we can lavish on ourselves to heal deep wounds that may be blocking us from our own inner resources. These practices help us build willingness. (For help in using active imagination to "alter internal history" and heal old wounds, see "Loyalty and Intimacy," Chapter 8.)

Even if we are already willing to let go, practice still remains a key to success. These simple techniques, like remembering to take a deep breath and learning to ground ourselves by breathing deeply and slowly into the body's natural balance-center (located just below the rib-cage); under stressful conditions are good practices that are easy to remember. Another good habit is remembering to say the Serenity Prayer several times a day. Making a habit to start the day with a few minutes of inspirational reading and reflection is time very well spent. A lot of 12-Step program members make a regular practice of reading one of the "a day at a time" books. A large selection of "a day at a time" reading (and tapes) can be found in most bookstores. It can be helpful to review the first three Steps every day, as a way to remind ourselves why we are in recovery and welcome spiritual power into our lives.

All of these practices build our inner connection. We join our conscious will with the spirit of Step 3 when we work to build these new habits in ourselves. New, healthy habits can be cultivated, and this includes the habit of turning it over! The key is keeping at it.

**

In order to feel really safe and welcome in this practice, we need to develop an unclouded sense of an inner spiritual connection that is ours to keep. Just as we are shown how to feed and dress ourselves and are taught to speak the language of our parents, we also learn much of what to think and feel about God or Spirit from our parents or from those who filled parental roles for us in childhood.

Traditionally, in healthy family systems, parents and elders in the community are there to teach us ways to recognize this spiritual contact. They demonstrate it in their own successful living. Alcoholism, drug abuse, sexual abuse and physical violence, however, are forms of disease. When these are present, they infect family systems with fear, grief, and anger, while, at the same time, they corrode the family's basis for trust, hope and love. In dysfunctional families there may be no elders to trust or respect whom we can turn to for guidance. Those we love the most may be victims — lacking the spiritual power and direction to save themselves or us!

Under these conditions, we may need to revamp our concept of God or Spirit in Step 3. We need a perception of God we can trust with our very lives. One of the tasks we may face is re-parenting ourselves as beings with certain very real spiritual rights. Before proceeding further in Step 3, it's a good idea to think over what it means to be spiritually centered.

**

Being spiritually grounded means having a sense of spiritual identity in a world where we have a place as a valued human being who has a right to be alive. We're not afraid that things might fall apart at any moment. We don't feel worthless or condemned. We feel we are a part of life.

Secondly, being spiritually grounded means feeling inwardly secure — within our family, with friends, at school or work, and in the community. We are able to trust our relationships to the care of our Higher Power, even under stress. We feel ourselves to be accepted—a spiritual being among other spiritual beings. We can ask for help or companionship, but we're not overly dependent. We can enjoy our own company and time by ourselves.

Finally, being able to draw upon a spiritual contact gives us power. We find the strength and confidence necessary to risk doing our best, out of self-respect and self-appreciation. We sense the joy that comes from realizing that no one else can do our part in life, and that no one can replace us. We can also draw upon this contact for the power we need each day to overcome addictions, to face the tough decisions in life, and to heal. Mistakes we make and injuries we suffer become the images, the vivid mural painted on the wall of the days and years we are alive. It's easy to see that having a sense of spiritual wholeness has a lot to do with living life as a strong, happy, and successful person.

Claiming these basic spiritual rights can be hard work. We may feel sad or ashamed when we compare these ideals to the ways we have learned to think and feel about ourselves and God. Fortunately, though, we aren't condemned to be lost or hopeless as a result of what we learned (or didn't learn) in the past. In recovery, we can learn to reparent our spiritual Child within, and to claim as much of the ideal as we are willing to accept.

If we were taught (or shown, by the way our parents acted) that "God" was mean, condemning or cruel, or that He didn't care about us enough to make a difference in our lives, we are free to toss that old idea right out on its ear! If "God" was a word without any meaning for us, we are also free to open up our minds to new ideas — read books, listen to tapes, explore religions — seeking a personal direction we can sense in our heart.

But can we accept this good, as something we deserve? A lot of us can't — or won't — at first. Often, there's anger in the way. It's O.K. to express anger or sadness or disappointment — even if it's directed at an idea of "God" we feel has let us (or our family) down. If it feels more respectful, we might try thinking of anger at God as anger directed at an "old idea" about God. Twisted ideas about God account for a lot of suffering. In dysfunctional families many hurtful behaviors may have been tolerated as God's Will or "forgiven" instead of stopped. But the spiritual truth that we find in recovery does not ask us to tolerate abuse. Before deciding to turn your life and your will over to your understanding of God, try going back and checking the three ways that a healthy spiritual contact shows up in daily living. Ask yourself: Does this understanding of God give me a good feeling about being alive? Am I willing to trust this understanding of God with the care of all of my relationships? Do I feel sure I can draw the power I need from this understanding of God to do the very best I can in life, a day at a time?

***

Affirmations are a good way to build a concept of God or Spirit which will give you hope, trust, and the power to live well. To enhance feelings of trust and confidence in your spiritual resources, experiment with affirmations. These are powerful but simple tools for replacing old failure messages we may have internalized with positive, life-embracing messages that build our inner bond with the spiritual. If negative self-talk about your own worthiness or ability to get well makes it hard for you to feel spiritually safe, affirmations are also a good way to replace these old "voices" with new ones. If you can, identify the voice and let yourself get in touch with any feelings or memories of sadness, anger, or shame you can remember from your past about whatever message it is abusing you with. You are free to tell old negative self-talk voices to leave the temple of your inner self.

Guided visualizations are good ways to get in touch with vague memories or feelings. Practice using affirmations to replace the harsh voices you hear in self-talk, while you are letting your imagination show you pictures of the past. (See the Exercise, "Replacing Old Tapes" in Appendix I.)

Affirmations can be especially potent when they are used to contradict and replace old tapes. Examples of old tapes include old parent messages such as: "You're no good!" or "Give up. You'll never make it!" or "It will work out for those other people, but it won't for you!" Use affirmations to create simple contradictions to these messages, such as, "I am a wonderful human being!" or "I can't lose. Everything I do is guided by the Spirit!" or "I win some and I lose some, and I cherish all of my experiences as parts of a rich life!" Then speak them (out loud) directly to yourself, especially when the self-talk is taking place. Doing this works to erase the old tapes and also adds a positive new internal message.

Step 3 is not a passive experience that just happens. It's a Step that asks us to take energetic action to find a way to open ourselves up to the power we have waiting for us, within ourselves. As we become willing to allow ourselves to have the power we deserve as wonderful spiritual beings moving along an important spiritual path, we receive the resources we need. This happens one day at a time as we do our share of the work.

Exercises

In Step 3 we acknowledge whatever resource we have tapped within ourselves that is powerful enough (and willing enough) to give us a direction out of the personal mess we found ourselves in, in Step 1. Here are some techniques for reducing internal resistances to tapping into Step 3's potential power source.

Exercise 1: The Serenity Prayer

God grant me serenity
to accept those things
I cannot change,
Courage to change
those things I can,
and wisdom
to know the difference!

Notice that all we are doing in this prayer (usually repeated at the beginning of 12-Step meetings) is cultivating our inner spiritual contact with the calmness of peace of mind, the power of courage, and the wisdom of clear vision and understanding. If the wording of Step 3 remains difficult, some newcomers may wish to begin working on Step 3 by repeating this prayer several times a day (perhaps substituting a more comfortable concept for God).

Exercise 2: Decisions

Practice making small decisions while staying in a one-day-at-a-time (or one-hour-at-a-time!) framework. Include the decision to trust the God of our understanding!

Exercise 3: Control

Write the name of a person (or a brief description of the problem) you are worried about on a piece of paper. Fold the paper once or twice and say, "God (Power of the Universe, etc.), I am turning this person (or problem) over to you. Thank you for being there for me!" Then, and this is the important part, consciously shift your attention to something else. If you fall back into your old worry rut, just shift your attention once again, and again, as though you are directing a child away from an activity that isn't good for him/her. If you don't have anything useful or interesting to do, consider taking on a Service responsibility in your 12-Step group. Give your Higher Power a little space and see what happens!

Exercise 4: Humor

Imagine yourself to be in the presence of God as you understand God. Visualize how it looks and feels, creating as much detail as you can. Tell God a joke. Does the God of your understanding laugh or smile or say S/He doesn't get it?

Exercise 5: A Collage

This exercise provides a way to open up communications between the thinking mind and the imagination, using art to bring our adult-self into better contact with the spiritual Inner Child.

1. Select a topic. General topics freely open up possibilities for images. Examples include: Authority, Intimacy, God-Goddess-Higher Power, Mother, Mate, My Identity, Goals, Wishes, Dreams That Can Come True. Any of these tend to elicit more than just one picture, feeling or memory.

2. Gather materials. It's a good idea to give yourself about a week to gather materials. Allow yourself time to let your imagination and your thinking mind open up to this project, bringing up images, memories, and incidents, while you make an effort to get together magazines and the tools you will need: scissors, glue, and a large sheet of construction board or paper. To stimulate your imagination and jog your memories, try giving yourself a few minutes just before going to sleep to think and visualize about your topic. Sometimes unexpected dream images may result.

3. Create structure for yourself (or decide you do not want one). Most collages and drawings end up as wadded pieces of paper in the trash because they lacked needed organization before the actual artwork even began. Before you begin pasting on your images, decide how you want to organize this design. You may wish to put images across the top of your paper or to arrange them clockwise or counter-clockwise down the paper.

Or you may decide to put your inner, more private feeling images toward the center of your paper and to arrange what you see as external to yourself toward the edges. Perhaps you see yourself as scrunched down in a corner, with various images or colors pushing in on you, or chasing you or moving away from you. Of course, you may decide to let your feelings take charge of your paper, and decide not to organize your art at all. No matter which way you go, you will have made a choice, and making choices tends to release feelings and ideas which might otherwise be blocked by the unspoken question, "Am I doing this right?"

4. Give yourself permission to go through with this project and have fun. Give yourself a whole afternoon or evening to have fun making your collage. Some people enjoy sharing this sort of activity with a few friends, while others prefer to be alone. Use a piece of paper which is large enough. Don't be cramped. However, it should not be so large that you feel intimidated at the prospect of having to fill it up! Let your feelings come up as you select and apply your images. You may wish to add to them, using crayons, markers, paint or colored paper. Seeds, grass, feathers, string or thread—any found objects around your home or garden— may be incorporated. Give yourself permission to get really involved. If words or sounds come up while you are doing this project, go ahead and let them out, speaking, singing or expressing any pent-up feelings out loud. Write them on the collage if you like. Let your inner child fully participate and engage in child-level self-expression. Give yourself permission to feel completion, too, noticing when the project feels complete and saying so: "Now this is done" (or words to that effect).

5. Value your creative effort. It is a good idea to mat and frame your collages. Put your collage up on your wall where you can appreciate it and interact with it as an ongoing communication from you to you! Note the emotions, memories, insights, and concepts that come to you. After a month or so, replace this collage with something else, if you like. It's a good idea to keep a recovery yearbook to reflect on, as you go along, to see your own development as it unfolds.

Questions to Ponder

1. What feelings (images or memories) come up when you read Step 3?

2. Does the prospect of making a decision seem risky or threatening?

3. Do you resist (have fears about) turning your will or your life over to the care of a Higher Power? Are there memories from childhood of feeling (or of being called) undeserving or unworthy?

4. Describe God as you understand God, today. Is this a God-concept you can trust with your life?

Personal Sharing

As a young child I had a strong spirituality, an inner sense of morality and justice. This was not from the teaching of others but seemed to be inborn. By the time I needed 12-Step recovery, however, I had become so disillusioned and embittered that I could not acknowledge any concept of a Higher Power.

When I became involved in 12-Step recovery, I considered myself an atheist. I put up with all the "God stuff" for reasons of survival. I knew that, for me, to drink was to die. I used the group as my Higher Power. I stayed sober at the meetings. I found it impossible to work the Steps, which I viewed as negative, self-condemning and humiliating.

For four years I remained free from alcohol, but addicted to cocaine. In an attempt to clean up, I joined another 12-Step fellowship. My habit lessened considerably, but I never stayed clean for more than 3 weeks at any one time. I had decided that I was an agnostic, not an atheist, but I still could not get past Step 2.

The following year my younger brother committed suicide, after a two-year struggle with mental illness. During those two years he told me how he shut down his feelings as a child, to avoid being beaten as I was. He acknowledged this as the reason he was unable to open up to his counselors but felt trapped and unable to change it. He was also shamed by our parents' denial of his illness, making it still more difficult for him to accept help.

As a result of this tragedy, I began facing my own inner child issues. My recovery thus far had been focused only on my physical addictions. Simply remaining clean and sober wasn't enough. I now saw that I was powerless, not only over substances, but also over the devastating effects of my upbringing.

Around the same time, I began studying the teachings of a metaphysical church. I found that their beliefs agreed with the inner spirituality that I had felt as a child. In my fifth year of recovery, I finally found a nurturing and supportive Higher Power.

I now believe in a Universal Spirit which dwells within everyone. This Loving Power is available to anyone who will acknowledge It. My Higher Power is not someone outside myself, but rather a Greater Power within myself. This Spirit neither judges nor punishes. It has always been one with me, whether or not I believed this. This has allowed me to work the Steps joyfully and without guilt or fear.

In addition to being guidelines for recovery, the Steps when read or spoken can also be experienced as a form of affirmative prayer. I find that I can pray much more effectively using words which I don't need to redefine as I say them. For this reason I have adapted a personal version of the Steps. I believe that this adaptation preserves the original power and purpose of the Steps while providing a useful affirmative alternative.

1. I acknowledge that I was powerless over the effects of my dysfunctional upbringing, and my life had become unmanageable.
2. I believe that a Greater Power within myself restores me to sanity.
3. I now turn my will and my life over to the care of that Power as I understand It.

4. I make an honest and thorough inventory of my life.

(In this inventory I include the things about myself with which I am content as well as those about which I am ashamed or dissatisfied. As I remain open to my Higher Good, the things in my life which need correction are made known to me. This Step is about self-awareness, not self-condemnation.)

5. Supported by Loving Spirit, I share my inventory openly and completely with another person.

(In this Step I do not admit to God. God already knows and goes with me, as I share my inventory with the other person. As a person with low self-esteem, I may tend to deny my assets at least as much as my character defects. It's very important that I acknowledge and express my worth as I rediscover it.)

6. I am entirely willing to have my Higher Power remove all of my character defects.

7. I boldly affirm that Universal Good removes my shortcomings.

(I do not humbly ask God for this as though I am unworthy. Instead I affirm that it is God's will for me to be perfect, whole and complete. Affirmative prayer is simply an agreement to cooperate with Spirit in order to bring about my needed healing. It is done unto me as I believe.)

8. I make a list of all persons I have harmed and am willing to make amends to them all.

(I include myself on this list when appropriate.)

9. I make direct amends to such people wherever possible, except when to do so would harm them or others.

10. I continue to take personal inventory, and when I am in error I promptly correct it.

11. I seek through prayer and meditation to improve my conscious contact with my Higher Power. I pray only for Divine Guidance and affirm the power to carry that out.

12. Having had a spiritual awakening as the result of these Steps, I carry this message to others and practice these principles in all my affairs.

—Anonymous

STEP FOUR

Made a searching and fearless moral inventory of ourselves.

> *It is plain that a life which includes deep resentments leads only to futility and unhappiness. To the precise extent that we permit these, do we squander the hours that might have been worthwhile.*
>
> —Alcoholics Anonymous
>
> ✳✳✳
>
> *"Drug Of Choice"*
> *What was my drink*
> *my delicious addiction*
> *that led to my oppression?*
> *My drug of choice*
> *I held in my hand*
> *was a glassful of depression.*
>
> —Carol Ann F., 7/30/90,
> Vashon Island, WA

In working the first three Steps, we start by admitting the troublesome issues that have made our lives unlivable. We then survey the resources we can tap as sources for inner power to guide us toward sane living. Finally, we commit ourselves to opening up to the care of a spiritual resource we are inspired to accept. If we have really gotten somewhere with the first three Steps, we are able to admit to ourselves why we are in recovery. We also will have begun to feel a measure of hope that growing to live successful, joyous lives may be a realistic possiblity.

Drawing upon this foundation of honesty and optimism, we now turn in Step 4 to considering those factors that have made us the unique individuals we are and have been in our lives. We do this with the view of celebrating what is unique about ourselves while at the same time we strive to become objective about our own dysfunctional behaviors and attitudes.

Ideally, then, we can approach Step 4 with an enthusiastic willingness to sort through our behaviors and attitudes with the goal of keeping what we like and (eventually) getting rid of the rest. If we are fortunate enough to have a strongly developed spiritual contact that provides us with a wellspring of serene confidence, the "fearless and thorough moral inventory" in Step 4 may feel like an opportunity to grow and to explore ourselves, rather than posing a terrifying and possibly overwhelming threat.

Many of us may not come to Step 4 as ideal examples of serenity, however. We may approach Step 4 with willingness and commitment, only to be engulfed by feelings of guilt, shame or even of disloyalty — as though being honest with ourselves is a challenge to deeply ingrained rules which have been internalized and buried below the conscious mind. Or we may feel driven to work Step 4 without feeling either confident or serene because of remorse or guilty secrets that torment us. Internal confusion, like a blanket of fog, can make it hard to see incidents in memory clearly. We may wonder if the inventory should be postponed until a more ideal condition of having internalized the first three Steps has been attained.

When we encounter these feelings and questions within ourselves about this Step, we can remind ourselves that the reason we are doing Step 4 is to find out who we are and who we have been in our lives. If we find out that we have buried fears or other feelings that spring out when we try to look at ourselves, that is definitely something to know about who we are! Likewise, if we have no peace, but are driven, haunted or tormented, we make progress in Step 4 when we admit these painful-but-true facts.

We needn't be at an ideal state of recovery in order to begin to make progress in any phase or Step of our recovery. If we did, few of us would have much of a chance! Perfection needn't be our goal. We can gain by taking Step 4 periodically, after cycling through the balance of the Steps and reaping the benefits of embracing the entire healing process. The spiritual side of the program, over time, tends to grow clearer and stronger. This makes it more possible to be fearless and thorough when we try to look into the deep waters of ourselves in the Inventory process.

✳✳✳

Step 4 asks us to cultivate fearless self-acceptance. Self-acceptance is not only necessary if we are to become willing to unmask behaviors we may have justified by blaming or fearing others—it is also needed to keep us from falling into the trap of self-attack.

An honest and balanced approach to facing ourselves as we really are today is what is wanted. We seek to be thorough because half-truths, rationalizations or too rigid points of view are all masks we wear that can hide us from ourselves. It probably won't feel comfortable admitting some of what is true about ourselves, but we must be willing to be honest anyway. The pain of coming out of denial is like the pain of undergoing physical therapy to overcome a serious injury; it's a part of the healing process. We've got to see ourselves clearly in order to heal. Glossing over the facts can lead us to repeat painful patterns in our lives and in the lives of those we love.

As we work Step 4, we are beginning a powerful process of transformation from deficiency towards self-mastery. Few undertakings have greater potential. We are eliminating mental and emotional ruts that may have immobilized us for a long time. We need to make sure we have the support we need to succeed in this important undertaking. Reading, participating at meetings, and making sure we get the diet, rest and exercise we need are ways to take good care of ourselves while we are engaged in the stress of self-examination.

Sponsorship and interaction with others in the program who are also working the Steps are also very nurturing. Step Study meetings can be especially helpful for rounding out narrow slants of looking at ourselves or others that we may not even realize we have. Working with others isn't competitive, though. We're always free to move at our own pace.

If we don't feel ready, we are free to step back until we're able to move on again. If timidity or the tendency to lose ourself in the opinions of others are major problems for us, it is important to work with a qualified individual. This can be a sponsor, a professional therapist, a friend or a spiritual advisor so long as it is a person we can trust.

Remember, we don't work the Steps to meet each other's expectations. The opinions of a sponsor or others in the fellowship remain suggestions only. The sharing at Step Meetings is one of the ways we seek to offer experience, strength and hope to each other, without attaching strings of control or manipulation. We each have a responsibility to take what we can use and leave the rest.

✳✳✳

The question of morals may be a sticking point for some in Step 4. The dictionary tells us that morals are a code of behaviors based upon value judgments as to the right and wrong ways to behave or to relate to others. Morals by this definition are simply the limits and boundaries we each set for ourselves, clearly defining what we feel is personally O.K. or not O.K. for us to do.

Some moral codes may, additionally, include value judgments as to right and wrong ways to think or even to feel. Most religions provide moral instruction as an integral part of their teachings. Sometimes these moral codes may be quite detailed, allowing for little personal choice. Many of us may associate morals with religion, perhaps with threats of punishment or social condemnation. If the idea of morals is painfully enmeshed with a rigid religious code we have chosen to reject, it's good to note that philosophies and social systems which are not religious also provide workable moral systems we can adopt or draw from.

What is wanted in Step 4's personal inventory is a system of moral standards and personal limits which will give us the boundaries we need to live without guilt and shame. We are no more bound by old, fear-based ideas in Step 4 than we are in any of the 12 Steps!

To dispel any mental confusion or feelings of shame associated with concepts of a moral inventory, it may be helpful to write a list of all the moral values we can think of and then go back over the list to determine which of these have roots within us and which are ideas we were given.

Once we get a sense of who we are, in terms of our own real values, we can put those on a list of Current Personal Values. These limits and boundaries are among the important internalized assets we can use to assess our conduct, past and present. Rules and expectations which have been imposed upon us by others can be placed upon a list of "Other People's Values (Not My Own)." These external sources of guilt and shame are usually among the most serious of our codependent liabilities.

In developing a list of Current Personal Values as principles to live by ask yourself where you really stand, or would like to stand, on such issues as:

1. **Isolation/Intimacy:** What is your ideal vision of being in touch with others? Is marriage or committed partnership an important value for you? How about your needs for privacy? Independence? Are you comfortable in one-on-one relating, or do you prefer group or family socializing?

2. **Control/Structure:** What are your limits and boundaries? What of yourself do you want to offer to others, and which others? Are you willing to ask for what you want?

3. **Obsession/Serenity:** What are your personal standards for moderation? What are the healthy sources of joy and pleasure that you celebrate in your life?

While we are trying to gain insight into our own standards, we need to cultivate the habit of noticing, at a feeling level, how we respond or react to our own thoughts, including our value judgments. If we've been in the habit of stuffing our inner feelings, the practice of noticing our own honest responses and reactions may open up new vistas. If we try to listen to ourselves, without making judgments about our reactions, we may quickly find a stronger connection to our Inner Child. We begin to develop more mental objectivity and at the same time we become more compassionate toward ourselves. We make a good start in developing a bond of self-trust between the Inner Child self and our adult self when we begin to accept ourselves in this very direct and practical way. We begin to free ourselves, too, from the burdens of shame and guilt we have carried that are based in trying to live by other people's values.

It may take some time to tell the difference between our own true values and the standards others have imposed upon us. It may well be true, too, that we find ourselves in agreement with some or many of the values we were taught.

***

In the next phase of the inventory, we try to glimpse the reality of how we have coped and survived so far in life. The patterns we find in this phase of the inventory are often deeply ingrained — and deeply painful. If we were influenced by dysfunctional family patterns such as threats of rejection, ridicule or abandonment, or by violence and financial insecurity, we may have developed powerful routines to protect ourselves or those we loved.

We now go back over the years, seeking to view ourselves as the survivors we are. We go back as far as we can remember, reviewing our lives, asking ourselves, "Who hurt us? Who are we mad at? How did we react?" If there are blank periods, we note those for future exploration. We may have coped by letting people down or by reacting defensively to what seemed to threaten us. Self-attack may also be a habitual coping behavior. We may have become our own critical parent to keep ourselves from taking on challenges.

Going back through the years, how have we coped? What were the circumstances that prompted us to go on automatic and lose the power of decision? It's O.K. to cry and it's O.K. to feel sorry about these incidents. We want to welcome whatever feelings may surface in this review of our coping and surviving behaviors, even the "bad" ones. Jealousy, rage, desires for revenge — all feelings are good feelings when it comes to working Step 4. Nothing is to be gained by lying to ourselves or screening our reactions to the past. Self-acceptance means giving ourselves permission to feel whatever we may feel.

Although we allow ourselves to get in touch with any feelings or fantasies involving figures from our pasts in Step 4, we are cautioned not to undertake action on these feelings in the reality of our lives. Steps 5 through 9 are necessary parts of the healing process that we are only beginning in Step 4. If feelings that come up are very troubling, talking with a sponsor or other trusted person who is not directly involved can help.

✳✳✳

We probably will find, too, that we behaved or tried to behave in ways that we can now see were actually pretty healthy, assertive responses to some of the pressures we encountered. Examples of affirmative responses to life problems are diagramed on the the the Freedom Wheel (Appendix 1). To get a sense of how healthy approaches can be defeated in dysfunctional family system, try moving backward, first locating a healthy attitude on the Freedom Wheel, then finding the corresponding spoke of codependency on the Victim Wheel on the previous page. If our healthy responses were attacked or discredited, we may find that we have suppressed a great store of rage and frustration. A sense of injustice is at the root of most resentment.

In this portion of the inventory, we note whom we are angry with, the ways we were abused or made to feel inadequate, what that we needed or wanted was interfered with, and how we feel as a result.

We must be as specific as possible about these incidents. If feelings are hard to contact, or difficult to name, look over A Checklist of Feelings (Exercise 5, this chapter). If we find we are contemptuous of ourselves for ways we have behaved, we place ourselves on our list — near the top.

It is helpful to construct a table such as the one below for this portion of the Inventory:

A Resentment Inventory

	Why?	Affects (Basic Needs):	I Feel:
Myself:	I wrote bad checks to cover expenses for food, utilities.	Identity, Survival.	Worthless, weak, and unable to take care of myself.
My stepparent:	Stole my share of family insurance.	Survival, Commitment.	Abandoned, ashamed.
Siblings:	Took heirlooms for themselves and wanted me to have nothing.	Identity, Gratification.	Rejected, ridiculed, used, betrayed, emotionally battered.

✳✳✳

In the next phase of the Inventory process, we go back over the Table above and make an effort to get in touch with our fears. Once again we ask ourselves, in each incident, what did we fear we'd lose or fail to get? We try to describe our fear in detail.

1. Do we find we are afraid that we won't survive? That we won't be accepted or cared for? Do we fear that we may be left alone (or trapped)? Does ridicule or looking like a fool strike terror in our hearts?

2. We look for the patterns created by fear in our lives. Have we been appeasers, losing our integrity in compliance, flattery, or by presenting a false front to those who we felt had power over us in some areas of our life? Have our deep fears taken over in some situations, trapping us into reactions that trigger crises and uproar in our lives? How much has fear colored our behaviors in transactions that involve the basics, such as family, sex relations, career and money-matters?

Often, feelings of shame, embarrassment, or arrogant self-justification may prompt us to minimize or gloss over these questions. Fears seem to have a life of their own. Tracking them down is always a challenge.

If we are inclined to sidestep this phase of the inventory, we remind ourselves that our unexamined fears usually control our behaviors, especially under stress. We may be living lives largely defined by our fears. It is by tapping ". . .the courage to change the things we can. . ." and facing up to our fears, that we begin to change our way of life.

✳✳✳

We complete the Inventory in Step 4 by setting up a balance sheet of our personal assets and liabilities. Our balance sheet is a thumbnail sketch of what works and what needs help in our personalities, a summary we can refer to easily as we move on to the other Steps. We sort through what we have written, first noting any characteristics we admire in ourselves. We look for courage, kindness, willingness to try, a spirit of adventure — any and all characteristics we see in ourselves as worthy, valuable or spiritual. We claim these assets, being careful not to leave out minor or "to be expected" positive qualities about ourselves.

Then, going back over all we have written, we try to be honest about what our real liabilities are. Do we tend to lie to ourselves rather than to admit to an unattractive bit of truth, for example? Do we get involved in crisis after crisis to avoid facing up to basic responsibilities? We seek to discover what the underlying weaknesses are within ourselves, not as an exercise in self-attack, but as an important step forward into new freedom. We remind ourselves that our goal is to build a starting place for self-transformation now.

Finally, we go back to our assets list and give ourselves credit for the assets we have earned by our work in doing the Inventory. We also remember to give ourselves credit for having survived and coped through the difficulties and trials of our past. We acknowledge ourselves as the unique expressions of life we each are and we thank ourselves for doing this work.

***

In conclusion, trying to get well in a 12-Step program without taking Step 4 is like trying to follow a treasure map without a starting place. Without first knowing where we started, we're unlikely to find the prize—no matter how carefully we follow the rest of the clues.

Recovery is a search for the personal treasure of rich, joyful living. In this treasure hunt there is no need for competition among the searchers. Instead, we help each other. Of course, we do want—and need—the treasure of addiction-and compulsion-free living. We aren't just playing a game. Still, working the Steps needn't be all hard work and pain. Among the best attitudes anyone can have for working the 12-Steps is a spirit of discovery and adventure. We need an element of fun. We also need the enthusiasm that comes of doing something exciting. One of the best testimonies of a living faith is to have the cheerful confidence to try something new and to do it with a light touch.

Instead of the old message we may have heard—that whatever is valuable is very hard—maybe impossible—to get the message in the 12-Step program is that the good things in life are attainable. We can cultivate the spirit of adventure to see us through the rough spots. Once we've established this attitude, we can use it on anything else we take on in life that's new or challenging.

Exercises

Exercise 1: Guilty Secrets

Shame about our guilty secrets can make us think we are losers or condemned people. What are these guilty secrets? We inventory them because in recovery we have the right to become healed of our pasts. We aren't stuck with our old lifestyles or even with our old personalities. If we don't like who we have been, we can decide to change.

1. Are we guilty of crimes?
2. Have we used others (or been used) in sexual situations that we are ashamed of?
3. Are there lies we have been living that, if they were to be exposed, we think might cause us to lose the respect and acceptance of those we love?

Exercise 2: Over-Responsibility

Another set of heavy chains we may be burdened with are guilt and shame about responsibilities we haven't been able to handle:

1. Have we felt responsible for but unable to take care of or to protect friends or family members?
2. Have we felt stuck in taking care of them, secretly wishing we had more time and freedom to be ourselves?
3. Have we stood up for someone out of feelings of intense loyalty that we sense may not be returned?

We can begin to break free of the emotional chains that have bound us to loser or victim attitudes by deciding to work Step 4 for the person we used to be. We can think of ourselves as a new person in recovery. Seeing ourselves as no longer bound to the ways we used to act can help to break chains of guilt and shame we may feel. This makes it easier to be really honest, too.

We really are free to create a new personality for ourselves. We can choose to be a new self that we appreciate, respect and love. We can look back on our old self as a sad, confused person who got a new chance.

If there are things your old self did that you find hard to accept, or if certain feelings tend to seep out of the past and threaten to drown you in a sea of tears, you can move forward in the Steps and begin the sharing of Step 5 with a person you can trust. You don't have to wait.

Exercise 3: Special Focus Issues

1. Turn to Appendix II, Issues in Recovery Inventories. Review any of the special focus inventories that you suspect may be factors in your history.

2. Review any special focus inventories you feel certain do not apply to you in any way.

3. Read the Affirmation/Meditation from any of the Inventories just before going to sleep. Ask your Inner Child to direct your dreams and allow you to remember what will be helpful when you wake up.

4. Keep a dream journal for one or two weeks while repeating the same bedtime meditation.

Exercise 4: Whose Value Is It?

Here's a test for determining whether a moral value is a personal standard we hold within ourselves or not:

1. When you read over each of the values on your list of "Morals," such as, "I always must answer direct questions truthfully," notice how you hear the phrase, in your own mind.

2. Whose voice is speaking? Is it your own adult voice, or the voice of a parent or authority figure from your past?

3. Place all the values you have internalized and hear in your own adult voice on a list of Current Personal Values.

4. Set any values you hear in a voice other than your own adult voice on a list of Questionable Values for further consideration.

5. You may feel O.K. about including some of these Questionable Values on your Current Personal Values list, but, before you do, ask yourself, "Am I comfortable accepting the voice of my mother, father, minister, priest, etc., inside the Temple of My Own Being directing my actions?"

6. Breathe deeply and slowly, allowing yourself to visualize yourself entering a Temple within yourself, bathed in rosy-golden light. Imagine this Temple as completely as you can, with details that make you feel safe, richly cared for, and at home. You may feel this Temple's location in your body, enclosed within your heart.

7. Know that it is O.K. to be entirely honest with yourself within your Temple and allow yourself to feel the safety and protection which is yours by right within your Sacred Inner Place of Peace and Refuge.

8. If you are O.K. with inviting the voice into your heart, then add the moral value in question to your Personal list.

9. If you are not entirely comfortable doing this, you may adopt the value, if you like, and speak it in your own adult voice.

10. If you find that you cannot either accept the voice as a spiritual guide or speak the value in your own adult voice, then it is a good practice to set the value on a list of Other People's Values (Not My Own).

Exercise 5: Reclaiming the Right to Feel

1. Are you among those who promptly get mad at themselves or who feel ashamed whenever they feel angry — no matter what is going on?

2. Have you been told that it is wrong to have some feelings, or that you should feel for others?

3. Do you find you are really afraid to feel frightened, or angry, or sad — as though the feeling may take over if you let it get out?

4. Do you have feelings you can't name? Or do some feelings seem frozen or just not there?

5. The following is a list of feelings most people experience. Can you get in touch with these feelings? Are there some you can't feel?

Checklist of Feelings

happy	surprised	hopeful	sneaky
joyful	shocked	accepted	seductive
carefree	pressured	confident	insensitive
playful	trapped	secure	horny
silly	anxious	relieved	wild
serene	worried	grateful	smug
content	tense	curious	extravagant
thoughtful	confused	inspired	rebellious
lazy	disappointed	empowered	contemptuous
bored	sad	enthused	disgusted
tired	sorry	devoted	frightened
exhausted	guilty	cherished	intimidated
depressed	embarrassed	sympathetic	terrified
empty	ashamed	protective	abused
indifferent	bashful	possessive	betrayed
hopeless	impulsive	insecure	rejected
helpless	passionate	suspicious	impatient
abandoned	loving	inadequate	irritated
lonely	caring	unworthy	angry
isolated	appreciative	jealous	hostile
frustrated	kindly	obsessed	vengeful
weak	affectionate	envious	aggressive
vulnerable	pleased	greedy	hateful
overwhelmed	satisfied	defensive	enraged

In recovery, we reclaim our right to feel all of our feelings, as whole human beings. We learn that actions can be wrong, that feelings are not actions, and that we can find ways to let our feelings out in safe, appropriate settings — where no one gets hurt or punished.

If you feel embarrassed or ashamed, or if you draw a blank when trying to get in touch with some of the feelings on this list, here is a technique for connecting with buried or frozen feelings, in a safe situation:

1. Give yourself permission to tell the truth. Imagine you are talking to someone important to you. Imagine that person sitting in a chair in front of you a few feet away. If you prefer, you can speak to yourself, looking into your own eyes in a mirror. Then say one of the following sentences, filling in the blank with whatever feeling you are finding it hard to feel or to express:

- "(Name of person), I feel (fill in the blank), and I want you to know it."
- "(Name of person), I'm afraid to let you see me feeling (fill in the blank)."
- "(Name of person), I'm ashamed to admit that I feel (fill in the blank)."

2. Then, add a few words to tell why. Say whatever comes to your mind right away. Examples:

- "(Boss), I feel (vulnerable), and want you to know it. You might eliminate my job!"
- "(Spouse), I'm afraid to let you see me feeling (weak). You might kick me out."
- "(Child), I'm ashamed to admit I feel (vengeful). I don't want you to see that."
- "(Myself), I feel (hopeful), and I want you to know it. I can live a better life!"

3. Give yourself permission to feel the feelings that come up for you when you make these statements, whatever they may be. Say, out loud, "I have a right to all my feelings!"

Exercise 6: Map Your Feelings

Here's a creative way for even young children to inventory and identify their feelings (Step 4) and then share them in a safe relationship and setting (Step 5). This Exercise was shared with us by Hannah S. (age 10), who learned it at the United Indian Health Clinic, Trinidad, California, in December, 1988.

1. On a piece of paper, write five feelings you sometimes have. (Step 4). Example:
       a. love
       b. excitement
       c. thoughtful
       d. anger
       e. happiness

2. Draw a different symbol for each of this feelings. (Step 4). Example:

love

thoughtful

anger

excitement

happiness

3. Now, write an opposite feeling that you sometimes have for each of your first five feelings. (Step 4). Example:

  a. indifference (un-love)
  b. bored
  c. embarrassed
  d. friendly
  e. sadness

4. Give each of these feelings their own symbol (different from the first five). (Step 4). Example:

indifference

embarrassed

friendly

bored

sadness

5. Now, using the only the symbols for these different feelings (no words), draw a map that shows how you have felt today (or during another time you remember). (Step 4.)

Example Feeling Map

(By Hannah S.)

6. Share your Feeling Map with a trusted friend or therapist. Let her guess how you've been feeling from your Map, and tell her whether or not she's read your clues correctly. (Step 5.)

7. Tell a story about your Feeling Map and the things that happened to make you feel the way you did. (Step 5.)

Exercise 7: Having Fun With Step 4

Does having fun with Step 4 sound impossible? Here are some brief, creative exercises to get in touch with your patterns and the coping behaviors that go with them.

Often, feelings of sadness, shame or anger lock us away from simple pleasures — daydreaming, playing with colored pencils or crayons, making things with our hands. If you find yourself getting diverted away from these exercises by a flood of feelings, try to name those feelings and put them on your Inventory as feelings that are blocking your creativity.

Just as facing our fears tends to be a big step toward becoming courageous, facing up to the feelings that are blocks to creativity tends to bring us closer to the creative Inner Child within. Keep at it. It does get easier if you will give yourself permission to be O.K. feeling all of your feelings!

1. This exercise requires you to make yourself very comfortable and relaxed. A cushy couch, a hammock, or a hot tub are all good starting places. When you're quite cozy, you are going to take a memory walk in time back to your childhood neighborhood, and stand across the street from where your family lived. Better yet, hop on board a passing space craft so you can look down from a long way away (like the moon) on your whole childhood community. You have a very powerful telescope and you can, if you like, turn up the speaker volume, too, and listen in on any conversations or other sounds. Imagine your family living in a glass house, and that you can see into the other houses in the community — like so many ant colonies!

• How does your family fit in the community or not fit in? Is your family accepted, ignored, admired or rejected by other families?

• How did your family see itself? What is the family myth that was acted out? Family myths include such family talk or non-verbal messages as, "We are better than other families"; "We can't help ourselves!"; "It's too much for us!"; or "We're no good!" (See What Are Your Family's Dysfunctional Myths?, Appendix I.)

• How did you act out the family myth? How did your personal style carry the family's message to the community?

2. Remember some of the highlights of your memory and draw your family as you saw it when you revisited it. Let your Inner Child do the drawing. (A good way to free the Inner Child is to use the hand you don't write with to do the drawing.) Use the colors and intensities that feel right. Notice any angry feelings that come up for you. Do you feel like scribbling out some of your family members or yourself? Do you feel like ripping up the picture?

3. Draw a design for the mask you learned to wear at home in your family, and the one you learned to wear out in the community. Were these the same or different? Using paper strips and flour-paste, make your mask, or masks, so you can try them on in front of a mirror. Give yourself permission to feel any feelings that come up for you.

Inventory Your Closet

Bring the inventory process to life in your household by inventory-ing your material possessions, especially the stuff you have accumulated over a period of time. Do a physical inventory as a part of Step 4. If you have a closet, basement or drawer crammed with items that have been saved for later, make time now to inventory those areas in your household.

1. Use the same techniques and procedures on these items that apply to the thoughts and deeds we inventory in Step 4. Decide what to keep, how to organize it, and what to discard.

2. What is valuable to you, not valuable because of other people's ideas or demands?

3. Do some of these items represent coping behaviors from the past? Are resentments or fears involved in what has accumulated in your life, physically?

4. Symbolically work through the rest of the Steps with your physi-cal inventory materials. Discuss them, or actually organize them, with a sponsor or trusted friend in recovery.

5. Work through Steps 6 through 9 with your physical inventory materials. Let go of whatever is to be discarded with careful consideration. If there are things which are worn out, broken or entirely useless, admit this and recycle them fearlessly. If there are projects and items that are no longer useful for you but which may be used by others, decide whether to sell or to give them away and do so. Allow yourself to experience recovery in the area of material resources.

Questions to Ponder

1. Can you feel your feelings, identify them, name them for what they represent?
2. Is there something that is a "guilty secret" in your past—crimes, sex behavior?
3. Do you have secret fantasies of love or revenge?
4. Do some behaviors or circumstances bring up memories from childhood, even very vague ones? Describe these memories or images as completely as you can, whether or not they seem to make sense.

Personal Sharing

"Here's how I heard it: Dad told me that Mom told Dad that Grandma told Mom that my cousin told Grandma that I said something derogatory about his brother." — This was the beginning of a letter to my grandmother last year. I was really angry to see a lie about me once again circulating throughout the entire family.

Grandma is the self-appointed judge of everyone in the family. She's committed to finding fault with others wherever she can, especially those who don't buy into her power addiction. She's also a master at indirect communication.

I called Mom and complained about Grandma's gossip. Predictably she defended her mother, so I called both my sisters. We belabored the issue and reaffirmed what a turd Grandma is. I called my sponsor about it. I called my cousin. I shared it at several meetings. I went back to the word processor repeatedly, and finely honed the letter to my grandmother. I never mailed the letter.

I can't control what others say or do. I can break my cycle of addiction to excitement that incidents like this provoke. Taking my own inventory I see that some of what I did helped me get in touch with my feelings. Most of what I did, however, simply fed my resentment. In the process I also communicated indirectly, and involved two more family members in the crisis.

—Anonymous

57

Incest Trilogy

I.
I Won't Leave Me

Can you help me with my problem?
No . . . I don't really want to help you; I only
want to feel ok myself . . . .
What's wrong with that?
I don't know really; you tell me.

I heard a woman telling what happens to a child
who is molested . . . . They are "eroticized" she said —
I said, Oh — so that's what it is called and after all these years
I finally know a word for what I felt when I was swept out of myself into
mystery and being one with an adult
It made me different — somehow —
I knew that much anyway!

So can you help me?
No . . . . I don't care about your old, old problem . . .
I just want a lover now, you see . . .
But I freeze up sometimes — when
I feel betrayed by unmet promises
and failed anticipation — and
I freeze up solid, heart
beating in fear, my stomach
retching — full of helplessness & rage
and such deep sadness —
Can you help me? No — I can
help myself. And so I will.

II.
Nobody's Baby

She was nobody's baby in the morning when her mom
just needed sleep — and so they gave her a bottle
on a pillow and left her by herself . . . .
She was nobody's baby in the daytime
when the rugs had to be cleaned and
the furniture all dusted spic and span
Nobody's baby when the sun went down —and they saw each other,
putting on a show — to make him stay

except he never, never did or if he
did, he didn't want to . . . .

And so she made a sobbing vow to always be
nobody's baby when she grew up — and so
she lived inward like a monk & occasionally gave in
screaming and crying in a memory of all
her angry time alone for no good
reason — just excuse after excuse.

Who cares?
She doesn't care . . . .
It's much, much more than
caring that she feels —
She boils or she freezes but
she doesn't ever, ever care . . . .
She can't afford to care —
and feel soft feelings
soft as a baby's whisper
or a need to snuggle and be safe . . . .

III.
My Dolls Committed Suicide

When I was three years old, I had
a teenage lover — my own goodlooking brother
who I loved and learned to associate
the feeling of excitement with his smell of sweat
dark rooms and keeping it a secret — even from myself . . . .

Except the sex was too much
of a secret for me to keep
my body acted out & so
my father tried to kill him — as a friendly act toward me . . . .
It didn't feel friendly though — and then
my brother went away . . .
my father had a heart attack . . . and I
was left a widow at age three — with no one to console me
and I clung to my secret hoping that it would all turn out all right,
somehow — in a fairy tale — the "happily ever after" part — as a child I didn't know
how vain a hope that was and no one helped me to find out.
I felt so sad I ripped the little heart out of my Raggedy Ann; my
china baby finally smashed herself and died on the cement.

It's a sad story, isn't it — and all of them dead now —
and me — not dead, not even dying — not even sad or sorry for
the life I've had so far — so far, so exciting and so powerful a life . .
All's well that lives in spite of history and fears no pain —
Pain's not so bad without the fear of it.
And all things have an end . . . .

—Raven, October 10, 1990, Humboldt ACA.

STEP FIVE

Admitted to God, to ourselves, and to another human being the exact nature of our wrongs.

Risks

To laugh is to risk appearing the fool.
To weep is to risk appearing sentimental.
To reach out for another is to risk involvement.
To expose feelings is to risk exposing your true self.
To place your ideas, your dreams, before a crowd is to risk their loss.
To love is to risk not being loved in return.
To live is to risk dying.
To hope is to risk despair.
To try is to risk failure.
But risks must be taken, because the greatest hazard in life is to risk nothing.
The person who risks nothing, does nothing, has nothing and is nothing.
They say they avoid suffering and sorrow, but they cannot learn, feel, change, grow, love, live. . .
Chained by their attitudes, they are slaves.
They have forfeited their freedom.
Only a person who risks is free.

—Anonymous, Submitted by Dave L., Fortuna, CA, & Joan N., Chicago.

In considering Step 5, we confront our vulnerabilities. We risk the possibility of personal rejection, ridicule, public exposure. To individuals who may have avoided intimacy, dreaded criticism, and distrusted authority, Step 5 poses a definite challenge.

We risk stepping out of isolation. We are asked to go beyond living inside our private theories and fantasies and take action in a larger world, a world which includes a concept of God, ourselves, and at least one other human being. Breaking old habits of spiritual, personal and social isolation and replacing these with fearless honesty is the purpose of Step 5.

Why do we take Step 5, if it asks so much of us and challenges so much self-protective armor we rely upon? The answer is that we don't take Step 5 until we've come to an inner realization that the old games, whatever they were, don't work for us anymore. If isolation were a tolerable way of life for us, most of us would not have come into a 12-Step program of recovery. If we could have lived happily with our secrets — or just gotten by in even relative comfort — most of us have to admit we probably would have done so, rather than completed Step 5.

Once, we may have successfully protected ourselves by shutting down, by shutting up or by running away. However, these self-imposed forms of isolation no longer worked for us. Feelings — guilt, shame, self-doubt, fears (with and without names), grief, bitterness — haunted us. We could neither shut them off nor escape.

With torment so internalized, we may have felt locked in an intolerable prison of loneliness and despair. This is a feeling of spiritual isolation so terrifying we simply had to find a way to be free. We couldn't live otherwise. For most of us, the willingness to work Step 5 hinges upon remembering how isolated and alone we felt before we found the hope of recovery. We become willing to risk sharing our secrets when we realize that this is what we have to do to rejoin the human fellowship and cease being creatures apart.

If we discover that we still fear a condemning, punishing form of Higher Power, we review Steps 2 and 3. We remind ourselves that, as a recovering person who has been directed to a 12-Step program, we have already been given evidence of our Higher Power's good will. We remind ourselves that we are a part of a spiritual universe. We say the Serenity Prayer. Ultimately, we share any fears of punishment or condemnation we have about God with the God of our understanding. After all, it's just another part of telling the whole truth.

Many of us discover that we are plagued by another form of isolation: the isolation of self-loss. We may be very much in the habit of snowing ourselves. Instead of communicating with ourselves by thinking over questions that come up and forming an opinion, we may be in the habit of simply parroting old, rigid ideas. We may, in fact, tell ourselves that we feel or believe in ways that we really don't.

Why do we lie to ourselves? Maybe we feel inadequate to think for ourselves. Maybe we fear if we were to let ourselves think or feel without using a stranglehold of control, that a monster of selfish, self-will would leap out of us. Often, we are in the habit of lying to ourselves because we really don't like ourselves very well. In Step 5, hard as it may be, we are asked to treat ourselves like people we can trust.

There is another type of problem we can run into when it comes to telling ourselves the truth in Step 5. We may have internalized some coping mechanisms that are entirely automatic and seemingly beyond our control. It is not unusual for people with addictive patterns to blank out under some forms of stress — pressured sexual situations, arguments about money or responsibilities or situations where there is fear of physical violence. Inability to feel feelings or to think clearly are not unusual reactions to stress. When, in Step 5, we are faced with sharing secrets about ourselves, these ingrained coping mechanisms may crop up, even when we are committed to honesty. We may get foggy or forget. If we have learned to protect ourselves by automatically shutting down under certain pressures, what can be done about it?

The AA "Big Book" states (chillingly) on page 58, ". . . Those who do not recover are people who cannot or will not completely give themselves to this simple program, usually men and women who are constitutionally incapable of being honest with themselves. There are such unfortunates. . . . They are naturally incapable of grasping and developing a manner of living which demands rigorous honesty. Their chances are less than average."

If we fear that we are among the unfortunates so cut off from ourselves as to be incapable of self-honesty, what can we do to improve our chances for recovery? Fortunately, there are many reparenting techniques we can apply to help us renegotiate even our deeply internalized coping mechanisms, if we are willing to do the work. Often, very early incidents which prompted reactions of rage, shame and grief in us are at the root of persistent fogginess or automatic shutdowns. If we will do the work, the Inner Child is always capable of self-honesty.

We may need to re-explore incidents from the 4th Step Inventory that were confusing, or that prompted rage or revulsion, utilizing Inner Child techniques. Shame and anger may also be trapped in our bodies — in chronically stiff joints or muscles. Body work, massage or movement work may also be very helpful tools for getting out of self-isolation.

Many of us may be inclined to skip over this aspect of coming out of self-isolation in Step 5. We may say that these innovative techniques aren't for us — that they have nothing to do with the simple business of telling the truth. We may be so used to relying on the rational, thinking side of ourselves that we are entirely distrustful of the prospect of opening up to the feeling side. Perhaps we think of our Inner Child as just a sniveler, a weak crybaby we want to leave behind. Denial, rigid ideas and pride are all barriers to self-honesty that can keep us locked in self-isolation. If we will take the time in working Step 5 to improve communication with our creative self, we can only gain as our capacity for self-honesty increases and we become more able to accept ourselves.

***

When we consider disclosing our secrets to someone else it's not unusual to experience a rush of defiance. We may be bitterly humiliated by memories of incidents where our confidences were abused. Waves of distrust, fear of rejection, of ridicule or of punishment may stir up a great deal of resistance.

In the face of these reactions, it may seem impossible to go further. Some feel so exposed at the prospect of taking this portion of Step 5 that they think of quitting the 12-Step program entirely — either to go back to the old lifestyle or to take up an alternative that eliminates or delays disclosure. Unwillingness to trust or to risk confiding in another human being may be a way of life for us. Social isolation can be a powerful habit. It may not yield easily to change.

We are thus faced with an objective barrier to continued recovery. We begin to realize that these issues of defiance and fear simply are not going to evaporate by themselves. At this stage of recovery, social isolation is not something imposed upon us by others. It's a condition we have internalized. Action is required to free ourselves. As with most kinds of objective problems, practical solutions are in order. Here are some practical strategies to overcome resistance to Step 5:

Reaction to authority is often at the root of problems of defiance or distrust. It may be helpful to go back to Step 3 and reconsider your concept of God. Ask yourself: When I say "I won't!" who am I defying? Is my concept of God or Spirit too weak or too mean to be trusted to protect me? We can afford the time to go through Step 3 again if it seems appropriate. A loving, powerful concept of God is essential to our success. Time we spend opening our hearts and minds to Spirit is never time wasted!

Using the Serenity Prayer may be helpful. We can ask that we be given serenity and courage necessary to go forward. We can ask for wisdom to choose a person who will not betray our confidence.

When we are spiritually grounded, we can set about considering whom we will share our 5th Step with. It's a good idea to put "principles before personalities" in this. Confidentiality is vital. Gossip is to be avoided. A good friend on a lunch date may not be right for the 5th Step. We owe it to ourselves to be thoughtful in selecting a person who understands the basics of the 12-Step process and will respect our trust.

A majority of 12-Step program members share their 5th Step with a sponsor. This is usually someone they have come to trust over a period of weeks or months in a relationship centered on working the program. Others may choose to share with someone outside the 12-Step program — a counselor, a priest or minister. It is usually not a good idea to share these confidences with a family member, spouse or lover who may be directly impacted or burdened by what is shared. Doing this may add more pain and confusion than it eliminates.

For a thorough Step 5, we will want to arrange sufficient time without interruptions. Feedback is important. Several hours — an afternoon or evening — free of ordinary distractions is in order. If you are working with someone who cannot give you such a chunk of time, or if your own schedule won't allow it, be realistic. Plan, discuss and commit to a sufficient number of meetings to get through all of Step 5 without rushing. Don't short yourself. If the person you have asked to work with you is unable to give you enough time to do a thorough 5th Step, it may be wise to find someone else instead of minimizing the project.

There is one more step in overcoming social isolation in Step 5: Don't put it off! Acting in new ways, even when we are convinced that these new ways are healthy, can feel pretty uncomfortable. Coming out of isolation requires courage. We need to guard against any tendency we have to say we aren't ready when what we mean is that we aren't willing.

Probably nothing does more for self-esteem than acting on convictions. Many feel that in taking Step 5 we change. When we take the action that Step 5 asks of us, we are demonstrating our ability to act with real courage. Our faith ceases to be hypothetical. We are living it. For many of us, this is a very great change.

***

Sometimes, there is a question of what to share. Some of our wrongs are easier to grasp than others. It's a fairly straightforward matter, for instance, to admit that we have robbed a filling station (if we have) or to admit that we've cheated on a spouse or partner. Nothing is to be gained by concealing any dark secrets in Step 5. Those who have tried to leave some things buried usually discover they have simply continued to bury themselves.

Neither is it advisable to work Step 5 with someone who you feel will censure you for aspects of your chosen lifestyle — such as sexual preferences — so that you are tempted to conceal some aspects of yourself. Step 5 is not something we undertake to expose ourselves to unexamined judgments and fears of others. It's important to be certain — before beginning the sharing that takes place in Step 5 — that the person we will be working with accepts us.

In addition to specific incidents, it is important to look at the wrongs caused by patterned behaviors. Do the incidents we feel shame and remorse about follow a pattern? If we have robbed a filling station, have we also stolen money (or goods) from friends, family? Do we feel so unworthy deep inside that we live out a pattern in which our basic survival depends upon sneaking and stealing? Are we locked in a pattern of envy or stealing to get even or to put up a front? These issues also must be discussed.

When we talk these matters over with a trusted person, we often are in for a surprise. Rather than the judgment and criticism we may have feared, we may find compassion and a sense of humor, which will help what we may have feared would be a pretty gloomy undertaking. The sponsor will probably ask that we explore our underlying motives. For most of us, these deeper patterns are what have made our lives unhappy and unsuccessful.

Most of us find Step 5 to be a miracle as well as a surprise. More than just social acceptance seems to flow into our lives when we have worked Step 5. Even concerns we may have brooded over for a long, long time may be affected in ways we could not have imagined in advance. It is not important that we have a sense of faith in advance to use Step 5 effectively. Just taking the action and telling the truth seems to be enough. No longer isolated outsiders in life, we find our fear of others and of economic insecurity tending to evaporate. Once we have begun, most of us find that we gradually enter a new world of hope and transformation.

✳✳✳

Exposing ourselves to abuse or punishment is not the purpose of Step 5. In this Step, we don't fight off our anxieties about exposure, or ridicule ourselves for being fearful. Instead, we find ways to do what it takes to get the support we need to go forward.

It may be that one of our problems is a tendency to expose ourselves to abuse. Some of us may have learned to be our own worst enemy. If we have completed an inventory and have admitted incidents that we are ashamed about, we still should not jump to conclusions about what we have to do until we have talked things over with a person we can really trust. Even if we feel certain that "we know what they will say," Step 5 asks us to risk checking out what at least one other person does say, when we talk to them. We are asked to do this to get out of living in our heads.

Taking Step 5 isn't like telling our secrets to a friend. The talking we do in Step 5 is a major step we take to change and heal our lives. This is very different from complaining or trying to get someone to help with a cover-up operation. One of the ways we can reparent ourselves in Step 5 is to be sure that the person we share with is thoroughly familiar with the 12-Steps and really understands the goals of Step 5.

If there are issues such as physical or sexual abuse which may be still ongoing in our lives, talking to a knowledgeable person, such as a professional counselor, is in order. Sponsors in a 12-Step program aren't meant to be substitutes for getting legal and other forms of appropriate help. We all have the right to safety and respect in our lives. This is true even though we may feel inclined to protect others or to minimize the injuries we may suffer. The power in Step 5 is lost if we insist on burying the truth about our situation, whatever it is. If we feel threatened, we owe it to ourselves to go to someone who potentially has the resources to help us out. If we will take the responsibility to go this far, it's the responsibility of a loving Higher Power to see us through to freedom.

Here are some warnings for working the 5th Step:

1. Don't share something at a meeting that would really hurt you or cause big trouble if it got out. This is true even though all 12-Step meetings have a commitment to the pledge, "What you hear here, let it stay here." 12-Step programs don't usually screen their memberships, though, so violations of this principle do sometimes happen. If in doubt, always share one-on-one with someone you respect and trust before talking in a meeting.

2. Don't share explicit details about sexual experiences at meetings, unless you are in a fellowship which focuses on sex issues. This is the sort of information that easily can be abused, especially in school, work, or a small community.

3. Don't divulge anyone's name when sharing your 5th Step, either one-on-one or at meetings. Protect yourself from revenge or gossip. It is definitely O.K. to share the name of a person who is molesting or abusing you, but only with a knowledgeable person who is qualified to help.

With these guidelines in mind, Step 5 becomes a pathway to support. When we share, we learn. We learn that we aren't alone and that others have had similar experiences and feelings. In sharing, we find solutions. We hear what others have to say. We feel their love. Step 5 offers us a new and different way of life.

Exercises

Honest communication requires the ability to be assertive — clear, definite, relaxed — not passive, servile or aggressive. Assertive communication skills can be learned. Practice is the biggest single factor in getting better. Here are some exercises designed to strengthen assertive "communication muscles":

Exercise 1: Become a Good Listener for Yourself.

1. While you are in a conversation — at home, at work or with friends — imagine you are listening to the conversation on a radio talk show. Listen with special care to yourself. It might be helpful to imagine the radio you have is a push-button model that you can program so that you can check in and monitor yourself from time to time. Imagine that your left thumb is the button, and that, whenever you squeeze your left thumb, you will be able to hear yourself as you are speaking. Regardless of what you are saying, do you sound rushed, irritated, afraid, or hopeless? Do you pause to take a breath as you speak? Do your ideas come across smoothly? How often do you fall into a pattern of blaming or complaining?

2. Do this exercise while you are talking to yourself in a mirror about your Step 5 issues. Look into your own eyes with love, patience, interest. Smile.

3. Do this exercise while you are sharing at a 12-Step meeting. Be willing to hear yourself, uncritically. Listen to yourself as respectfully as you would listen to a sponsor or a guest speaker.

4. Use your push button radio to monitor yourself in the exercises that follow. Imagine (visualize) yourself radiating interest and understanding to yourself, as you listen.

Exercise 2: Take Time to Feel Before You Speak.

1. When someone asks you a question, practice taking a breath and breathing it out before you answer — even if you have a ready answer — and consciously notice your feeling-response, whatever it may be. Do you feel challenged by being asked a question? Do you feel responsible for the person who asked the question? Do you feel confused? Are you unsure you understand what is being asked? Do you suspect manipulation or put-down motives? Instead of responding with a "thought-answer," consider responding with a "feeling-response" instead. Does it feel safe to expose your feelings to this person? In this situation?

2. Before asking a question yourself or making a request, take in a deep breath and let it out slowly. Allow yourself to feel whatever feeling(s) you have in the area below your diaphragm (just below your rib cage). As

you speak, stay in touch with those feelings. How does it feel to ask for information you need, or for behavior you prefer?

3. Imagine (visualize) your feelings as areas of colored light. Breathe in the color and then speak, allowing the words you say to be colored by the feelings in your breath. Breathe your feelings into the room as you speak. Visualize your feeling-words splashing colors on those who are hearing you.

4. Imagine you and the people you are talking with are filling up clear balloons with the colored air of your feeling-words. These can be any size or shape. Draw a room full of the balloons that have been blown up. Visualize you and the others taking your balloons outside and letting them float free — or popping them.

Exercise 3: Speak from Personal Experience.

1. Notice any tendency you may have to speak in "you-statements," such as "You must think . . ." or "You always want me to . . ." Change all "you-statements" to self-disclosure "I-statements," such as "I feel afraid of being judged . . ." or "I'm unwilling to do . . ."

2. Notice tendencies you may have to rely upon others or authority to justify your feelings. Watch for statements such as, "Everybody feels . . ." or "My therapist (or the Bible) says that healthy (good) people feel . . ." Remember that we need not justify our feelings. Practice owning your feelings by changing these to "I feel . . ."

3. Notice tendencies you may have to repress or "stuff" your own input in family, social or work activities. Risk verbalizing your ideas, impressions and creative fantasies about projects you are involved in, in a clear, calm voice. Your input is valuable.

4. Practice validating your own experience in everyday situations. In problem-solving situations, search your memory for experiences that were similar, or felt similar, in your past. Share what you did or how you felt then. If you have had no previous experience that is similar, risk sharing that information, too. Your participation is valuable.

Exercise 4: Speak Only Truth.

1. Listen to yourself as you are recalling an experience and sharing it with others. Do you exaggerate details or the emotions that were expressed? Do you find that you add "facts" that didn't occur to spice up the story? Do you leave out elements that might be unflattering to yourself? Practice retelling experiences exactly as they happened.

2. Do you become selective in what you say or how you say it, strictly to avoid ruffling feathers? Do you repress important insights or disguise information that you are afraid might be unwelcome? Do you adopt different points of view, so that you are supporting several (possibly

incompatible) versions of reality, depending upon whom you're with? You don't have to appease others to be accepted! Make a commitment to yourself to risk telling as much of the truth as feels safe, and to tell no lies, in all of your relationships.

3. Do you lie about your behavior — where you go, what you do? Consider renegotiating your relationships and your activities so that lying becomes unnecessary.

Exercise 4: Act the Truth

1. In front of a large mirror, do a pantomime of a portion of your 5th Step (using no words, only actions) while you watch yourself. Express first the actions, and then the feelings involved — as though you were doing two scenes from a non-verbal play. Which is harder for you to act out effectively, the feelings or the behaviors? Use props, if you like.

2. With your sponsor present, go through the above exercise again. Try to communicate your issue without using any words at all until your sponsor understands non-verbally. How does it feel to communicate something of yourself non-verbally to someone you trust? Does your sponsor get your actions or your feelings more easily?

3. Using something that you are comfortable sharing, try this exercise with a group of program friends. Do you have trouble staying "real" in front of others? Does "clowning" take over? Try to build humor into the process without losing the other feelings that are there to be expressed and received as well.

Exercise 5: Truth in Color

Use color crayons or felt markers for these free expression exercises in telling the truth. Start each exercise by drawing a circle on a piece of paper.

1. Take an incident from your 5th Step and, using colors and shapes only, represent the action that took place and how it affected you. Consider yourself at the center of the circle. If the incident involved you acting on another person, draw a shape to represent you at the center of the circle and another to represent them — inside or outside the circle. If the incident involved being acted upon by someone else, use a shape outside the circle to symbolize them. Use colors alone to show the actions.

2. Draw the same incident using only colors to represent the feelings involved. Stay with your own feelings and don't project feeling-colors on the other person (or people) involved. Give yourself permission to color all of the feelings you experienced.

3. Share your drawings with your sponsor. Does it feel riskier or easier to share creative work than sharing words?

Questions to Ponder

1. What do you fear that God as you understand God won't forgive?
2. What are you ashamed or afraid to tell anyone about yourself?
3. What isn't "important enough" to bother with, or to share?
4. Who do you know accepts you just as you are?

Personal Sharing

Letting Go, or,
Who Reframed Roger Rabbit?

STEP SIX

Became entirely willing to have God remove all these defects of character.

Mary had a doll she loved very much. The doll had lost an arm, so Mary asked God to fix the doll. Nothing happened, so she again asked God to please fix her doll's arm. Still nothing happened, and finally Mary cried out, "God, why haven't you fixed my dolly's arm?" God answered, "I was waiting for you to let go of her."

—Anonymous, submitted by Martha H., Blue Lake, CA

***

I've come to see that relationships are something you have, not something you are . . .

—Charlie T., Humboldt ACA

We may start out a little puzzled at the focus of Step 6; we may be used to thinking more in terms of problems than character defects. Isolation is a problem, for example — not a character defect. We may be sharply aware of several problems we face in life, but only dimly conscious (if at all) of our character defects.

Step 6 reminds us that we can solve problems only by becoming willing to change something about ourselves. If we are isolated, for instance, what are we doing to keep ourselves that way? We have to bring the focus to where it can do us some good — back to ourselves — if there is going to be a change.

The character defects we work to release in Step 6 are the behaviors and attitudes that keep us bound to our problems, whatever those problems may be. Since most of what we do that causes us (and others) pain we do over and over again, these character defects will generally be found among the habitual behaviors and ingrained attitudes we have. Habits are the limits we really live by, whether we're aware of them or not. Habits may account for how we spend nearly every moment of our day. Our lives may fairly dance or drag along, structured by the routines we have.

Many of our identified life problems, especially those that reoccur, are bound to us by our own habits. Many problems simply cannot go away until we become willing to let go of the thinking and acting that ties us to them. If recovery is to be a living experience and not just something we read and talk about, we're probably going to have to become willing to say goodbye to a lot of our old, habitual behaviors.

A present character defect may be a former coping behavior that once was an important part of our survival kit. But, in recovery, it becomes excess baggage. We usually aren't aware of the routines we don't need any more until they begin to cause trouble.

It is said that people don't change behaviors that work. Take, for instance, habits of appeasement or defensive touchiness which may have been lifesavers when we had to fend off threats in dysfunctional relationships. These reactions can — and usually do — hang on into recovery. We may continue to placate or to bristle in relationships and situations where no comparable threat exists. We may also continue to feel and act more vulnerable than is actually necessary. If we do this, we suffer needlessly as we negate our own power in situations where a more positive role is possible for us.

***

Step 6 is another action Step. The first action in Step 6 is review. If we have done the Steps that lead up to Step 6, we will have made a written Inventory in Step 4 of issues that brought us to recovery. This is a good place to start. Now we look at our inventories again to see, as well as we can, how the issues we have pinpointed as troublesome still hang on and have power in our lives. Are we strengthening the values we found in ourselves by our present habits? Or do our habits undercut our vision for the future?

It's a good idea to continue the practice begun in Step 5 of sharing these insights with someone we trust. Honest interaction with a sponsor can be very helpful. Without rationalizing, we seek to examine our day-to-day behaviors. We want to seek out any indications that we may be dragging our old miseries, in the form of habitual reactions, into our present lives. Are we still defending ourselves from threats that were once quite real, but now are behind us? Are we objectively still being threatened or do we just feel threatened? Do we continue to act from habitual fears, habitual suspicions, or other defensive patterns? On the other hand, do we continue to expose ourselves to threats that we now know will do us harm?

In Step 6 we need to become aware of ourselves in the present. What do we actually do, think, and feel? We want to try to see ourselves in terms of all of our habits, not just the most glaring or flattering ones. From the time we open our eyes in the morning until our final sleepy yawn at night, how are we living? Which side of the bed do we get up on? Which shoe goes on first? Do we eat breakfast? Meditate? Exercise?

***

This self-scrutiny may seem like a pretty silly idea. We may be tempted to skip part — or all — of it. We may ask, "What's this got to do with my becoming willing to have character defects removed?" Some of us may become more belligerent, feeling that this sort of inquiry is nobody's business. "What am I supposed to do — ask my sponsor if I'm brushing my teeth in a spiritual way? I did Step 5. Let God decide what my defects are."

We may feel we are too busy or that we already know how our Inventory liabilities show up as character defects in our lives. But do we? Often we may be more willing to inventory our problem behaviors in Step 4 than to actually let them go. We may be inclined to speak of our issues in general terms or to characterize them as past mistakes, as though they are no longer a part of our lives. Insight alone, however, doesn't heal compulsions or remove ingrained fears. We have to become willing to actually change and let go of our old ways in order to move closer to our inner potentials.

Why do we seem to be so attached to our old ways, even when they directly interfere with our hopes and goals? Do we have to admit finally that we are addicted to wrong-doing and are therefore morally weak? There is another way to look at it. We now know that the grief process isn't exclusively about death or separation. It's also about change.

Change in our lives — even the change that comes with victory and triumph — is commonly associated with a feeling of loss, anxiety or sadness. We move on in life, stage by stage, day by day. Feelings of sadness or loss can come upon us with success as much as with failure. Change, especially sudden change, may bring up memories of other events which were painful or frightening. We may remember times, too, when we risked something and suffered disappointment. It's also not unusual to feel near-panic at the prospect of letting go of old defenses. We wonder what will we do, instead. We may feel we face a loss of identity if we let go of a strongly held defense. Indeed, to the extent that we've lost ourselves in codependently seeing ourselves in reaction to others, this feeling can seem very real. But we really are not these fear-based behaviors. We are the inner self these behaviors have been set up to protect. We need to ask our Higher Power to give us the willingness we need and to help us move to reclaim who we really are and can be. In Step 6, as we become willing to allow for the possibility of gradual change, we slowly move out of the reactions that have kept us anchored to the past.

It takes time to become willing to accept the feelings that come up for us when we face change. We have to give ourselves time to gradually let go of the past. But, as we give ourselves permission to feel and let go, the changes heal us and carry us forward to a brighter future free of our old ruts.

✳✳✳

When we realize that we need not be bound by our old habits and reactions, a more positive self-image becomes possible. Limiting self-concepts such as, "That's just the way I am," can be challenged by consciously choosing to behave differently. The more we exercise the options we have to change, the greater this freedom to change becomes. Instead of a passive or defiant "That's the way I am" stance of the past, we can adopt an attitude of "This is how I choose to be today."

No matter how much a behavior may have helped us cope with the impossible in the past, does this behavior serve us now? If it doesn't, then it's up to us to become entirely willing to let it go.

We must remember that we are not in recovery to meet other people's standards — just our own. If we find that we aren't willing, today, to let go of some behaviors that we might ideally like to eliminate, self-honesty remains the best policy. We can ask our Higher Power for the willingness to change, if it is in keeping with our highest good. We can help ourselves become more willing by picturing alternatives to behaviors that remain in the way. Alternatives and the willingness to accept them will come.

If there are behaviors that we choose to keep, even though others may object to them, we are honest about this, too. Success is to be measured in terms of how well we can accept and live happily with ourselves. We want to live up to our own ideals, not other people's. With self-responsibility comes genuine independence. Codependent reliance upon the approval of others is gradually replaced by trust in the guidance we receive from our Higher Power. If we can accept ourselves and we are willing to live with the consequences of the choices we make, who's to act the judge?

We do, however, need to remind ourselves to come back to this step periodically to review our own progress. What may be useful and comfortable in our lives today may become excess baggage tomorrow. Recovery is a dynamic process of continuing change. Rather than a steep staircase we climb once, the 12-Steps are more like stepping stones that lead along a path we can follow, day by day. When we take Step 6, we have the opportunity to act, not react, as we choose to release or reaffirm behaviors. The freedom to choose is a blessing of recovery.

Exercises

Exercise 1: Dysfunctional Patterns and Low Self-Esteem

1. Review the inventories of special focus issues in Appendix II. Have any of these issues patterns impacted your life or your family?

2. Do any of the questions seem directed at you or at patterns others seem to perceive in you?

3. Are there special focus issues you are unwilling to relate to or even read? What are these?

Exercise 2: Addicted to Excitement

Some of the most persist character defects are the habits that keep us living "from crisis to crisis." Here are some exercises to track down and replace habits associated with crisis living.

1. Go over your daily routine activities from the time you wake up. Identify the areas and activities you tend to skip, skimp on, or neglect. Is your crisis-living the result of accumulated neglect?

2. Are you willing to become willing to re-orient your priorities so that this sort of crisis situation can be replaced with routine attention?
Example: I get up at about 7:30 a.m. I always take vitamins, drink coffee and meditate or reflect for half an hour. I brush my teeth, but I don't floss. I have no regular plan for dental care and I often put off or postpone appointments with my dentist. I tend to live from crisis to crisis in the area of taking care of my teeth. I want to become willing to give myself better personal care in this area of my life, even though I am not

*entirely willing today. I now have dental insurance that will
pay part of the cost of regular checkups.*

3. Review your communication habits. Identify situations in which
you tend to react with panic or aggression. What can escalate a conversation into a crisis?

What alternatives would change your communication style?

*Example: When there doesn't seem to be enough money, I feel
frightened. Last week, I shared my concern with my partner,
but he didn't seem interested. I mentioned how little money we
had for bills again during the week, but my partner changed
the subject. Last night, he wanted to go out to eat and I didn't
argue, but this morning, I snarled at him when he tried to help
me with something I was doing. I'm in the habit if underplay-
ing my fears and then getting aggressive later. I'm in the habit
of escalating minor irritations into fights when my fears seem
ignored. I can imagine myself showing more of my fear in my
communications, and not channeling it into later outbursts of
anger or hostility. I'm willing to push myself toward this new
personal ideal.*

4. Go over your outlook on life. Do you have moods that set up a
baseline for generating a crisis? Can you visualize yourself going through
your daily activities free of these moods?

*Example: I wake up calm, but I often slip into worrying soon
after. I am tense and anxious a lot, no matter what is going on.
Sometimes I eat to feel calmer, and then I feel angry at myself
about that. I sometimes feel like I'm in a crisis when there's
nothing going on but my own inner fears and the anger I direct
at myself. I can imagine myself feeling calm and having trust in
my ability to work things out in life because when I remember
to meditate and turn my life and my will over to the care of my
Higher Power, I do feel much calmer. I am willing to have the
habit of worrying removed and replaced with greater serenity
and trust. I will say the Serenity Prayer when I notice myself in
my old worry rut.*

5. What patterns of behavior show up in relationships you create? Do
certain kinds of crises reoccur in some, or all, of your relationships? Are
you willing to release the codependent patterns that keep you hooked to
these crises?

*Example: I make friends with people I meet in recovery. I want
to build lasting friendships, but often the other person may not
be willing to make — or to keep — commitments. When others
have less commitment to a relationship than I do, I often create
a crisis by expressing strong feelings of betrayal and hurt. I
can see that I am trying to control the other person with my
anger and pain — a codependent pattern. I'm willing to release this character defect. Instead of creating a crisis by*

venting my feelings to the person who has disappointed me, I
can express them to a sponsor. I don't have to stuff my feelings,
but I don't have to throw a tantrum to express them either. I am
willing to stay in touch with my heart when I speak, even when
that's painful.

Exercise 3: Draw a New You

1. Draw a picture of yourself (or start with a photograph) exactly as you are today. Show the way you feel by the expression on your face, the body language you display, and the colors you choose.

2. Modify your picture by drawing or pasting images and symbols around you to show how you are living. Show the things that are in your way in life by placing them in front of you, or in between you and a goal you'd like to reach.

3. Now, modify your image so that it becomes free of any personal or social habits you are entirely willing to have removed. Redraw, trace or start with another photo and show how it looks to be free of these habits.

4. If the things that were in your way are removed, show how it feels to reach your goal, using color or whatever you choose to express the feelings that come up for you.

Exercise 4: Change Something

A backwards way to work Step 6 involves changing a few harmless behaviors as an exercise in finding out how it feels to let go of a habit. Often, changing simple, innocent habits can create a chain reaction that begins to break up denial when a habit may mask a hidden liability.

1. Change the way you do three of the things you do every morning. If you always sit in one chair to eat breakfast, sit in a different chair on the other side of the table. Change which shoe you put on first. Change what you say when you greet your mate (or your goldfish). Change any three harmless acts. Keep up the changes for a week. Notice how it feels to alter a habit, and what thoughts and memories come up for you. In a safe situation, talk about your feelings and the thought associations you experience.

2. Go back to doing things as you did before. Keep that up for a week before deciding whether to stay with the old or go with the new. What were the other habits that were linked to the habits you changed?

3. Try this exercise again, changing three different innocent behaviors that are part of your routine at work or socially.

4. Try it again, changing three simple habits of self-care or personal priorities.

Exercise 5: Saying No

If we have admitted that we are addicts or codependents, we have acknowledged that there are at least some patterns that we have found impossible to say no to on willpower alone. For this reason, when we say we are entirely willing to see a bad habit removed, we may find it hard to believe ourselves. A good way to build up our credibility is to practice saying no to behaviors we are willing to let go of. If we're going to be changed by the process of recovery, we need to be able to believe in ourselves. Here are some exercises to build confidence in our sincerity:

1. **Saying No to Active Behaviors.** When we are entirely willing to stop doing something, we can say no by resisting going through with the action, whatever it is. Say *I am entirely willing to have this bad habit removed* and take several deep breaths until the impulse to do the act passes. It may be helpful to do another action that is positive, instead. Active bad habits can be defined as any behaviors you would like to eliminate. Examples might be impulse buying, snacking, aggressive driving, or nagging other people.

2. **Saying No to Passive Behaviors.** If you are entirely willing to break habits of neglect or habits of putting up with unacceptable behaviors, practice saying no by taking assertive action. Say *I am entirely willing to have this low self-esteem behavior removed* and take a step in positive, direct action. Examples of passive bad habits include neglect of personal health, non-assertive withdrawal, depression, appeasement, listening to gossip, letting your rights and values be trampled on, or failing to share your ideas.

3. **Saying No to Negative Thinking.** If you are entirely willing to have a self-defeating pattern of thinking removed, practice saying no to this pattern every time you notice it. Say *I am entirely willing to have this negative thinking habit removed* and actively switch your thinking to something positive. Picturing a simple image like a fragrant flower or a bird in flight can be very helpful and quick. Affirming something that anchors a feeling of security in your Higher Power's care is also good, such as, "I am safe in the care of God," and can break up ruts of worry and fear of other people. Examples of negative thinking include worrying, rehearsing conversations, self-attack thoughts and thoughts of "showing someone" or "getting even."

Questions to Ponder

1. What old behaviors that used to serve you don't work any more and are now in your way?

2. If you let them go, stopped doing them, what might happen?

3. What do you want for yourself instead of your old habits, behaviors, or attitudes?

4. Is it worth the risk to let go now?

Personal Sharing

I remember the day a therapist took us through a group inner child exercise. We each went back to our home of origin and found our little child. We then had the child pack her things and asked her to leave with us. My little girl was playing in her room down on the hardwood floor all alone. She smiled when I entered the room and knelt down to give her a hug. She was beaming as she grabbed her baby doll to take with her. She took my hand and skipped down the hall and out the front door.

We had to walk past my family who had gathered on the front porch to tell us goodbye. She didn't want to hug anyone. She just kept skipping away, never looking back. The therapist's voice reached out to me, telling us to move on away from this place and look down the road to see who was waiting to greet us.

I heard a voice loudly calling out to me, and I turned my head to look back. There stood my mother next to a little girl about seven years old. Tears streamed down the child's face as she called out to me, "Please don't leave me here with her. You've always taken care of me. She hates me. Who will take care of me if you leave me here?"

I heard the voice of the therapist insisting that we turn from our families and go with our child, down the road and around the bend. I felt a terrible pulling at my soul to go back and get my mother's little girl, but the therapist's voice said, "Don't go back! It's time to leave those people and move into the light of your new life. Look now, further down the road. We've got to get around this bend. Now look closely and see who is waiting to greet your little child."

I turned back to the road and felt my little girl's hand tightly grasping mine. As I looked around I saw Glenn, my husband, kneeling with open arms, waiting for us. My little girl ran freely to him. She threw herself into his arms and just hugged him and cried. As I approached them, I, too, got down on her level and was enveloped by their loving embrace.

This is where I remain today, with my little girl ever-present with me. I take care of her and protect her and we both remain close to those who want to love us. God has blessed me with an abundance of individuals who believe in me and want the best for me. Most of all they love me for who I am—Josie, a child of the living God.

Peace has entered my life, a serenity I never knew existed before. I still have the long journey to travel as do we all, but I'm not alone on that road. There are friends waiting to help me in times of trouble. They want to share the fun times, as well as the sorrows. Surely I am not alone. I feel so blessed and at peace with God and with who I am.

—Josie E., Dallas, TX

The Hurt

I wear my sadness
Like a shroud.
It is my death.

My skin is white
And pale and soft—
Underbellied—
Not tough enough.
Not enough exposure
To the sun.

I feel wrong. On guard.
Ready
For attack.

But I am safe in my cloak;
Dagger in its sheath.
Hidden in my hood,
I go into this world
Unseen.

If I unwrapped myself,
Who would
I be?

—Sue O., Summer 1989, Humboldt ACA

The Heal

STEP SEVEN

Humbly asked God to remove our shortcomings.

> *For the whole earth is a point, and how small a nook in it is this thy dwelling....*
>
> —Emperor Marcus Aurelius, Roman (121 - 180 A.D.)
>
> ✳✳✳
>
> *Dear God,*
> *Help me turn*
> *my stumbling blocks*
> *into*
> *stepping stones!*
>
> —Carol Ann F., 7/3/90, Vashon Island, WA

If we've managed to come this far in the Steps, we've learned much about ourselves. Probably we have discovered unsuspected assets in ourselves, as well as liabilities. We've started to use powerful new strategies for self-change in our lives. Now, in working Step 7, we are faced once again with the question of whether we still need a spiritual boost to see us through. Answering this question brings up the concept of humility, which is central to Step 7.

The purpose of Step 7 is not to rob us of confidence or to humiliate us as incompetent. The issue instead is one of balance. The concept of humility we are asked to cultivate in Step 7 is a genuinely positive quality, one that is potentially of great help to us. Step 7 asks us not to overcommit ourselves by relying too much on self-reliance. When we ask our Higher Power to remove our liabilities, we are giving Spirit a chance to become active in our lives.

Humility allows us to look at situations realistically. How big or small a task do we face? It also allows us to be honest about how powerful or weak we and our resources are in relation to that task. A professional consultant such as an engineer is actually being humble, in the sense that we mean it, when s/he says "Yes, I can build that bridge. We'll need these materials and helpers to do the job." The engineer is simply looking at the situation honestly for what it is. S/he doesn't gloss over the difficulties or inflate them. A competent engineer takes responsibility for knowing where to get what's needed to complete the job.

An unqualified person might try to bluff. They might underestimate the materials or fail to set up the necessary help. The project might fail and someone might get hurt. A bluffer deserves to lose credibility. In recovery, we are our own trustworthy experts. Humility is a tool that we need to cultivate so we can see our own situation clearly and realistically. We must reach out for whatever help we need to realize our vision.

In the previous Steps, we sized up the project. We learned to turn within, to draw upon our spiritual resources. As we learned self-honesty and self-acceptance, we probably began to trust ourselves, perhaps for the first time. What we have done so far stands as a foundation for the lives that we want to build. To the extent that we have gotten to know ourselves — with both strengths and weaknesses — we have learned humility as we mean it in Step 7.

Now we take a look at our liabilities and bad habits. We admit the limits of our present powers. What can we do for ourselves? Where are we stumped, powerless to change? As our own trustworthy experts, we need to know when to reach for help. If we were to try to rely on a bluff, the structure of our lives can become shaky. This is the spirit of balanced humility in which we turn to our Higher Power and ask God to remove our shortcomings.

✳✳✳

The asking for help in Step 7 isn't hysterical pleading, nor is it a matter of giving detailed instructions to God. Just as we have done our part in taking the Steps that lead up to this one, we now are asked to trust that our Higher Power will transform us for our highest good. Just as we've become willing to "Let go. . ." through the exercises in Step 6, we now take a deep breath and ". . Let God!" For Step 7 to be accomplished, we must actually release the shortcomings to God's care and will. The asking that occurs in Step 7 is grounded in the conviction that our Higher Power is present, available, and willing to mold our lives to our highest good.

As we grow in the inner perspective necessary for success in Step 7, we may notice a release of tensions that is directly physical, whether or not help with a physical problem is an issue with us. When we succeed in really "letting go and letting God," inevitably a burden is lifted from us. It is a good practice, for this reason, to link verbal practices of asking that our shortcoming be removed with the practice of techniques for relaxation. As we remind ourselves to associate a physical sense of relaxation with ". . . letting God," we can actively cultivate the healthy humility we seek within our bodies, as well as within our minds. We become more peaceful and serenely confident physically as agitation, tension and timidity within the body is released.

Relaxation practices need not be complicated to be effective. Taking in some long, slow breaths is a simple, effective practice. Other relaxing practices include taking a warm bath, listening to music, swimming, taking an unhurried walk or having a massage. Yoga and other disciplined approaches to relaxation are also fine ways to cultivate Step 7's harmonious release of stresses in body, mind and spirit.

✳✳✳

Another method for cultivating humility while building self-respect is to school ourselves to remember where we came from before we found recovery and to count the blessings we have already received. Techniques for developing an attitude of gratitude are easy to learn. If we are feeling inclined to take personal credit for all that we have accomplished since we started getting well it may be helpful to remember how we were at our first meetings. Were we confused? Frightened or in pain? Were we insecure in some ways that were utterly unacceptable? If we hadn't come into recovery, what might have happened? What happened to help us? Did that help come from self-sufficiency?

We want to contrast how we were with how we are, today. How much of this is due to what we've learned in recovery? We own the benefits we have already received from being in a fellowship along with what we've gained from tools we've learned to use in our lives. When we count the blessings we have gained and contrast these with the pain of what might have been, not only do most of us feel grateful but current difficulties may lose a measure of their terror and their sting.

It is humble to acknowledge the progress we have made. It isn't humble to minimize the positive change in our lives, nor is it humble to put ourselves down. These are very dysfunctional concepts of humility. They are tied to false ideas that our Higher Power wants us to humiliate ourselves, which just isn't true. When we rejoice in recovery, it's a form of praising and celebrating the presence of living Spirit in our lives.

Exercises

Exercise 1: The 10-Day "Worry-Loss" Diet

Here's a crash diet that really works — to eliminate unsightly lumps of worry or bulges of anxiety! Start with the character defects you have decided you are willing to have removed.

1. Ask God to remove each one of them, as it suits God's purpose for your highest good.
2. Visualize yourself handing over each and every defect on your list to the God of your understanding. Visualize yourself letting go.
3. Then, visualize yourself moving on to other things. Consciously shift your attention:—concentrate on an activity, think about a topic you are interested in—anything of interest, so long as it doesn't involve whatever was on your list.
4. For the next 10 days, practice abstinence from worrying about anything that was on your list. Practice a day at a time (or an hour at a time) in which you don't think about the character defects you have asked God to remove.
5. If you slip, simply go on. Shift your attention to something useful or fun. Don't worry — keep at it. It gets easier.

Exercise 2: Take a Deep Breath

To get into the habit of ". . . letting God," practice taking a deep breath, feeling the air filling up your lungs and then letting it out again slowly.

1. Say the Serenity Prayer, taking a deep breath between phrases:

> God, (breathe) grant me serenity (breathe)
> to accept the things I cannot change, (breathe)
> Courage to change the things I can, (breathe)
> and Wisdom to know the difference. (breathe)

Take two or three deep breaths after finishing this prayer.

2. Take a deep breath before asking, or answering, a question.
3. Take a deep breath before expressing a fear or a suspicion about the motives of another.
4. Take a deep breath before engaging in gossip.
5. Take a deep breath before asking for what you want. Remember to ask for all of what you want, and then take another two or three deep breaths after you have done so.
6. Take a deep breath any time you remember to think of it, anywhere you happen to be.

Exercise 3: Practicing Gratitude

To build an attitude of gratitude, review your progress in recovery on a regular basis — daily, weekly, yearly.

1. What situations are you free of today, as a result of your recovery?
2. What hasn't happened to you (or to those you love) that might have happened if you hadn't gotten into a 12-Step program?
3. What has changed for the better?
4. What or whom do you feel joy or love toward in your life today?

Acknowledge all these things and give thanks for them.

Center yourself by breathing into your solar plexus (the area just below your diaphragm) and let go. Feel how it feels. Take another breath. Feel. Let yourself explore this experience.

Questions to Ponder

1. How has recovery affected you and your life already?

2. What are some of the fruits of recovery you are experiencing now?

3. Do you feel you can trust the God of your understanding to mold your character?

4. Center yourself by breathing into your solar plexus (the area just below your diaphragm) and let go! Feel how it feels. Take another breath. Feel. Let yourself explore this experience.

Personal Sharing

In studying Jin Shin and other physical techniques for balancing the flow of vital force in our bodies, I have found the following exercises simple and useful.

1. **One-Brain Acupressure Exercise.** This is a way to release the emotional charge built up around stressful situations to take you out of the place of victim and bring you to a place of empowerment. Use both hands to apply a firm continuous touch to the places shown on the Pressure Points Chart (below) while you do the visualizing part of this exercise. Hold two fingers of one hand on your frontal eminences (pressure points on your forehead) and place all fingertips of the other hand over your occiput (base of your skull).

a. First, visualize the stressful situation as it happened from beginning to end, noting all the details. Imagine you are watching it from outside, as though it were seen through a window or on video. Take a deep breath and let it go.

b. Play the situation back again, once again noting all the details. But this time, let all of your senses come into play. Remember sounds, sights, smells, temperature of the air, feelings in your body . . . Allow yourself to be in the situation as completely as possible. Take a deep breath and let it go.

c. Play the situation back once again. This time, however, imagine the situation changed in any way you wish. You may simply change your attitude about it or you can completely change the details and outcome. The mind doesn't differentiate between what really happened and your new made up version; it just accepts. When we hold the acupressure points we are using for this exercise, the blood flow within the brain moves away from the reactive paths that already existed toward the center that is capable of creating new choices. This technique can defuse past situations and make new behavior patterns possible in similar, stressful situations.

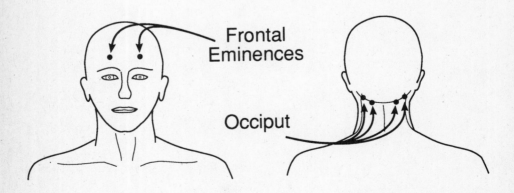

Frontal
Eminences

Occiput

2. **Rebirthing Breath Release.** Rebirthing Therapist Leonard Orr is the originator of this circular breathing technique. Books by him and others give more details on these techniques and, in many parts of the world, classes and therapy using these methods can also be found. This exercise is a powerful way to get a physical sense of release beyond just a mental visualization. The breath moves you from the mind into your body and emotions.

a. Build a rhythm of deep, fast, powerful circular breaths, not holding the breath in or out. Bringing it in and letting it fall away . . . when it is out, bringing it right back in again. Keep this powerful breath moving through you in a continuous circular manner for 15 minutes.

b. While you are breathing, allow yourself to move whatever it is you wish to release out of your body. Let any parts of your body — arms, legs, head — move freely as they are led. Allow your emotions to move your body. Feel the issues flowing out of you through your dance.

c. You can also bring into your body new, desired character traits or behavior patterns while continuing to breathe. Move them through your body — stepping, dancing forward in your new path and ways.

—Aradhana T., Arcata, CA

STEP EIGHT

Make a list of all persons we have harmed and become willing to make amends to them all.

The pain of one is the pain of all; the honor of one is the honor of all.
　　　　　　　　　　　　　—Native American proverb.

***

As much trouble is caused in this world by taking offence as by giving offence.
　　　　　　　　　　　　　—Morry S., Trinidad, CA

In Step 8, we undertake the work that heals our relationships with other people. This may sound like a very big order — and, for most of us, it is. Some of our personal relationships may have become the focus of frustration, heartbreak or confusion, perhaps for a long time. Indeed, some individuals entwined in our histories may have died or exited from our lives. Healing change may seem, at first glance, impossible.

Our purpose, however, in Step 8 is to build ourselves a gateway into a bright new world where functional relationships are possible for us. Working Step 8 is a spiritual undertaking, like all the Steps. We seek to bring a new dimension of spiritual understanding to bear in the relationships we have, or have had, so that healing becomes possible in us. Persuading other people is not the goal of Step 8, and we are careful not to take on that responsibility. We remind ourselves that, in a spiritual universe others, too, have the option to heal, if and when they are willing to accept that option. We keep the focus on clearing our side of the street, even as we reconsider the feelings and needs of those we love, and we trust the outcome of our efforts to the care of our Higher Power.

***

Just what do people have a right to expect from each other, anyway? In the 12-Step programs of recovery we accept ourselves as being worth healing, as the spiritual children of a Loving Parent. As worthy, valued individuals we have spiritual rights including the rights to feel secure, accepted, cared for and appreciated. The promise of recovery is the promise of having these deep basic needs met, by the action of God as we understand God in our lives.

Just as we joyfully claim and affirm these rights for ourselves, we must, logically, affirm them for others — all others — whether we are acquainted with them or not, whether we like them or not. If any of us has the right to heal and be whole, then each of us has that same right. Human beings harm each other in direct relation to how much they ignore or lose sight of this underlying spiritual common ground.

All relationships, then, are at core spiritual connections between spiritual beings. As people with God-given value, we can expect to have our basic worthiness acknowledged in the many forms of care and support we receive and give to others. If we are tempted to deny this, we remind ourselves that, though these expectations may not always be met by others, it is still our right to have them. Self-respect and respect of others are really other names for acknowledging the God-centered nature that's within us all. In practical terms, however, unreleased anger or fear tends to cut us off from feeling our underlying connection with some individuals or groups. Nothing is to be gained by denying such blocks where they exist; the path free is the path through. (See Exercise, "Releasing Terror & Rage," in this chapter.)

We receive practical survival-help, guidance, affection and/or companionship from others. This starts before we are even born, or we wouldn't survive. What we do for each other ranges from a little to a lot, depending on the relationship involved. In turn, we are instruments in the lives of others. Acknowledging some degree of spiritual "common ground" is implied in every contact with others. All interactions involve honoring each other's spiritual identities.

***

Of course, we don't have the same degree of responsibility toward all people in our lives. Neither do all people have the same degree of responsibility toward us. Personal commitments and responsibilities depend on the kind of bonding we feel, along with other more contractual responsibilities. Parents, for example, not only usually feel deeply bonded with their children, but a contract of responsibility exists from the moment of birth, which is in part enforceable by law and is a powerful social custom. Among friends, employers and employees, however, our connections include a mix of stated and implied agreements worked out in advance or over time. Greater and lesser degrees of intimacy depend on factors such as how much trust and contact exists. We also have many brief or superficial contacts with others — store clerks, public figures, neighbors — where not much bonding is felt. What we get from them or give them is more or less a matter of routine — a smile and money in exchange for goods, applause for a song.

We all vary in our relationships. One person may be deeply bonded with people or pets, while another may be surrounded by generations of relatives. Some may feel a strong sense of obligation and commitment toward family members, even if all feelings of bonding are strained or broken. Some acknowledge only a very few strong connections—one or two relationships—and prefer to have only superficial contact with everybody else. What satisfies and fulfills one person may seem bleak fare to someone else.

How, then, do we determine what is reasonable to expect, of ourselves and others? What do we say to those who vocally insist we owe them, whether we like it or not? Where do we draw the line?

One of the goals in Step 8 is to develop a sane present perspective on the relationships we have, and have had with others. What's needed is a spiritual standpoint that makes it clear, at least to us, where we stand in relation to others. If we don't have this, we can only guess at our responsibility — or remain a pawn to the demands of others.

In Step 8, as in all of the Steps, we focus on our own experience, and we review the boundaries of intimacy and commitment we learned and rehearsed growing up. However fuzzily they may have been stated or understood, we did learn some boundaries and limits on what to expect from others in our family system. What were they? And did we get what we needed to be whole and healthy spiritual beings by using that set of rules? Were our spiritual rights to feel loved, nurtured, included and recognized respected and celebrated — or were they violated, neglected, denied?

✳✳✳

We come to see the spiritual underpinnings of each one of our relationships more clearly, past and present, if we imagine ourselves at the very center of a circle that includes all of our relationships. Everyone in our circle is a valuable, unique spiritual being. No matter how distorted our relationship may have become due to the effects of addictions, compulsions or codependencies, this is still true.

If we are willing to think of ourselves as having entered life at the center of such a circle, grounded in universal goodwill, we will be able to evaluate our relationships, thinking in terms of what we had a reasonable right to expect, and of what we did, or didn't get. All those within our circle, we think, have some degree of responsibility to us, and we to them, even if it's only to acknowledge our mutual right to be alive.

Our job in Step 8 is to determine the boundaries separating the different kinds of relationships we have and have had, to admit where we've been let down or where we have failed others, and then to become willing to act in the present based upon this new perspective. We aren't dependent upon others in doing this. From the center of our own circle, we are free to investigate and to act — whether others do or not — to heal our circle of relationships.

Let's look at the kinds of relationships we have as human beings. First, there were those who were our primary caregivers — our parents or those who took that role. We had the deepest need and right to expect unconditional love, nurturing, guidance and companionship from these individuals from the very beginning of our life. Later, as parents, we become the primary caregivers to our own children and in some respects to our partners. From these relationships we gain or fail to gain the strongest validation of our authentic selves. This is our primary circle.

Beyond the boundary of these primary contacts, but still very intimately involved in our lives, are trusted intimates — siblings, grandparents or others who are deeply committed to us. Trusted intimates have a great influence in our lives, too. They are expected to give us practical help as well as dependable loyalty. Although they are committed to us, they aren't our primary caregivers. They have other responsibilities and interests that we must recognize and accept. If these limits become blurred, issues of authority and abandonment result. As adults, our trusted intimates probably include our closest friends and family members who are committed to stick with us.

Outside the boundaries of this circle there are those who have some influence on us—aunts, uncles, cousins, family friends and, later, the friends we make for ourselves.

These are secondary, extended family relationships. Limits of commitment in these relationships vary, depending on a range of factors including which ethnic group we identify with. Generally, these people aren't responsible for meeting our material needs, except for perhaps an occasional helping hand. Mutual loyalty and companionship are the important responsibilities in this circle. So are shared activities and voluntary cooperative efforts. As adults, relationships we form at work, church or other places where interests are shared may become, in effect, part of our extended family ties. We practice recognizing, negotiating, and respecting each other's limits and boundaries in this circle. If we lack an extended family growing up, then we may tend to isolate ourselves from groups as adults. We may also confuse the companionship of shared activities with deeper commitments. This can lead to social confusion. Overcommitment, inappropriate disclosures, and/or a tendency to impose, overreact to or flee from social stresses can result.

Finally, there is a fourth circle, made up of non-intimate elders and authorities in our community. These are our role models. They inspire our confidence and respect. Teachers, doctors, ministers, and heros such as athletes and public figures are within this circle. Although little day-to-day companionship may be involved in these relationships, we still learn from them. We give respect and learn to earn respect through relating to these leaders and the ideals they represent. If our family system boundaries cut us off from or restrict our identification with this fourth circle, we may feel we are part of an underclass group.

✳✳✳

Now we reflect on our own situation—our family and other relationships. Did we have all four kinds of relationships growing up, or were there some holes? What about today? We're interested in seeing just what we learned, or missed, about receiving and giving care, support and recognition in our childhood environment. It may be helpful to create a chart, like the example on the next page. Substitute the actual relationships you did have, in each layer, with real names, rather than categories.

Sample Relationships Chart

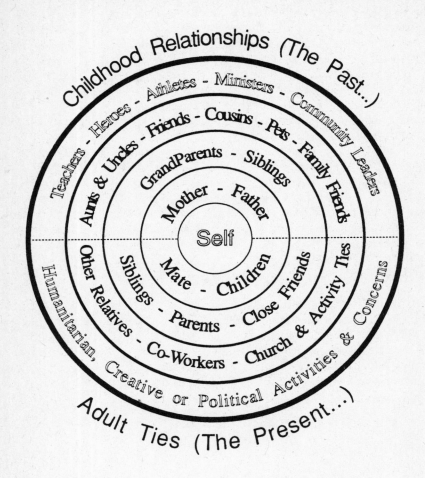

Childhood Relationships (The Past...)

Teachers - Heroes - Athletes - Ministers - Community Leaders

Aunts & Uncles - Friends - Cousins - Pets - Family Friends

GrandParents - Siblings

Mother - Father

Self

Mate - Children

Siblings - Parents - Close Friends

Other Relatives - Co-Workers - Church & Activity Ties

Humanitarian, Creative or Political Activities & Concerns

Adult Ties (The Present...)

Levels & Limits of Care & Responsibility

Sample Relationships Chart

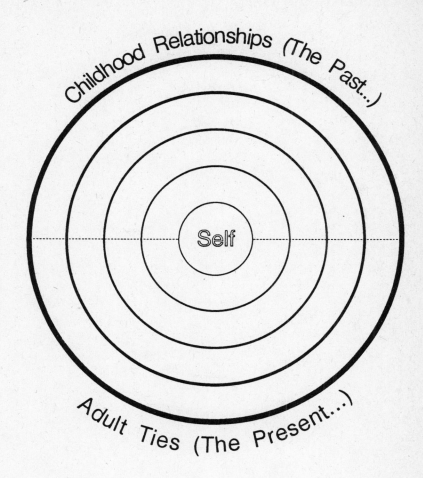

Levels & Limits of Care & Responsibility

Sample Relationships Chart

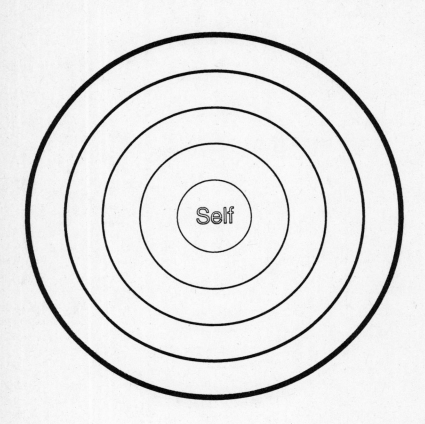

Levels & Limits of Care & Responsibility

If we see that our primary circle was weak—parent(s) absent, toxic, or abusive — did someone else (a grandparent, sibling, babysitter) act as a primary parent? Did a parent demand that we take care of them, and do we now avoid commitments or continue to lose ourselves in others? Did we learn to do without intimacy? Are we still practicing that pattern, by withholding ourselves from those who have a right to be closest to us? Who are we the primary caregivers for today? Are we a consistent source of unconditional love to them?

In our childhood, was there a shortage of trusted intimates? Were we socially isolated, or did we become vulnerable to peer pressure? Did we instinctively try to fill holes in the family by over-depending on friends or community role models? Were we, as a result, rejected or used? Are we still inclined to impose or to set ourselves up to be used in close voluntary relationships? Are we workaholics or otherwise inclined to escape human contacts with compulsive activities? Or have we become, in effect, users ourselves, terrified of commitments?

Did intimates vent frustrations upon us, break promises, lie, or use up resources that, by right, should have been used to nurture us? Are we, as a result, suspicious, selfish, manipulative or unavailable?

Do we see where unresolved stresses within a dysfunctional family—severed ties, lapses of contact or communication, long-distance moves—cost us the support we deserved within an extended family or in the larger community? Did family secrets cut us off? Have we been inclined to continue those patterns, functioning as loners, or lacking the skills to clear up conflict or repair a damaged sense of trust?

Layer by layer, as we take time to place each name where it belongs within our circle, we begin to see where patterns of distorted, misunderstood responsibilities between ourselves and others have contributed to hurt and bitterness in our lives and in the lives of others. Some relationships are, admittedly, confusing or complicated. Some people who may have been very close to us during one phase of our life—for example, former sweethearts, childhood friends—may later have become less important or drifted away. If we are unsure where an individual fits in our life-circle, now or in the past, we ask our Higher Power to show us. If we are willing to allow our Higher Power to restore sanity to our circle of relationships, the guidance we need will come to us.

***

If, in reviewing our family ties, we see that we were born into a family system where the boundaries between the various circles of caring weren't understood, or became blurred, it follows that we too, became confused. To some degree, we have lost touch with our authentic spiritual inner self. Without a strong sense of our own inner identity, we probably adopted the dysfunctional family system, whatever it may have been, even though we may have instinctively rebelled or tried to escape. As dependent children, we remained enmeshed, involuntary trainees, learning the family rules that infected our whole circle of caring relationships. We later, as adults, become the perpetrators of these or similar patterns in the lives of others.

Fortunately, the 12-Steps of recovery give us an opportunity to learn and to practice new, healthy patterns. We can be free, even if our family or social histories happened to be disastrous. As we become clearer on what we received and did not receive in our childhood relationships, we can finally grieve these losses and injuries — perhaps for the first time. In giving ourselves the opportunity to be honest about these wounds and about our feelings, we finally are able to reclaim our authentic self, the Inner Child within.

We may have been gravely deprived or hurt then, but now in this phase of our recovery we realize that we need no longer depend upon those people, whoever they were or were not to us. We are free to turn within, to our Higher Power, and to ask that these deepest needs be met at last. We ask that even unmet needs and distortions going back to infancy be healed in us, and that our Inner Child be freed now, to live in the present. We have always had this spiritual right, but now, in Step 8, we have the clarity and faith to begin to claim it.

As we become willing to grieve and be healed by spiritual power, we discover a path out of the maze of vain attempts to fill old, unmet needs by unfairly burdening present relationships. We cease living life as confused, enmeshed victims, and begin living as whole people and adults.

✳✳✳

From this standpoint, as people who are no longer victims, we reconsider those who have harmed us, past and present. Without justifying their misbehavior or neglect, we consider how they, too, may have been spiritually lost, addicted, confused, or misinformed. These people were also the hapless victims of addiction or codependency — perhaps without ever seeing a way out of the maze.

Haven't we been harming these people by blaming them for not giving us what they didn't have or know how to give? Now that we have found a sane perspective and a way of life for ourselves, are we willing to let go? Wrong and hurtful as they may have been (or still may be), our bitterness is like a chain that binds us to dysfunction, whatever form it took.

We need to recognize our needs as valid and ask God to see them filled. Without denying what we needed and still need, we are free to detach ourselves from other people's abusive or neglectful behaviors, and to hand the relationship over to the God of our understanding so that we are healed. Manipulation of others, or overcoming their resistances and denial isn't our role. They, too, are free to adopt a spiritual point of view. That's their choice. Our responsibility is to own up to our end of the relationship, and become willing to do our part.

We are free to ignore dysfunctional family rules without being in any way disloyal to the genuine bonds and ties we have with our loved ones. We honor what is genuine in our relationships as we continue to live our daily program free of the distortions of addictive or codependent relating.

As we become willing to stop harming others with our blame and hatred, we may find a flood of sadness stored behind the barriers we built with fear and anger. Even a great flood of dammed up feelings, however, may be seen as a symptom of our healing, like a storm that brings a long-parched desert into bloom at last. At this stage of our recovery, we realize that we no longer need to hold on to old fears and anger to protect ourselves. In the care of our Higher Power, if we are willing to release the chains that bind us to the past, we can go on to live a free life.

Finally, we consider those who we admit have been our victims. Perhaps we will see where we have been neglectful or selfish, or have tried to impose upon others for care that was inappropriate or impossible to give. Perhaps we've been so needy and hopeless that we have stolen from our friends or family, or so insecure and threatened that we've lied and deceived to protect ourselves. We may see where we have perpetuated patterns of abuse, contempt, or rejection in a desperate attempt to keep control.

Reflecting on the whole fabric of our past and present relationships, we ask ourselves if we are willing to rebuild each of these relationships as is appropriate, acting as a sane and spiritually centered adult. Perhaps we will not have a clear plan for making amends yet, but that should not stand in our way. The question we face in Step 8 is: are we willing? If we are willing to make our amends and to accept — and live — from the sane perspective of our recovery in our relationships from this day forward, we can trust our Higher Power to provide us with the guidance and opportunity necessary for success.

Exercises

Exercise 1: An Inventory of Harms

Reexamine the materials from the 4th Step Inventory, placing each name on the Relationship Chart, in this chapter, as a childhood or adult relationship. Setting aside any injuries done us by these people, we now list the kinds of harms we have done each of them:

1. **Violence.** Have you physically or verbally attacked this person? Intentionally threatened them? Betrayed a confidence in gossip? Told lies or presented a distorted version of events to make them look bad?

2. **Imposition.** Have you tried to make this person feel you were their only resource? Have you deceived them or tried to make them feel guilty or ashamed in order to get them to do something for your pleasure or gain? Have you lied about how you feel or how you see them to get them to give you something?

3. **Control.** Have you set up a system of rules to keep yourself on top with this person? Has getting this person to do things your way (the right way) led you to lie, conceal facts or feelings? Have you withheld things or denied your true feelings to try to force compliance?

4. **Rejection.** Have you treated this person like a throwaway, someone whose existence meant nothing to you? Have you ridiculed this person? Have you created a clique that is basically a hate group directed at this person? Have you justified taking this person's things or cheating him/her?

Exercise 2: We Only Harmed Ourselves

After we've completed the Relationship Charts, we may notice some holes in our circles of intimacy (or see that we have magnified one level of commitment to make up for holes in other areas). By avoiding some levels of commitment to others, who's been hurt? Have we been so preoccupied with some relationships that we've been distracted from accomplishing some of the goals for which we have a valuable talent or an aptitude? Have we harmed only ourselves or have we made the lives of others a little or a lot poorer as well?

Talents wasted, joys not shared, misunderstandings not cleared up — these are among the large and small omissions that separate a poor life from a rich one. What could we have been putting into life — and what has that loss meant, at least potentially, to others or to our community? Each of us can only answer these questions for ourselves.

1. Of the four circles — Primary, Other Intimates, Extended Family, Non-Intimates — is there one or more kinds of relationship you skimp on or lack? Which one(s)?

2. Imagine yourself living a day, week, month of your life with only the kinds of relationships you are now avoiding or neglecting. What kinds of conversations or interactions do you imagine? What feelings do you experience? Do you dread these contacts or want them but feel you are obliged to forgo them? Take 20-30 minutes, and give yourself permission to say, think and feel anything that comes up without restrictions.

3. Write a short play, poem or create some art with yourself as the subject as you imagine life would be with only these relationships in it. Share this creativity with someone and talk about your feelings or fantasies about these kinds of relationships.

4. Based on your writing/art and sharing, develop a plan for adding these relationships to your life. What will you have to do, learn, change in order to make this happen? Or are there kinds of relationships (or activities) that take most or all of your attention, time and money that you will have to cut back on? How will you benefit? Which others will benefit?

5. If you are resistant to making a definite commitment of time to putting this plan into action (Step 9), consider whether unreleased fear or rage is at the root of your unwillingness. Do the names of specific individuals come to mind from the past? Memories of embarrassment or abuse? Ask your Higher Power to give you the guidance needed to release these memories and the strength to take initiative in reclaiming this aspect of relationship-healing.

6. Are you tempted to justify avoiding certain kinds of emotional risks by thinking you are hurting only yourself? Do you abandon people or break commitments to shield yourself from real or projected possible problems? Are you complacent about being shy, timid, or sensitive?

7. Do you justify these behaviors or reject those who give you critical feedback about them? Which social circles are most affected — Primary, Other Intimates, Extended Family, Non-Intimates?

8. Imagine yourself acting brazen, aggressive, or coarse (or whatever you imagine is the opposite of shy, timid, sensitive). What feelings come up? Memories?

9. Draw a picture of an incident you remember when you were hurt, battered, humiliated. Write a news story about the terrible thing that happened to the innocent child (you) to go with the picture. Name names and put in all the facts. Tell how unfairly the perpetrator acted. Make sure you interview the victim (you, the child) and put down how angry and outraged s/he feels.

10. Paste the picture and the story on a large piece of paper, and write a headline at the top, in bold block letters, "Extra! Extra! Read All About It! Rotten So-And-So Exposed!" Imagine this story appeared on the front page of the newspaper in the town where you grew up and was read by everyone. Imagine the feedback and support you got from the community.

11. Share your story with someone. Take your Inner Child through this exercise, as though you were reentering the incident, in the here and now, and living it this way. Leave the guilt where it belongs!

12. Take action to overcome shy, timid or sensitive demands you are making on present relationships due to these old injustices.

Exercise 3: Emotional Clearing—
Releasing Terror and Rage

If we are honest with ourselves, many of us have to admit that we are deeply unwilling or unable to forgive and forget some incidents. They may have been too devastating, humiliating or lasting in their effects—or they may be ongoing behaviors, still a threat and a source of irritation in our lives. We may feel rage or terror every time we think of some people, or so defensive we behave as automatically as wind-up toys whenever we encounter them. Not only do we find we can't wish away these reactions, but we feel like we don't even want to!

What's to be done? Are we up against a limit to the healing possible for us in recovery? Do the bad guys win—leaving us permanently the prisoners of our terror or fantasies of revenge—and prove we're still the same old victims, poisoned by our own spite, envy, and vengefulness?

Without willingness to try some new behaviors ourselves we are stuck. But if we're open-minded enough to try some new tricks, our situation is far from hopeless. Fear and rage, we remind ourselves, are not just mental experiences; they have a physical component which is bound up with certain chemical processes in our bodies, triggering involuntary fight or flight reactions. We can't just think them away! We have to release them, physically.

Here are some simple and effective exercises for gradually releasing physical components of terror and rage. Don't be afraid that you are hurting the actual person when you do any of these exercises; these aren't intended as voodoo. You are only releasing the anger that is trapped inside you.

1. **Sock It To A Pillow.** Beat, kick, punch, and/or strangle a large cushion or pillow. See it as a specific person you are mad at and imagine you are hitting or kicking that person. If you have privacy — scream, cry, call the person names. Direct all the rage, fear and frustration that's in you at that pillow. Keep it up until you feel a release, or, if that doesn't come, for at least 3-5 minutes.

2. **Chop It Up.** If you have a woodstove, release terror and rage by naming some of your pieces of wood, and then chopping them into kindling! Or name some celery sticks or carrots and chop them up into bits. This is especially helpful in releasing irritation in on-going relationships.

3. **Kill A Picture.** Draw a really ugly, exaggerated cartoon picture of whomever you fear or hate. If you are mad at a bureaucracy or other non-person, make a cartoon monster out of them. Use strong colors and let out lots of physical energy while you make the picture. Take 5-10 minutes to make this as detailed and as ugly as you can, but don't put yourself in the picture. Then, crumple the drawing up. Throw it across the room. Jump up and down on it. Scream and swear at it. Tear it up, shred it, burn it to ashes. (Do this until you feel release, several times, if necessary, or combine this exercise with the Pillow exercise, above.)

Exercise 4: Loyalty and Intimacy

1. Referring to the Victim Roles Wheel and the Freedom Wheel, (Appendix 1), ask yourself what the difference is between Imposition and Support, and between Dependence and Trust. Be as specific as possible. What is different about what gets said, body language, possible repercussions, etc.?

2. Review your experiences in childhood and as an adult with these issues as your focus.

3. Imagine you are surrounded by a sphere of protective, healing light, and deepen and expand this review to include all of your feelings, along with the memories.

4. Have you had experiences where you had to choose between honoring your Inner Child's real values and sticking with an important person in your life?

5. In each instance, how did you feel (a) toward the important person, (b) toward yourself, (c) toward the outsider?

6. As your own loving parent, rescue your Child from painful incidents in the past. Imagine you reenter the situation, exactly as it was.

Instead of being a victim, support your Inner Child as s/he expresses her/his feelings completely, stating her/his limits. Make sure those feelings and limits are acknowledged and respected. You can imagine any sort of help you need to make the situation safe.

7. Do you have a present sense of conflict between loyalty to persons and loyalty to principles in your life? How do you feel, right now, about this issue?

8. Develop affirmations which reflect your goals for loyalty and commitment for your life in recovery. (See Appendix 1 for help in creating affirmations.)

9. Draw or write down these affirmations and put them on your mirror or walls where you will see them.

10. Offer them to your Inner Child as tools to use to build a healthy new reality in recovery. Ask your creative Inner Child to guide you to live up to these values.

Questions to Ponder

1. Who let you down? Who hurt you? Who taught you to be a victim?

2. Whom have you carried these behaviors over to in your life? Whom have you let down, abandoned or abused?

3. Is there someone you can't forgive?

4. Is there someone you can't forget?

I am an adult child of an alcoholic and drug addict on a journey to a place within myself where forgiveness is moot. I believe that, through a process I am unable to fully explain or prove, I chose to be born into my nuclear family; I chose my father and mother. Similarly, I chose and continue to choose all of the people and circumstances that fill my life. Today I look at these circumstances and personal relationships as challenges or lessons that I have chosen, consciously or unconsciously, to engage in to attain my highest spiritual awakening.

As I view my past, I see my own pain and confusion. Throughout my life I blamed others for inflicting this pain. I felt I was unfairly treated, or insisted that I was the surprised victim of circumstances beyond my control. Now, I see more clearly. The people (parents, husbands) and the circumstances (death, suicide, addiction, divorces, illness) are not to blame. They were the instruments of my self-created divine plan of growth. They were the actors and stage setting that I chose. A good student does not blame the lesson-giver but is grateful for the lesson and takes responsibility for the need to learn it. The fact that my lessons were difficult attests to my need to learn them and the great potential they hold for my advancement. This theory also helps me to understand the phenomenon of repeat lessons. For if I choose to ultimately learn a lesson but refuse to learn it at one point in time, I will continue to choose similar people and circumstances to provide the opportunity again and again to learn it.

This brings forward a challenge to me, in a way greater than any other in my recovery. It is the challenge to fully accept myself and my life, which means an acceptance of the lessons I have chosen to learn. The challenge is to fully forgive myself for the misguided blaming of others and for the lessons unlearned and repeated. Perhaps the greatest effort must be expended in order to forgive myself for the suffering I have allowed myself to endure throughout these lessons.

In the past, I experienced pain because, in part, of my misunderstanding that people's actions or circumstances were directed against me personally, without my consent. A clearer perspective dictates that people's actions and the circumstances they created were not a personal vendetta against me. I chose the lesson and the other person cooperated in its execution. Within the lesson, the other person expressed herself in the highest way possible at the time. In fact, the person's actions were probably a manifestation of her/his growth process in lessons s/he chose for herself. Each situation or relationship brought to awareness lessons for one or all parties and a corresponding opportunity for growth and understanding.

At this point, I question the transformation of my painful feelings into judgments, such as blaming others, which requires a determination of what is or who is right or wrong. I need to and want to experience my feelings in every experience, but do I need to accept emotional injury that limits my future? Can I see other people's actions as their soul's attempt to move into a position of perfect spiritual awareness, the soul's innate perfection? If I can be accepting and grateful for these lessons and willing to learn and move on, there will be a change in my perspective. Like the vast open sky that allows storms to move in and through it without influencing its embrace of the next day's weather, I can allow myself to move through each lesson and to embrace—

without judgments or prejudices based on past experiences — future lessons. For like the sky, I remain, and the stormy experiences pass. With such an understanding, my choice is not to accept emotional injury for other people's actions. My choice is to set myself and others free from the past through an increased understanding of my life's process.

An important ingredient in forgiveness is release. In this case, I release the lesson, the lesson-giver and myself. Emotions that were present and helpful throughout the lesson need not be clung to when their usefulness has passed. Release is the final step. This is the magic that allows me to move on with maximum freedom to the next lesson in my progression in spiritual unfoldment. This, the substance that gives final form to the lesson well learned. The joy at the end of a long, hard road. The final gift that I give myself.

—Susan S., Springfield, Il.

Recovery

I weep for the sadness my soul has known
and leap for the Joy I have now

I honor the spirit inside of you
and the spirit inside of me

Side-by-side we have traveled this gnarled road
not sure of which turn to take

But the depth of commitment my soul has made
will be sure at journey's end . . .
it was rewarded with Sanity

—Carol Ann F., 7/28/89, Vashon Island, WA

STEP NINE

Make direct amends to such people wherever possible, except when to do so would injure them or others.

> *A newcomer asked me, "When am I going to get happy in this program?" I said, "Nothing to it. Just stop doing whatever it is that's making you unhappy. That'll do the trick."*
>
> —Clay S., AA "Oldtimer"
>
> ***
>
> *In recovery I no longer run to Mom—knowing she'll invalidate me. I also resist calling everyone who may be sympathetic, when my real motive is simply to stimulate my own outrage. As I remain unwilling to contribute to my family's dysfunctional dynamic, it ceases to affect me one day at a time.*
>
> —Charlie T., Humboldt ACA

Making amends—to ourselves and to others—in recovery always means taking appropriate action. Appropriate action, as defined in Step 9, is never manipulation or revenge, nor does it involve the loss of self-respect. Whether the end result is acknowledging a debt to be repaid or requires substituting honest communication for hurtful defensiveness or appeasement in a relationship makes no difference. Step 9 challenges us to act in ways that take courage. It also asks us to let our Higher Power guide us when it comes to timing our amends. If we are willing to meet the challenge of Step 9, our very willingness takes us to fuller selfhood of sanity.

In Step 9, appropriate actions are always actions that build self-esteem. Even when they may involve making a difficult choice or may not produce an immediate healing in our relationships, making amends still produces feelings which are deeply satisfying and empowering. When we act appropriately in Step 9, our actions are the acts of our recovered inner self. They are initiated in our hearts and carried out with the deliberate courage of a clear mind guided by a loving God. This is very different from merely making apologies or reacting to pressures.

There are three factors we must balance in each amends we will make.

1. All of our amends should reflect our own innermost values that we've identified.

2. When we make amends, we must stay within the healthy limits we have

established for ourselves.

3. When we reach out to others, we need to remember to honor and respect their boundaries and values.

Even though each of these goals is simple, putting them into practice can take some planning. If we have a plan, we'll feel more assured when we approach people. We will see Step 9 as a process with a beginning and an end. Not only will we be less inclined to approach Step 9 in a secretive or haphazard way, we'll be much less likely to skip over some people on our list or to drag the process on indefinitely.

Step 9 is the final act of the work we began with the inventory process. If we have worked the Steps leading up to this one, we will have a pretty clear idea of who we are and where we want to go with our lives. In Step 8, we made a list of those who were harmed by our old way of living. Now in Step 9 we consider what is appropriate to share with each of them, in terms of offering amends.

It's a good idea to go over our entire list with a sponsor or trusted ally as we begin this Step. Usually, it simplifies matters if we separate the list into several classes of people: those who are still a part of our lives; those who have moved on (or died); employers or other more or less impersonal authorities; those we still don't like.

There may be some on our list whom we have already approached — those with whom we have close ties or those whom we have felt a keen sense of remorse toward. In working a formal amends Step, we review what we have said and done already in these cases. Have our amends up to this point been in any way haphazard, self-attacking, appeasing, or manipulative? Have we honored the boundaries of others in making these amends? Have we been insensitive? Having worked all of the Steps that lead up to amends now, do we see anything that needs to be changed, reconsidered, or revised? We do ourselves and our loved ones a kindness if we reconsider positive new ways that recovery can impact these relationships.

Now, going on to others on our list, we consider how we can straighten out our end of the trouble. Are feelings still raw? Is a letter more appropriate than a visit? Is the timing right?

If we are considering amends where undiscovered secrets or criminal activities have been involved, it's desirable to discuss the whole matter with a sponsor before taking any direct action. What sort of crime or secret is involved? What role did addiction or codependent patterns have in the incident? Were others involved or would others be implicated if the whole matter came out? What is the path of greatest healing? It is wise to wait until clarity prevails before taking any drastic action in such cases. We need to listen for spiritual guidance so that healing, not added injury, comes from the amends we make.

In cases where we have slandered or abused the trust of others, especially those we still dislike, delay is practically never justified. Tempted as we may be to write off these wrongs, taking an easy way out really defeats the purpose of Step 9. We only retreat into old habits of isolation when we try to justify ignoring some of the people that we've hurt.

Our purpose in making amends is not to take the inventories of those we've hurt. We don't have to expose ourselves to further injury if they are unreceptive to spiritually centered communication. We are offering amends to acknowledge the ways that we have acted out or reacted codependently to them. When we do this, we are unhooking ourselves from those old errors that we now see clearly. If we are to move on, free of the accumulated burden of past errors, nothing short of direct action guided by a loving God will do. We have to live our recoveries so that our ideals become the substance of experience in our lives. Step 9 is the way we unify what we believe with who we are. "Faith without works is dead."

✳✳✳

We may be very willing to go ahead with the amends process but, as long-time victims, we may still be inclined to guess at what it means to be "normal" in some, or many, areas of living. We may feel that we lack the necessary footing to make balanced judgments. We may also lack confidence and be inclined to give in to the demands or opinions of others. How are we to decide between our own wishes and the pulls and tugs of others who may want more than we are prepared to give? We may wish that we could find some sort of formula for keeping our balance when it comes to interacting with others.

The Victim Wheels and the Freedom Wheel (Appendix 1) offer some helpful guidelines to separate codependent attitudes from those which are rooted in a healthy identity. It's a good idea to review any plan for amends by consulting the Freedom and Victim Wheels, to make sure that the planned action is free of manipulation, rejection, or appeasement. Also, on the following pages, two Wheels to illustrate good judgement versus judgmental reactions in Step 9 are included.

Judgmental Locks

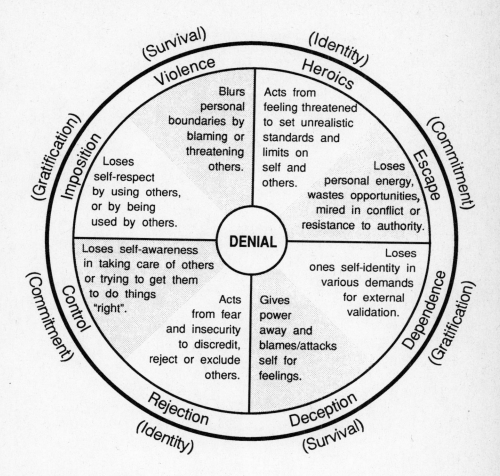

Good Judgment Keys

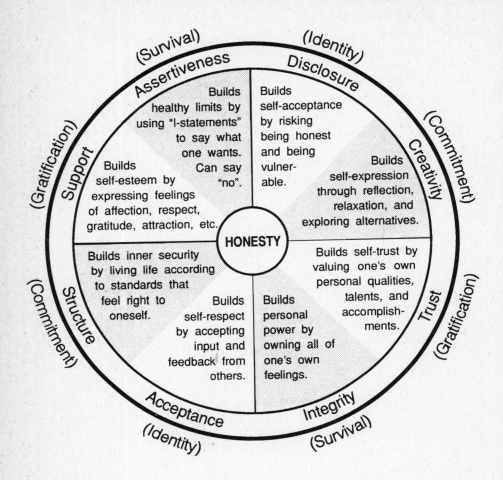

Notice that the exercise of good judgment produces actions which affirm strong, spiritually centered identities. Using good judgment means acting from a basis which is in touch with the principles we have today, but which leaves us room to learn something, too. When we become established in a genuinely functional way of dealing with life, we feel secure and not so threatened by others. The self-respect that doesn't depend on being "one-up" is rooted in this security. We feel independent, not isolated. We can care for people and appreciate them for who they are.

On the other hand, being judgmental is a fear-based reaction where we try to enforce our idea of what's right on others. Most often, we become judgmental when we feel threatened. Situations that put us in touch with losses of the past often feel confusing for this reason. When we are making amends with people who share painful history with us, it helps to stick with some definite communication goals, at least at first. If communication during an amends starts to feel threatening, affirming something positive can help. Sticking with "I" statements is also a good bet. Fear of other people tends to lessen as we get more comfortable communicating from our end. And as our lives and relationships begin to heal, making amends becomes a way out of trouble that feels good instead of a source of anxiety.

***

Finally, what do we owe ourselves, in terms of direct amends? For one thing, we probably had pretty limited ideas about what is desirable, or possible, for ourselves. It's likely that we've taken in some nasty, judgmental attitudes toward ourselves. Perhaps we've acted out the negative messages we got from others. For instance, while addicts are poisoning themselves with drugs or alcohol they are usually telling themselves that they are no damn good. Codependents tell themselves that they're to blame or that everything would be fine if only they were perfect. These ideas are poison, too.

Certainly we owe ourselves amends for all these putdown messages. Most of us will say that when we stop the abuse we are making amends to ourselves. Surely, this is true. But don't we deserve something more than an end to taking some form of poison? Aren't there some positive acts we can take to make up for having undercut ourselves?

If we missed out on something in life that we wanted, do we love ourselves enough to reach out for it now? Perhaps we want to go to college or we want to relate in a way that we've been afraid to risk before. Can we do it now? Or if it's something that can't be reclaimed, is there something else we want? If we are going to forgive ourselves for whatever we've lost or missed out on, we must actively seek to bring renewed joy and contentment to the lives we now create. If we ask our Higher Power's help, we will surely be guided on such a path. A most important amends we owe ourselves is our willingness to let go of limited ideas of what is possible.

Some of us will come to see that we were, indeed, very badly treated by others who, at one time, had power over us. What can be done about these old harms? Injuries from abuse, neglect, or lack of commitment from parents or mates may seem impossible to forgive. Maybe we've been victims of prejudice or discrimination. We don't try to justify the injuries others have done us in Step 9. That would be as unjust as trying to rationalize the abuses we have passed along ourselves. We don't go back into denial about the problems that really did exist and may still. But we need not leave these old tyrants in control of our destinies. Even if they remain sick or abusive, we can make amends to ourselves by beginning to draw our validation directly from God.

We perform a generous act of amends to ourselves and to those who have done us harm when we go ahead and heal. It's a kind act not to let ourselves be destroyed by the diseased actions of others. It's even kinder when we are able to fully embrace success as something we can accept in our lives. This is true, too, for the effects of social prejudices and abuses. When a healthy life becomes "normal" then we have healed, no matter how bad things may have been once. As we free ourselves, we also lighten the burden of those who let us down. This is a very kind thing to do.

We have only to claim success, joy, health, and abundance and turn to our Higher Power for it. As we do this—and it may take a little persistence to get used to the idea— we find that no one stands in our way. We may feel a measure of grief as we begin to give ourselves this new outlook on life. We may wish we had taken action sooner and not missed out on opportunities or wasted years of our lives. To some extent, feeling remorse is unavoidable if we've been making mistakes in our way of living. But we can do a lot to make amends for time we feel has been wasted by sharing our stories with others. Maybe someone else won't find it necessary to re-invent the wheel in the same way we have! In this way, even our failures become resources in the lives around us as we share ourselves in the fellowship of the spirit.

Exercises

Making amends means more than just admitting that we've made mistakes. Making amends means communicating—actually talking to people—sometimes to people we may not like and who may not like us much, either.

For those who have been conditioned to stuff feelings, to lose themselves in concern for the reactions of others, or to deny their own needs, undertaking to make direct amends in Step 9 may be entirely unfamiliar behavior. We may freeze and feel unable to speak, or we may draw a blank and forget what we have to say.

Practicing direct communication techniques in a safe setting, using the humor of exaggeration, helps. Here are some brief practice exercises to put an end to our shame-based communication in relationships. Do these with a sponsor or with others in a recovery setting. These are good exercises to use toward the end of a retreat weekend, to bring insights into greater focus by means of practice. Introducing humor tends to cement the spiritual to everyday reality as well as engage the Inner Child's delight. You may also do these on tape, in front of a mirror, and later go over your tape with a trusted ally. Since direct communication is the goal of these exercises, sharing them is crucial.

Exercise 1: No More Mr. Nice Guy

1. Think of an incident where you have not gotten what you've wanted from someone. Perhaps this will be an ongoing pattern with another person. It can be a big or a little thing, as long as it's something that you've appeased the other person about, denying your own needs.

2. Describe the other person's behavior to your partner (or describe it on tape). Describe your own past appeasement behaviors and what you have been afraid might happen if you asked for what you want from the other person.

3. Now play out the scene. Let your partner be the person you need to confront. If you are doing this with a mirror, play both parts and record the scene so that you can share it later. Tell your partner the lines to say or the actions to take. Walk right up to him/her and say, "No more Mr./Ms. Nice Guy! I want you to (fill in the blank) from now on!" Be sure to ask for all of what you want. Notice how you feel when you say this line. Are you able to say it forcefully, or do you whisper, choke up? It helps to use props to exaggerate the situation. You might have a white hat and a black hat, for example. Try coming into the room very quietly, looking at the floor, wearing the white hat and then throwing the white hat on the floor, putting on the black hat, stamping your feet and making eye contact when you say your lines.

4. Play the scene again. This time, have your partner act out what-

ever you were afraid might happen in an exaggerated way. If, for example, you're afraid that the person won't like you anymore, have your partner act out a charade of someone really not liking you—making faces, using body language to exaggerate the rejection in an extreme way. When they've finished, do a charade to show how you react to that kind of behavior, letting your feelings out. Be sure that no physical contact takes place in these charades. It's good to have some pillows or a chair that can represent people and to direct the actions at these.

5. Play the scene again. This time, stand on a chair when you say your lines and have your partner sit or lie on the floor. Use extremely dominating body language. Say your lines several times, louder and louder, until you are shouting them. How does it feel?

6. Play the scene again. This time, let your partner be you and you be the person to be confronted. Say what you'd like the person to say to you. Give yourself the experience of getting what you want. How does it feel?

Exercise 2: No Longer a Hostage to Hurt Feelings

1. Think of a relationship where you have been controlled by someone who claims to have hurt feelings whenever you tried to express your own feelings honestly. Describe their behavior and yours, as above, to a partner.

2. Play out the scene, as above. This time, say whatever you have to say in as mean a way as you can. Exaggerate it. Say it harshly. Say it loud. Use any words that come to your mind, including swearwords. Be completely unreasonable. Notice how you feel. What does the other person do, say? How do you respond?

3. Play the scene again. This time, wear a mask (or put a bag over your head) and say whatever you have to say. Perhaps you'll want to shout it from the next room, or speak with your back to the person. Does this seem easier? How does the other person react?

4. Trade roles with your partner and play the scene again. Act as you would like the person to act. Come out of denial. If this has been a person who has left (or died), have them return and respond as you would like them to respond.

Exercise 3: No More Walking on Eggshells

1. Imagine an incident where you have been controlled by fear of other people's anger. Describe this, as above, to your partner.

2. Play the scene, as above. It's good to have popcorn or crumpled paper (to represent eggshells) on the floor. While your partner remains passive, stomp on the paper or popcorn while you say whatever you feel like saying to the person your partner represents. Express your frustration. Express your love. Express all your feelings toward that person. Jump up

and down, making as much noise as possible, shouting what you have to say. Smash as many eggshells as you can. How does that feel?

3. Play the scene again. Use props such as water guns or shields, etc. This time, let your partner act out the behaviors you are afraid of. If, for example, you're afraid the person might blow up, have your partner act out a charade of someone literally blowing up using a balloon. Keep stomping eggshells while the other person acts out. If you have a water gun, you can shoot them, if you like.

4. Play the scene again, reversing roles.

Exercise 4: An End to Living Like Clark Kent

1. Maybe the real Superman had good reason to hide his identity under the unassuming disguise of Clark Kent, but most of us would like to get credit for the efforts we make. Imagine a situation where you do most (or all) of the work and don't get credit for it. It may be a situation where you are simply taken for granted or one where someone steals the show and focuses the attention on themselves. Share this incident with your partner, as above.

2. To do this exercise, it's good to have a superhero tee shirt to wear under a loose-fitting shirt or jacket. Batman, Wonderwoman, etc., may be substituted for Superman, so long as the character has a secret identitiy much of the time. (If a decal tee shirt isn't available, you can make one by pinning or gluing a large nametag to an ordinary tee shirt.)

3. Play the scene, as above, but this time imagine that you are doing so in front of a large audience or a TV news camera. Have your partner describe whatever achievement is involved, in detail, while you stand there. At the end of the story, throw off the shirt or jacket, revealing your superhero tee shirt, and say, "And it was me, (insert name of your super-hero), who did it all!" Notice how it feels to say this. (It's O.K. for anyone present to applaud.)

4. Play the scene again. This time, stand on a chair, table or ladder and tell the story yourself, in detail, wearing the teeshirt. Finish with the same line, as above. How does it feel to describe an achievement?

5. Play the scene again, reversing the roles. How does it feel to hear someone claim an achievement?

6. Play the scene one more time, with both you and your partner wearing superhero tee shirts.

Exercise 5: Self-Nurturing

1. Tell yourself you are welcome in new or stressful situations.

2. Give yourself the things you want to receive from others.

3. Make a list of what excites you, makes you feel loved, or inspires you. Put this list up where you will see it, and give yourself these

experiences.

4. Take a candlelight bath, or a bubble bath. Float some flowers in the water. Listen to favorite music while you enjoy the luxury.

5. Read a book you like.

6. Take yourself on a walk.

7. Cook yourself a tasty, nourishing meal.

8. Buy something just because you like it.

9. Do something that feels good.

10. Draw a picture (or take a photograph).

11. Do something you've been putting off.

12. Write yourself a love letter, and mail it to yourself.

13. Write yourself a forgiveness letter, or a commendation, and mail it to yourself.

14. Do something that might seem silly, or dumb, but FUN.

15. Buy yourself some flowers, or pick some from your yard.

16. Watch a sunset or sunrise with yourself.

17. Take yourself out—on a date, or to visit a friend.

Questions to Ponder

1. What appropriate actions can I take now to heal or repair the past?

2. Is this action free of appeasement or manipulation?

3. Is this action free of self-righteousness?

4. Is the timing right?

In personal relationships, there is a question those engaged in recovery must inevitably address, which is, "At what point does another person's dysfunctional behavior require me to take action to protect myself?"

In relationships, there is a strong tendency for intimacy to increase with time. However, dysfunctional patterns get in the way of intimacy, forming barriers against intimacy. There comes a point in time when the level of intimacy will no longer grow, without the removal of these barriers through working an active program of recovery. When the relationship has grown to the point where a deeper level of intimacy is called for than the other person's dysfunction will allow, the person in recovery must face whether to get out of the relationship in order to preserve their own serenity, or to hang in there, hoping that the desired changes will come in time.

There is only one real answer to this question. The hang-in-there approach is really only codependency and cosigning the other person's denial. The relationship can grow no further without some real recovery taking place. To indulge in theories to the contrary will only jeopardize one's own recovery. A good thing taken as far as it could go and left there is better than a good thing taken over the hill and dragged along for several miles after it has died. There needs to be a real commitment to recovery in relationships. Maintaining and enforcing this high standard isn't being judgmental or holier-than-thou; it's just setting limits that are compatible with sticking with recovery.

—Jim W., Eureka, CA

There's a part of me that's a baby in a high chair, eating mush. There's learning how to latch a button, standing on tip-toes to barely turn a doorknob, reaching out for something that was "no!" My first authority was a woman. I was putty in her hands…and Mama let me down.

My mom was deep in lies, so deep she lost us both in them: the happy ending fantasies that kept exposing me to violence and hopeless disrespect…the "you should feel" invalidations that twisted me to self-contempt…the endless games of "you guess how I feel"…

And still, she had my heart. I always wanted her to win those family fights. I stood by her—and she'd appease the raging fool she cared for more than me, and let me be abused. She'd turn on me and lie while I stood there like a tiny, soft-eyed fawn, betrayed. The next day, it would all begin again—pulling me back. Of course, I hated her. Mama was a bitch! And all the time, I had a sad, sick fear inside, that I was doomed to be just like her…

But, I'm glad to say, it hasn't happened as I feared. Thanks to reparenting, to recovery and to living by the Steps, Kathy doesn't have a childhood full of nightmares anymore. She's been rescued, healed…restored to sanity. Her history has been bathed in light so pure and golden it's become a kind of tapestry for her. Threats and tears and losses woven to a tale of hope…a tale of courage…finally, of joy…

I live now in the sun. My Inner Mom who loves me wears long braids and laughs like windchimes or like seagulls wheeling on the tide. The temple of my Inner Self remains a fearless place. Filled with sunlight, laughter, and the songs of birds...Knowing that I have a Mother now to trust...a Mother who will stay...

The cartoon is wryly sexist...and I smile. The woman in authority isn't me. I am a child among children, living a child's life of wonder. I'm secure enough today to smile as an adult. I love that silly, soft, confused and often sadly lost sweet woman who was there for me—sometimes—and sometimes let me down. There wasn't a program then, you see. And today, today there is...So, thank you, Mama, after all, for bringing me to this!

—Kathleen W., Eureka, CA

The Evolution of Authority

   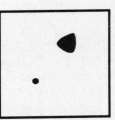

STEP TEN

Continue to take personal inventory, and when we are wrong, promptly admit it.

> *The idea that we can be possessively loving of a few, can ignore the many, and can continue to fear or hate anybody, has to be abandoned, if only a little at a time.*
>
> —*12 Steps and 12 Traditions*
>
> ✳✳✳
>
> *When it seems like the same things are happening again, it's important that I remember I'm not the same, vulnerable, three-foot-tall little person I was then.*
>
> —Brenda, Maui, HI

Step 10 is the first of three maintenance Steps in recovery—along with Steps 11 and 12. These three Steps encourage interlocking practices which help to safeguard our recoveries from complacency and forgetfulness. These Steps help us to stay spiritually fit, a day at a time.

The first one, Step 10, asks us to stay self-aware in the present. It also asks us to be willing to act in the present, based on our awareness. Step 10 serves to remind us that recovery is a way of life, not an event that happens and is left behind.

No matter what we learn, it seems true that we keep only what we practice. This is as true of the self-awareness skills we learn in recovery as it is of a tennis backstroke. In recovery from addictions, compulsions or codependency, we have to continue to build habits of self-scrutiny to be applied on an as-we-go basis. If we don't, old behaviors and attitudes—ruts worn by years of practice—soon begin to creep back into our lives. Our vision of personal freedom may quickly become blurred. Despite all insight and intentions to the contrary, we may find ourselves making the same mistakes all over again, reacting as we did before recovery.

As people in recovery, we have to learn to live life on life's terms. Life wouldn't be life if it did not include challenges, surprises, reminders of the past, even some sadness and tragedy. Daily events and the pace of life can chip into serenity, leaving us agitated, fearful, frustrated. Before our recovery, we may have had a front of dishonest behaviors we used to create a false appearance under stress, stuffing our honest feelings and disguising our motives. Now that we are no longer content to stuff our feelings or to lie to ourselves about our motives, we may feel unsure how to act. Do we act from feelings or not?

Of course, basing actions on purely automatic, impulsive reactions to daily events and stresses can get us into trouble. We come to realize more and more that feeling our feelings and acting them out on others are two entirely different things. Impulse may prompt us to react from fear, projection, jealousy, spite. Honest as these feelings may be, acting on them is likely to cause pain and confusion. Most of us, too, have personal sensitivities that make us more prone to react unpredictably. We may be inclined to justify becoming touchy and defensive in some areas.

If we are resolved to take off our stuffed-feelings masks and become more honest communicators in recovery, a process of trial and error may be expected. And any time we change and grow, we can expect to make mistakes.

In order to minimize the accumulation and impact of the wreckage of the present we create in our lives, we need to find ways to keep an eye on our own conduct. Working Step 10 helps us to take responsibility for both our successes and our failed attempts in the present. We learn to "take our own inventory" on an ongoing basis. We own our progress, as we admit and correct our failings and missteps. In doing this, we accept responsibility for monitoring our own conduct. As we become increasingly aware of our own vulnerability pitfalls, we find ways to walk around them in the present. Self-inventory provides a "self-rescuing kit" to get us back on the path that leads in the direction we choose.

✳✳✳

Self-inventory involves engaging in a kind of constructive self-criticism. Many of us feel fearful and defensive under any form of real or implied criticism, however, even if it's coming from ourselves. We may still have painful memories of criticisms being used against us, as justification for abuse or abandonment. We may not have a clear sense of the role constructive criticism plays in skill-building or in achieving goals.

Constructive criticism is a key factor in the learning process. When we establish a goal for ourselves — whether that goal is personal recovery or something more specific, say, learning to drive a car — then a strategy needs to be set up for achieving that goal. A goal without strategy and objectives for achieving it remains only a fantasy.

In the goal of learning to drive, talking about wanting to learn to drive is not a strategy for learning to drive. An effective strategy involves something definite, such as signing up to take a driver's ed. course. Driver's ed. is a strategy for learning to drive. If it's a good course, it will be laid out in a series of smaller objectives that are designed to help us move, little by little, toward our goal. If we want to succeed and become licensed drivers, we have to be teachable and make use of the feedback we get as we go along. Utilizing feedback, including feedback in the form of constructive criticism, is an important part of getting where we want to go.

In the 12-Step programs, our goal is sane and balanced living, and the program is a strategy designed to help us achieve this aim. The Steps are markers along the path, even though we each move independently and make our own choices. To stay on the path, we have to pay attention to how we progress. We still need to be teachable. We

118

need to give ourselves permission to claim our progress and validate our feelings. At the same time, we need to remain as objective as we can about how our behaviors match up with our recovery goals.

Developing the habit of constructive self-reflection does, admittedly, take practice. But once we accept the idea that this act of self-discipline is not intended as torturing self-attack, then we can begin to view Step 10 as an act of self-protection and personal care. Choosing to keep up a discipline we have taken on voluntarily builds self-respect and deepens self-trust. We come to experience ourselves as persons capable of commitment, which is a big factor for building confidence and personal security. Instead of a dreaded and dreary bout of self-attack, the reparenting we give ourselves in Step 10 gives us clarity about our own motives and keeps us focused on our goals. Getting realistic about ourselves usually makes us less sensitive to the critical feedback we receive from others, too.

***

Resistance to Step 10 often shows up as resistance to doing the inventory now. We may be inclined to put it off. Won't we, some ask, squelch all spontaneity if we have to watch our every move, worry about our every word? But taking a spot-check is not intended to stifle creativity. Overcoming this sort of resistance to Step 10 is largely a matter of taking the actions we believe will serve us in recovery and trusting that our feelings will catch up later. When we get in the habit of regularly doing Step 10, usually more creativity becomes possible, not less. Structure is healthy self-responsibility, an antidote to codependent control. (See the Recovery Wheels, Appendix 1)

When we take an inventory depends upon circumstances. Taking a spot-check of our feelings and motives is an option, not an obligation. When stress or hostility begins to dominate a situation, we can immediately choose to take a few deep breaths before we speak, while we examine what we are feeling. We bring the focus back to ourselves: What is our goal in this situation? Do our present feelings prompt us to want to act in ways that aren't in line with our goals or commitments in the situation? Are we communicating honestly—asking for what we really want, offering what we actually want to give? What are some options? Can we, for example, act to refocus the interaction in a more positive way? Does wisdom dictate that we temporarily remove ourselves until emotions settle? Taking a few seconds to spot-check is an exercise of our freedom to choose.

***

There are periodic inventories that can be very helpful, too. At day's end, we may take a few minutes to reflect, with a notepad, on how our day has gone. If we are inclined to do so, even 15 minutes of journaling or sketching can be a very helpful form of inventory. Buried feelings may often surface when we give our Inner Child a few minutes for free expression.

It's a good practice to ask ourselves a few questions aimed at the areas where there may have been difficulties or triumphs:

1. Have I isolated myself today? Have I taken a communication risk?
2. Have I been obsessed with something— a person, food, drugs, power? Have I been relieved of an obsession?

3. Have I felt like a victim today, weaker than or controlled by others? Have I held my own?

4. Have I appeased or injured someone today? Have I acted from my inner loyalties today and kept my boundaries intact?

5. Have I been dishonest—stuffed or denied any feelings today? Have I been willing to feel all of my feelings?

6. Was I distracted today—did I lose touch with my Higher Power due to stress, anger, or fear? Did I trust my Higher Power under difficult circumstances?

We are careful to own our progress in these areas of daily living. It's as important to give ourselves credit for the gains we make as it is for us to admit where we have fallen short. In owning our progress we are giving credit to the power of healing in our lives.

It is also helpful to do a periodic review of our progress over a longer time frame — a month, several months, a year. Many find that a few days of retreat, taking some special, personal time for deeper reflection, is a form of self-care that is very nurturing. It is often the case that our here-and-now issues have roots that can be traced back to past incidents. It's a good practice to return to Step 4 periodically when previously undiscovered aspects of the past begin to surface. Often, we are given new insight as recovery progresses and we become spiritually grounded to deal with deeper levels of truth about ourselves and our histories.

✳✳✳

Step 10 is a here-and-now action Step. If we are to gain the benefits of this work, we have to remain willing to act in the present. If we avoid or postpone taking action now to correct the errors we uncover in Step 10, we are getting in our own way. We get to keep only what we practice. If we don't make progress in building a new, positive way of life, as compulsive personalities, we tend to revert rapidly to our old, latent behaviors.

We needn't fear that we will fail to meet a false, perfectionistic standard in Step 10. It is not an outside authority that we answer to when we act with honesty to clear up our end of a problem. Our Inner Child's awakened conscience prompts us to act.

Sometimes, the ways we have been wrong may be in the acts we haven't taken. We may have been afraid to risk asking a question or exposing a caring feeling to someone because we feared rejection or thought we might look foolish. Perhaps we haven't given someone something of ourselves out of self-protective fear. Our strengthened Inner Child may prompt us to take action to extend ourselves in ways that are new and wonderful — and also risky. We have to remember to be patient with ourselves in this phase of our recovery. Our Inner Child deserves to be parented with gentleness. It's important that we take only the risks to feel and share that we are prepared to leave in the care of our Higher Power. If we find that we are afraid to trust the outcome to the God of our understanding, then we may not be ready to take the risk.

We are careful not to sabotage ourselves by needlessly setting ourselves up for invalidation or abuse. But we remind ourselves that recovery isn't a fantasy or a fairytale, either. Some of our risks and disclosures may be rejected or misunderstood, or we may not be able to communicate as we hoped we could. In living life on life's terms, honest action combined with trust in a loving God will see us through. A sense of humor is a form of faith that can be cultivated, too. Our aim is to heed the guidance of our Higher Power as we feel it in our heart, and take the action our awakened conscience dictates. If we take action to make working Step 10 a part of our lives today, we can safely leave the outcome of our efforts in the care of a loving God.

Exercises

This is a good kick-off exercise for Step 10, especially if you have a tendency to bog down in routine. It often provides a connection to feelings that may be suppressed. If it is done regularly over a period of time, it may help to bring up buried memories to be inventoried in Step 4, as well.

Exercise 1: Reparenting the Inner Child

1. The object of this exercise is to write constantly for at least ten minutes. Write anything that comes to your mind. Don't concern yourself about whether or not it makes sense. Just keep the pen moving—writing words. If you get stuck, write, "I'm stuck . . . " Just keep writing anything. Set a timer and go.

Example: How do I know about reparenting if I don't know about parenting I always feel like I can't do anything because I don't even know where to begin and it always seems too overwhelming. Keep writing, keep writing, I'm stuck, I'm stuck, the feeling is "I'm not doing it right," oh yes— Reparenting the Inner Child—my fearful inner child, the child who wants to play, not work, not do chores, not get beatings— the Inner Child who feels lost and afraid—the Inner Child, the Inner Child, the Inner Child—I have to keep writing. I feel scared. I'm not sure of what, but I feel scared. I won't do it right, I know I won't. I'm not right now. My hand is hurting. Oh—Creativity—It sounds exciting and wonderful, but not for me—only for others who are talented and rich and can go to schools and have parents who love them and each other.

2. Read the writing back to yourself. How do you feel, reading this? What memories come up? If you got stuck, what had you written that preceded getting stuck? What came after it?

3. Do you notice any messages in what you have written? Are these your own messages, or are they the messages of others? If, so, whom are the messages from? Are there key words in these messages that help you recognize these as your own thoughts or the thoughts of others? How does what you've written relate to the way you are living?

Exercise 2: Getting Really Stuck

Feeling stuck? Depressed, immersed in self-pity? Here's an exercise for self acceptance when we aren't at our best and brightest!

1. Start by giving yourself permission to be honest. Don't intellectualize or analyze — just admit the whole truth, whatever it may be.
Example: *I'm having a rotten day and I don't know why. I am in a dark mood — hating myself, my life, the whole structure of society. I don't fit in. I'm certain, I'm not doing it right. I have no motivation. My progress must be slipping. Oh, no! I shouldn't feel this way!*
2. Instead of fighting off a bad mood, try to exaggerate it. Make a commitment to yourself to go with it. If this sounds like just what you don't want to do, ask yourself this: Has resisting your feelings done any good? Give yourself permission to feel however it is you feel, right now.
3. Describe how you feel. Either speak out loud into a tape-recorder or write it all out. List every single thing in your life and about yourself you cannot stand. List everything you are unhappy about, everything! Your clothes, home, lover or mate, job, the world. Don't leave anything out, and don't allow yourself to write about anything good. Stick to what you don't like, period.
4. Read this all back to yourself while you're in front of a mirror. If you have taped it, look at yourself in the mirror while playing it back.
5. At the end of the exercise, simply admit to yourself that this is the way you felt, at the moment, without judgment. Don't analyze. Give yourself a break. Look into the mirror and say, "I love you, and I accept you completely. All your feelings are O.K. with me!"

Exercise 3: Self-Esteem Inventory

In the evening (or another time you set aside):

1. Name three things you acknowledge yourself for, today.
2. Consciously express thankfulness for the good you have experienced in your life, today. (Nothing is too small to be acknowledged.)
3. Forgive yourself for three mistakes or things you might have done better, today.
4. Have you judged yourself, today? Forgive yourself for judging yourself. Let go. Relax. Learn. Plan to try something different, next time.

Questions to Ponder

1. Review today (so far) and notice how you have felt, or if you've been stuffing any feelings. Feel those now.

2. Which issues are involved? (Be as specific as you can.) If you are in the midst of your day, make yourself an affirmation for the area (or areas) that are giving you trouble and repeat this to yourself several times, perhaps alternating with the Serenity Prayer or other favorite.

3. When you have time, explore the issue or issues involved. Do memories or feelings from the past come up for you?

4. Are you powerless in some respects involving this issue? Is this an issue that takes you back to Step 1, or 4 or 6?

5. Review any of the special focus inventories in Appendix II, answering all of the questions honestly.

Personal Sharing

Sometimes there is tremendous fear when I have to speak in front of people. I just shake and shake because the child in me was beaten, screamed at, told she wasn't good for anything except hard work. The fear is terrible but I can't run away. I just pick up that little child inside me and I hold her. I just have to hold her and keep telling her that I won't ever leave her or let them abuse her again. And I keep on holding her and holding her and finally, I go ahead and speak.

—Pam H., McKinleyville, CA

Recently, I had to deal with the IRS. I owed them money because my company had dissolved a pension plan and I had been advised to pay off my bills but not warned to save some of the money for Uncle Sam.

They certainly weren't fun to deal with! When I made a call to arrange payments, the gentleman on the line really sounded disgusted with my inabilities. I kept saying to myself, "He's just doing his job; don't react. Don't fear him." Of course, I wasn't going to cry on the phone.

As soon as I got off the phone I put on my headphones and listened to part of a Louise Hay tape about, "I've done the best I can!"

That night, I had been asked to do a lead on Step 10 and I realized I had really practiced Step 10 that day. A part of me wanted to concentrate on the IRS person on the phone and not look at myself. Instead, I was able to share this and also tell how I made amends to me.

Thanks to my program, today I take risks even if sometimes I might appear to be a fool because I want the freedom that risk-taking gives. Even as I write this all down I realize I've handled things the best I can. It's a lot easier when I remember to turn it over to my H.P.!

—Joan N., Chicago, IL

WAIT, WAIT, WAIT! STOP THAT EMOTION
IT FEELS TOO MUCH LIKE LOCO-MOTION
IT FEELS TOO MUCH LIKE CO-MOTION.
EMOTIONS ARE BAD, THEY WON'T LIKE ME
EMOTIONS ARE BAD, THEY'LL ALL LEAVE ME
THEN WHERE WILL I BE . . IN THE DARK AND ALONE.
Heart beating too fast. Breath shallow and weak.
Why do I do this? Just a dummy with a stupid streak?
Maybe I fell on my head once too often . . .
Maybe on purpose trying to fill up a coffin.
Hello? Anyone there? Gather 'round. Let's talk.
After all, it's my life being tossed around.
Not what I think, but what do I FEEL?
It's been a long while, but there's something real
Way down deep inside a locked gate.
If I try real hard, pray and meditate,
I can find those feelings
I can contemplate.
I am a good person, not the best, not the worst.
Can't I make mistakes? A perfectionist's curse?
Big deal. I can learn from mistakes and go on with my life.
People do . . . and I'm people too.
I don't have to push. I don't have to shove.
I can get back to living! I can move on to love!

—Joyce B., Tsimpsian Tribe (Alaska)

STEP ELEVEN

Seek through prayer and meditation to improve our conscious contact with God as we understand God, praying only for knowledge of God's will for us and power to carry that out.

Nan-in, a Japanese Zen master, poured tea for his visitor. He filled the cup, and then kept on pouring. The visitor watched until he could contain himself no more. "Look! It's overfull. No more can go in!" "Like this cup," Nan-in responded, "you, too, are full of your own speculations. How can I show you Zen unless you first empty your cup?"

— Muju, Japanese, 13th Century.

***

Well, you see: once upon a time there was a blazing fire inside me. The cold could do nothing against it, a youthfulness, a spring no autumn could touch. . . . There was an enormous energy there . . . . A force, it must have been the life force, mustn't it? . . . And then it grew weaker and it all died away...

— Eugene Ionesco, French (Born 1912.)

Personal recovery in any 12-Step program can be described as a spiritual journey from a kind of spiritual death back into life. We who were the lost people — victims of addictions or codependent patterns — rediscover our authentic, inner selves again. We move from the bleak, barren landscapes of a failed existence back into a fruitful way of life, full of challenge and opportunity.

Connecting with our lost inner identity, the magical Inner Child within, is a spiritual process. However much therapy, medical treatment, hard work and good sponsorship may provide, the actual experience of healing requires connecting with a deeply spiritual core within ourselves. What makes recovery a reality is the fire of vitality that is reawakened in us. As much as we may gratefully acknowledge the skilled guidance and support we receive from others, it still remains that all of this would count for little if no spark of fire within ourselves existed to respond.

To build a strong connection to the resources we have within, the flame of spirit within us needs to be fueled if it is to burn with a steady light. Working Step 11 is a way to feed the contact between our ordinary awareness and our spiritual power source within. Making regular use of prayer and meditation is a maintenance practice that helps keep us in touch with personal inspiration.

∗∗∗

Even if we are willing to acknowledge the importance of spirituality in recovery, we may still have a certain amount of resistance to the idea of prayer — or to the systematic practice of it. In order to begin to integrate the practice of prayer into our daily lives as Step 11 recommends, we may need to reconsider the meaning and purpose of prayer. What has prayer meant to us in the past?

Painful associations can easily block the way to utilizing prayer or wanting to take time for it. Perhaps we associate humiliating memories with prayer — memories of begging God or of trying in vain to strike a deal with God to stave off a disaster. Why weren't our prayers answered? Weren't we good enough? Or did we fail, somehow? We may feel unwilling to try prayer again — as though we are facing the possibility of a kind of soul-rejection if we do.

Maybe we were exposed to prayer in a household where appearances were everything and emotions were suppressed. We may have memories of prayer as a ritual smothering the Child within. We may have come to look on prayer as an undertaking intended mainly to impress others or to keep from being criticized. We may remember prayer as a mechanical repeating of mere words, hollow rituals devoid of meaning, feelings or power. If we experienced much religious hypocrisy in the past, we may fear that turning to prayer represents a kind of self-negation.

If we are tormented by these or similar associations with the idea of prayer, our first response to Step 11 is likely to be a form of inner resistance — avoidance, defiance, or denial. We remind ourselves that resistance is often an indicator of a need to unbrick more inner walls and feel the feelings that have been stuffed away. We may need to begin working Step 11 by giving ourselves permission to grieve the pain of confusion and loss that is locked inside ourselves and that is associated with old ideas about prayer.

∗∗∗

We can help ourselves by redefining our understanding of prayer now. We can take the initiative to reparent our Inner Child with a more realistic understanding, one that is no longer hooked to vain pleading or self-abasement. The New Century Dictionary (1957, Appleton-Century-Crofts, Inc.) tells us that prayer is "communication directed toward God [including] . . . asking, praising, adoring, confessing." Regardless of any confusion which we may have associated with the idea, prayer really isn't so complicated, after all. Prayer is the act of extending ourselves toward the God of our understanding. It's a matter of how we conceive of God and of our relationship to the spiritual that determines if and how we pray and what form those prayers will take.

If we work to replace any old conceptions we might have of a weak or mean God with a kinder understanding, then reaching out to our Higher Power becomes easier. A Higher (or Inner) Power that is both capable and willing to support us is an ally that we want to reach. When we pray, we affirm our personal right to communicate with the God of our understanding. Few rights rival this one, in terms of power in our lives.

***

How and when we pray is up to us. We may or may not feel it is appropriate to get down upon our knees in prayer. Rituals such as ceremony, dance, assuming particular postures or going to special places — shrines, churches, grottos — are all left to individual conscience in 12-Step programs. Praying in a group, including saying the Serenity Prayer at the beginning of 12-Step meetings, is never an obligation. These personal decisions are always a matter of free choice. In all 12-Step programs we are assured of our right to a personal relationship with the God of our understanding. As we develop that relationship, we pray in words, dance, ritual ceremony, song or whatever comes from our hearts. If we don't have a positive association with forms of prayer we learned in childhood, Step 11 is an opportunity to explore new options.

We may find ways to claim as prayer some activities that we may not have associated with concepts of prayer before. Affirmations, for instance, are a positive form of prayer that asks by affirming that God is willing and able to see us made whole. Affirmations, many find, are a spiritual antidote to many old ideas about God and about prayer. Repeating (or writing) affirmations directly contradicts old behavior hangovers we may carry. We no longer beg an external force when we pray in affirmations. Instead, we join ourselves with the God/Spirit that dwells within us. (See "Creating With Affirmations," Appendix 1, for more on utilizing this important form of prayer.)

Rejoicing in our blessings is another form of prayer we may not have claimed. When we express (inwardly or outwardly) our gratitude for the good things we see around us—the pleasures of restored health and sanity, the joy we feel in fellowship— we are doing what the dictionary defines as praising and rejoicing. When we appreciate a sunset or feel awe in the face of nature, talent or courage and we acknowledge the spiritual basis of these wonders, we are also praising God.

If we begin to claim these forms of prayer and worship, we may find that we have always been pretty spiritual folks. Many of us find, when we review memories of childhood, that we praised the beauty of life, even if we had no words to express the reverent feelings within our hearts. What little child has not, in his/her peaceful moments, delighted in life? We can choose to count among our prayers our appreciation for a waterfall, or for a bird's song, the sounds of children's laughter, the smell of dinner cooking. We can choose to see the work we do as a prayer of offering we make with our bodies and our minds, a praise to our Higher Power that gives us energy and direction. The love we give to others can be a prayer if we see it as a validation of spirit that flows from heart to heart.

Once we have come to understand prayer as a right we enjoy, rather than as a burden or an obligation, then the whole activity begins to take on a natural harmony in our lives. We find building and improving a conscious contact with the God of our understanding is no longer an activity that takes us away from life. Instead, prayer becomes an integrated pulsebeat that gradually comes to underlay much of what we do.

***

Step 11 also asks us to practice meditation to improve our conscious contact with the God of our understanding. If prayer is the act of reaching out to God, then meditation can be seen as the act of letting Spirit in. When we take time to meditate, we

127

make a conscious decision to open ourselves to guidance and inspiration.

One of the classic methods of meditating is the practice of clearing the mind of all thought. All distractions, including emotional responses to thoughts, are gradually released, dismissed. The object of classical meditation is emptiness, stillness, complete one-pointedness of being. Achieving this state of poised detachment may be the goal of years of discipline.

But meditation need not be so formal nor so thoroughgoing to be effective. Our goal, in Step 11, is just to make some space and time available in our schedules to receive new direction. Meditation involves making a decision to set aside our projects, goals, and other commitments for a few minutes and to use that time receptively. Rather than attempting to become entirely devoid of all thought, most find it easier to simply replace the usual preoccupations of the mind with something else. Inspirational reading or repeating a brief, affirmative statement (mantra) can refocus our awareness and create a quiet space within. Making a decision to suspend action and worry while listening to a piece of music or a meditation tape is another good approach. Yoga, rhythmic programs of exercise, jogging, drawing, making pottery, lying in the cool grass contemplating the clouds that sail across the sky — any of these practices can be used in meditation, so long as we make a conscious decision to release our everyday cares and ambitions while we do them.

✳✳✳

Once we see that meditation need not be the rigorous practice of a demanding discipline, the practice usually feels less intimidating. We may, nonetheless, still be inclined to postpone or forget to give ourselves quiet breaks.

Keeping ourselves distracted — out of our bodies to a greater or lesser extent — can be a defense. We may have learned to stuff pain, fear or grief by focusing on something else, on something outside of ourselves or on a different feeling. When we lived lives that were dominated by addiction, our Inner Child within simply had to escape from the pain of a present that s/he was powerless to change. Without necessarily making a conscious decision, we found ways to escape. We coped and survived.

Coping by escaping from the now is a habit that, once established, often dies hard. Individuals in recovery may admit that they have been more or less addicted to excitement — to anger, to silent rehearsals of dialogue with people who aren't present, to fantasies of fear, worry, domination or conquest. These distractions cut us off from experiencing the responses of our authentic selves within. To compound the confusion, we may also have become magnets generating or gravitating toward real crisis in our lives and relationships. We may act out our fantasies, live out our fears.

Meditation is a practice that directly contradicts all these forms of distraction. When we meditate, we give ourselves permission to be 100% in the present, here and now. We give ourselves over to the care of God as we understand God. We consciously release our hold upon everything. For those of us who have carried self-protective excitement habits along into recovery, meditation may threaten something near and dear to us — our ability to escape from feelings in the present.

Rather than blaming ourselves as failures who are unable to work Step 11, we need to see our old coping mechanisms for what they were — the way we survived an impossible past. Under past circumstances, escape was probably in order. We lacked other tools. Now, if we are willing to use them, we have tools available to us. We don't have to run.

A good beginning is simply to take a few minutes to breathe deeply while we go over the ways it is now safe to be in the present. How has our life changed? How are we different? We may still feel like rebelling, but gentle, persistent reparenting will usually succeed better than insistent demands. As we note the ways that we are now safe to be our undefended selves, we reassure our Child within that the experience of recovery is lasting and trustworthy. This may take a little time, but, fortunately for us, the Child within wants to be present in the now. The Child within has gifts for us: creativity, innocence, a sense of fun.

Re-entering the present as an undefended, vulnerable human being is risky but essential. Playful forms of meditation are good ways to rebond with our inner self. As we gradually replace distraction with meditation, our Inner Child returns.

$$***$$

Seeking to discover and live out "God's will for us . . ." is basic to recovery. We who lost touch with our authentic inner self find that this connection is restored as addictions, compulsions and codependent patterns fall away. What is most authentic about each of us is primarily spiritual in nature. In the continued practice of Step 11, we seek gradually to reduce the inner conflict that interferes with contact with our authentic self. When momentary goals take us away from this larger goal, we remind ourselves of the purpose of Step 11. Lasting success depends upon sticking with our truest selves. We need to remember not to abandon ourselves. When in doubt, we ask, "Is this goal (or impulse) in keeping with my highest good?" We seek direct validation by means of prayer, along with the power to live by what we discover is written in our hearts. In Step 11, we seek guidance so that our actions cease to be rooted in reaction to forces outside of ourselves. We move in the direction of balance and poise, toward being in touch with a comfortable sense of purpose and inner harmony.

As we become more and more willing to practice Step 11 and to live from the guidance we receive, we tend naturally to experience a growing feeling of confidence. We usually notice increased tolerance toward others. Finding inner validation, we no longer feel so fearful of making or acknowledging mistakes. We no longer have to guess at what to do or say, nor do we second-guess others to gain their approval or divert their wrath. Even sadness and pain eventually lose some of their force in our lives. Fear of these feelings or shame about having them begins to evaporate in the strong light of Spirit.

As we come to live more on spiritual power, directing our will toward conscious contact with the God of our understanding, we find more of the courage necessary to face our lives with honesty — and humor. After all, spiritual power is an inexhaustible wellspring that has been made available to us, a day at a time. We come to understand that we needn't fear — or hate. With prayer and meditation to keep our contact with our Source, we may truly come to walk in peace. And as we accept ourselves as worthy of this peace, we may discover previously unrecognized talents and gifts within ourselves.

Exercises

Exercise 1: Guided Visualization

Guided Visualization/Active Imagination is an effective form of meditation for tapping deep inner resources of personal spiritual power. This form of meditation allows us to contact memories and feelings while it empowers and heals from within. It is also a process that encourages internal unification to continue even during sleep or times when our conscious attention is directed toward other interests, since we bond it with such basic functions as breathing and heartbeat. Here is an exercise for developing this skill.

1. Read over the following Guided Visualization. Allow yourself to become comfortable with the images and with the idea of allowing yourself to experience this form of healing meditation.
2. Tape record the meditation, or have a friend read it to you. Allow yourself to relax and go with the suggestions.
3. Play the tape (or listen to someone read it) every day for a week or two.

We begin now by taking in some deep, deep relaxing breaths of sparkling fresh air. Allow yourself to let your breathing become rhythmic as it slows down and becomes a deeper and more peaceful feeling.

Feel the air around you — the fresh sweet air that sparkles with a silverygolden light that fills it. Feel it as it flows smoothly, deep into your lungs. Allow yourself to see the light, sparkling and silvery as stardust. Breathe it in and breathe it out. Visualize your breathing as a stream of sparkling silver, surrounding you with healing light.

Allow your lungs to carry this silverygold light to your pulsing, flowing bloodstream and flow throughout your body. Feel the silver sparkle in your legs and feet. Feel it flowing up through your thighs, your hips and swirling pure relaxation in every organ of your body. Experience it tingling down through your arms into your finger tips. Allow this silverygolden light to spread healing and relaxation into your neck and head, moving effortlessly throughout your entire body. Feel yourself entirely filled up with healing, gentle, glowing light.

If you like, you can move this soft silverygolden light around like a sparkler of healing, releasing tensions or discomforts in any of your organs or muscles in your body. You may wish to notice especially your neck, or in your shoulders, anywhere at all that little knots of tension may accumulate. Using your fingertips to direct the flow, imagine yourself dissolving each and every knot of tension with a sparkler of pure light. Let yourself relax and float in a sea of light and healing.

Now, imagine that you have flexible, metallic, grounding cords of pure earth energy extending from the bottoms of your feet into the very molten core and center of the earth. These cords do not in any way restrict your movements. Instead, they create a constant flowing pulse of metallic, glittery bluegreen energy that circulates up from the very center of the earth into your body. This energy from the center of the planet is power- fully magnetic and very, very strong. If you are willing to let go of painful memories, you can let this bluegreen energy mag- netically attract any toxic-feeling memories from anywhere within you, and then take them deep into the center of the earth, down into the molten core where everything is liquid fire. The pressure in the earth's core is very great: so powerful it takes all of those toxins and impurities and it turns them into jewels — pressuring these experiences of toxic thought into beautiful sparkling diamonds, sapphires, rubies, and other riches — treasures that are yours to keep. You can use them for adornment or exchange them for the nourishments you need or as gifts you wish to give.

And now expand the light that fills you, mixing the silverygold light that you breathe into your blood with the magnetic bluegreen energy of your grounding cords. Connect- ing yourself to the center of the earth, experience yourself entirely surrounded with healing light and energy available to you. Breathe in and surround yourself in a circle of radiant, healing, bluegold light. This light protects you totally. Only that which is for your highest good and healing can enter now. Anything not important to your healing and wellbeing is sent harmlessly away. Experience feeling completely safe, secure, protected within a radiant fountain of bluegold light. This circle of pure light is strengthened with every breath you take, waking and sleeping, day by day.

Imagine yourself living your life with this circle of light around you. What is best for you seeks you out. What is harmful cannot reach you. You are free to direct the flowing into all of your activities, into every relationship, past and present. As you direct the light around you, you move easily, always expe- riencing your connectedness and safety as you breathe the light, deeply peaceful and relaxed. Pause now, for a minute, and feel the power of connectedness and safety all around you. It is a fountain of healing that cascades around you endlessly, nourishing and healing every experience and memory.

Taking a deep breath, allow yourself to experience this

power and protection. And every time you choose to do so, you can feel this sense of safety by taking in a deep, relaxing breath. Your metallic cords into the center of the earth are yours to keep. You can feel yourself becoming centered, connected through the force of gravity to the center of the earth. Breathing in the bluegold light of air and earth, experience the healing. And with every breath you take, this process of self-healing becomes more and more a natural and integrated aspect of your Inner Self. Every time you pause to contact this deep process, consciously taking thought to breathe in clean, fresh air, it becomes easier and easier to experience and to direct this healing to yourself, or to the others in your life who have a deep connection in your heart.

Now, returning to normal consciousness, you feel the energy of relaxed, centered awareness flowing through every part of your body. You come into full, normal consciousness awake, alive and alert, ready to go on with your day, knowing that you can contact and experience the safety, peace and confidence that is yours to keep by simply taking in a deep, relaxing breath. At the count of three, you are back, fully awake and refreshed, and ready to go on with your day. One. Two. Three.

When you have become comfortable with this meditation, you may wish to use this safe place within as a personal inner temple, a safe place to go to ask for guidance and direction from God as you understand God. Remember, you always have a right to peace and safety in your inner temple. Only that which is there for your highest good has a right to be there with you. If an attacking image or voice disturbs you while you are involved in meditation, confront it. Ask it, "Why are you here? You can only be here if you are working for my highest good." Within your temple, this sort of question has to be answered honestly, when it is asked. You will either be shown what the healing gift for you is, or the voice or image will have to leave at once.

Exercise 2: Have a Talk with God

If you are troubled by ideas that praying is limited to repeating certain set prayers, here are some brief exercises to expand your horizons.

1. Look over a familiar prayer, such as the Serenity Prayer, and rewrite it in your own words. Say the ideas out loud, speaking directly to your Higher Power.

2. Tell your Higher Power how you feel right now, using your own words. If you feel good, thank your Higher Power. If you feel awful, ask

your Higher Power to give you the help you need, in a way you can clearly understand it along with the power and willingness to act. If you don't feel very willing, say that, too. If you're angry with God as you understand God, say that, too. Try telling God the truth, whatever it may be, and see what happens.

3. Go somewhere beautiful and talk to God. Go to the ocean, or to a lake, or waterfall. Talk to God while you are walking along a friendly path.

4. Talk to God while you are at a movie, or on a date. Ask for guidance to be the person you are meant to be in every situation you are in. A simple request, like, "Guide me, please!" is usually enough to make a real difference.

Exercise 3: Reflections on My Space

Here's an hour-long creative process designed to get in touch with suppressed emotion. Try it as a cure for the a case of the blahs, when life seems to be nothing but an endless string of identical routines. Do it periodically — every few months or yearly. It's a good way to check on progress in recovery and it's both objective and fun.

1. Sit down in a comfortable place where you can look around your environment at home. Imagine you have left all of your other interests and concerns in a large secure trunk somewhere safe, and have locked it. Everything will be there when you come back. Take in three deep breaths and let them out slowly, stretching your arms, shoulders and neck to release any tension as you breathe out. Relax.

2. Ask your Higher Power to guide your imagination. Study your house from an objective point of view, as if you were analyzing a dream. Loosen up and let yourself listen to your imagination freely, without screening your impressions. Imagine the stuff of your home as symbols appearing in your dream. What does the room you're in tell you about the person (or people) who live there? How are things organized (or not organized)? Do the pieces of furniture relate to one another in style or placement? What is the atmosphere created in this particular room? How do you feel about this room?

3. Write or speak into a tape recorder as you respond to the above questions. Give yourself about five minutes. Don't edit or pass judgment on your impressions. Be thorough and honest.

Example: I feel O.K. about this room. It doesn't really excite me, but it's O.K. I like the artwork on the walls, but I hate the color of the carpet, and it's pretty worn. I enjoy the plants, but they are looking a little drab, like they need some care. I actually don't care for the way the furniture is arranged. It is a little too cluttered and the space isn't used as well as it could be. There are a number of things that are just in the way, not *useful at all, just taking up space.*

4. Review this description as if it were yourself that had been described. Give your imagination complete freedom to use everything you've noticed as symbols about yourself.

Example: I notice that the overall feeling present is "O.K., but. . . " The description is lacking in emotion or excitement except for the word "hate" (referring to the carpet). Am I generally lacking in emotion, except for what I hate? Do I like some aspects of myself, such as my creativity (artwork on the walls) but hate my inability to maintain steady, sufficient income to meet my basic needs (carpet on the floor)? Am I looking and feeling a little drab, as though a day in the sunshine would do me some good? Do I need vitamins, exercise or care (plants)? Do I feel I'm carrying around excess emotional or mental baggage from the past and remaining unfocused in the present (clutter and poor use of space)? Do I have some habits or thoughts about myself that are not useful, or are actually in the way of my growth and development (useless items)?

5. After interpreting your dream, ask yourself what you want to do to change the situation. Act on the room.

Example: I look at the room again: I would like to replace the carpet with a plush Persian rug. I notice I selected the one thing I have the least ability to change today, the item I described with the strongest emotion. Do I do the same thing in my recovery? Do I look at the most difficult area and then feel frustrated that I can't effect an immediate change? Admitting that I may be quitting before I start, taking this approach, I consider small changes: Maybe I can't go buy a Persian rug this afternoon, but I can get rid of some of the clutter and useless items. Maybe I have a friend who would enjoy some of them? I can rearrange the room more to my liking. I can dust the plants and give them some love and water. Is some of the stuff I feel is useless clutter actually someone else's? Do I need to communicate with them?

6. Coming back to me, I ask these same questions: Do I want to change? Do I have time for the process? If I don't, what is more important? What are my priorities and values at present? Do I have the energy and tools to make the changes? Where am I using my energies? Do I need more support? Do I have old tapes running about my life and my priorities based on someone else's values or desires for me?

7. If at all possible, make changes in the room as part of this exercise. Give yourself an experience of change and progress. Let the changes you make in your environment be a form of prayer in action, a testimony to your willingness to accept guidance from within and act upon it.

Questions to Ponder

1. Is prayer a word with meaning for you?
2. Do you feel you can meditate?
3. What does conscious contact feel like? How does it show up in your life?
4. Is knowledge of God's will something you sense inside yourself? How about power?

Personal Sharing

I was feeling tired and sick this evening, so I went and took a sauna by myself. It's been a sad time for me, with friendships ending and much of the old hostility cropping up at home — perhaps due to stress? I don't know.

But in my sauna tonight, I was not worried or upset. I was musing, instead, that I never had a living grandmother. Both of my grandmothers died very young of asthma before my parents were grown up or met each other. I often use time in the sauna for meditation, so I asked God to bring me in touch with old women-spirits, like the grandmothers I never had or knew.

The sauna is a small, wood-lined room with high benches for lying in the extremely dry, hot air. It gets up to 180° F., and I pour eucalyptus oil on the hot stones, so the air becomes tangy and penetrating. It's very relaxing and peaceful.

Toward the end of the session, I felt guided to relax on a low bench, where it wasn't quite so hot. As soon as I lay back there, I had the experience of having Nan-Mother, Lorena, become present — a delicate presence, but quite assured. She shared that she felt somewhat sad and confused about her own unresolved issues, even now that she had died. She showed me a dark place in her heart, where her first husband was in her past, with a lot of unresolved hurt and sadness (over his drinking and his running out on her and her two babies, almost sixty years ago). She saw him as an old, drunk beggar calling to her from deep shadow. He reminded her of a young man she once loved so much and missed so bitterly. She couldn't walk freely past him into heaven. She felt angry and also somehow afraid.

Her second husband had a lot of unresolved anger toward her first husband, too. She felt she had to do something to resolve this conflict between them, or else get caught up in this sad old business again. She didn't want anyone to suffer, no matter how badly they had acted. But she couldn't deny the truth, either, and so she felt stuck.

While I was seeing all of this, it was as though she were working a program with me. I just accepted it as a gift from my own Higher Power. In the meditation, I shared the idea that Lorena invite both these spirits to move toward the light with her in peace and harmony. And, as far as resolving the old hard feelings, what about seeing both men as little children, instead of full-grown men with all those grudges?

When I made that last suggestion, she suddenly became a little girl, herself, sitting, golden and curly, in a real old-fashioned garden, behind a cozy-looking white-

135

frame house. She was playing with a little spotted cat, laughing a very hearty belly-laugh, as she sat there in the soft grass and white clover. All the feelings of conflict just vanished, dissolved in a sudden burst of sparkle, warmed by the friendly sun.

Little Lorena had some friends who were hugging her and telling her how glad they were to see her, and how much they'd missed her. And she and I both started crying — in that warm, sunny, fragrant garden, with a big pink rose bush on the back of the house, and smells of clover all around. Two boys who had been stuck in errors and resentment as big men who'd tried to be her husband were climbing in a tree, each about six or eight years old. They were all restored to being children, innocent and safe — and finally there to stay.

—Raven

Stage III Recovery

I woke up with a smile
feelin' good about life
I'm an integrated person
a Mother and a Wife.
I woke up with a grin
feelin' like a sage
I'm a whole person now
at this wonderful gold age.
I woke up with a sigh
and grabbed my "writing book"
I'm feelin' wonderful
and think how good I look.
I woke up with this joy
and peace within my heart
it took me so very long
to find this final part.
I woke up so peaceful
feelin' in "the pink"
I hardly ever worry now
what other people think.
I woke up with gratitude
and abundance I can share
I can take my life and live it
I know now...anywhere!
I woke up with a smile
feeling great love in my heart

I turned 50 yesterday
am ready for the next part.
I woke up with contentment
and respect for this past chapter
I'm having such fun now, God
could you postpone the "forever after"?
I woke up in love with life
on my face a full-blown smile
I'm feelin' such peace now, Lord
let me stay here a long, long while.

Carol Ann F., 7/29/90, Vashon Island, WA

STEP TWELVE

Having had a spiritual awakening as a result of these Steps, we try to carry this message to others and to practice these principles in all of our affairs.

People of genius are rarely content browsing upon the greatness of their own thoughts... More than most, such people are called by the mighty herd instinct; their searchings, their findings and their calls are inexorably meant for the crowd and must be heard.

—Dr. Carl Gustav Jung, Psychologist (1875-1961)

***

Perhaps one day I may even make a commitment to serve a group, and even (gulp) get involved and active... I'm beginning to understand that the Area Meeting Schedule, the office, and the phone system don't happen by magic.

—Anonymous , Portland ACoA.

Human beings depend upon each other. We are born tiny and helpless. Our families and community must sustain us during a long period if we are to survive at all. As adults, as parents and productive members of our societies, we assume the roles of providers. Living long, we at last come to depend again upon the care of others as vitality gradually fades. Our lives move to a nearly audible pulse of changing needs, changing goals, through a life dance that is linked and entwined with the lives of others.

Coming to recognize ourselves as a part of life's interdependent dance is a mark of maturity. If we accept ourselves as valuable, we come to see ourselves as worthy of the love and care necessary for our well-being. We cease to feel shamed by our needs. We accept what we need to be whole from life and from others, and we also come to accept ourselves as having the capacity to give. We come to see that we share a responsibility to put something back, if what we have received is to be there for the next person or for the next generation.

Much of the maintenance work that we do in Step 12 is about putting something back. It is not based in a joyless sense of obligation, though. We offer to share the way of life we have found in the give and take of life's dance. What we give, we give voluntarily, offering to reach out our hand to the next person who reaches out for help.

Our Service and 12-Step work is based on the realization that spiritual insights quickly lose force unless these insights become the basis of action in our lives. We do the work of Step 12 in order to keep what we have, by living what we have learned. As we share what we have gained through recovery, we reaffirm the changes that have taken place in our lives.

✳✳✳

"Spiritual awakening" in 12-Step programs starts with learning something about humility. In 12-Step programs, we come together in a healing process that begins with admitting what we can't do for ourselves. The price of admission to our fellowship is a depth of honesty that is painful to accept. We each must face a question we'd rather not answer: Has physical, mental or emotional addiction rendered us helpless—powerless to stop doing what is harming us, while we are at the same time unable to go on as we were?

The willingness to even consider the question of Step 1 requires reflecting on profound spiritual issues. Addictions, after all, are defined as life-threatening conditions. If we admit we are powerless over some form of addiction, aren't we facing the possibility of our own death or a kind of living death? Stripped of denial, we feel naked. We are powerless, out of control—as vulnerable as newborns in a new world.

A spiritual awakening begins when, despite our reluctance and fear, we actually take Step 1. Starting with our first honest admission that we really do have a problem, we begin to move out of self-loss. Admitting an unattractive truth that is threatening to our inner sense of security and our image takes courage. We can't know in advance if we will recover. We face the terrors of uncertainty. Risking action in the face of uncertainty, when life itself may be at stake, requires acting in faith. This combination of honesty, courage, and the willingness to act in faith is the basis of a spiritual way of life.

✳✳✳

Spiritual awakening develops as we reconnect with our authentic inner self, the Inner Child. All of the Steps include some of what we mean in Step 12. From the first time we share at a meeting, we are beginning to carry the message. We share our experience, including our pain, our unflattering insights into our own motivations, the feelings we fear others will not accept. Others who haven't found the courage to face similar features in themselves may be helped by identifying with what we've shared.

When we speak from our hearts, those who share a common problem hear us and are comforted. Whether it's a common experience or shared feelings that run through dissimilar events doesn't seem to matter. Without attempting to impress anyone, we always have something to give when we share our truth. And in the act of personal sharing, we awaken more and more to our spiritual identity, validating and claiming ourselves.

Having this spiritual awakening is an ongoing experience. Usually, we become aware of growing unification over time, as we gradually come to know and accept ourselves. Our understanding of recovery develops as we apply the principles in the 12-Steps to the events of our daily lives. As we become more established in this way of life, we see that working Step 12 is not an activity to be postponed. It isn't something to be undertaken only after we have finished with ourselves.

Through the daily practice of honesty, courage and willingness, our lives undergo a process of change. Circumstances and personalities that once seemed to dominate us gradually cease to do so. New opportunities present themselves because addictions no longer cloud our thinking. Through living in recovery, a new strength and hope grows in us.

Strength in recovery no longer depends on only us and our personal power. Strength now is fashioned from the spiritual tools we are learning to apply in our lives. Going through the Steps, talking to a trusted friend, reaching out for spiritual help — these are the sources of power that come to replace the dogged resistance or defiant attitudes of the past.

Hope, too, ceases to be a kind of wishful thinking to avoid facing reality. Nor is it the fanatical, closed-minded dedication to ideals it may have been in the dysfunctional past. The hope we share in recovery is realistic. It's based on what we see demonstrated in our lives and in the lives of those around us. Hope is restored, becoming a quality that radiates through us as our lives become meaningful and sane. In recovery, we can share hope because our lives are living proof that hope is warranted.

***

One of the ways we directly share our experience, strength, and hope with others is through sponsorship. Sponsorship or co-sponsorship is a committed relationship with another member of a 12-Step program, focused on applying the 12-Steps to daily life. Sponsorship involves making a commitment to working the Steps and supporting another in doing the same.

In the original 12-Step program, AA, sponsoring someone usually meant starting with prospects who were still practicing alcoholics and sticking with them as they sobered up. In the early days, it was not uncommon to take a newcomer home, as part of sponsoring, and then to take him to AA meetings until he got the program. Such practices still occur. But going to this extreme is not a requirement for sponsorship — nor are such practices necessarily wise or helpful under most circumstances. Facilities and professionals in the field are generally better equipped to handle intervention or direct treatment than private individuals. Sponsors don't sober people up, get them off drugs, or get them to face a self-defeating, codependent pattern. Sponsors share what they have learned with people who already have made a decision to work on their issues. We do not lead each other, in 12-Step programs; we travel side by side.

In 12-Step programs today, there are many kinds of sponsorship relationships. Some contain very structured agreements to meet or talk on the phone a specified number of times per week or month. Others arrangements may be less specific, with phone contact on an as-needed basis. Often, regular attendance of a group may be a part of sponsorship commitment.

Because individuals who have already worked the Steps may be in short supply in newer groups and because sponsors may easily become authority figures, some 12-Step programs advocate co-sponsorship relationships. In co-sponsorship, two or more people establish an agreement to work through the Steps together even if neither has done so before. Step Study groups, in which a definite commitment (usually six months or a year) is made to meet regularly to work the Steps, are typically co-sponsorship arrangements. (A format for Step Study is included in Appendix III.)

Sponsorship is a form of putting something back, that is a major feature in 12-Step programs. Working through the Steps alone is not as effective as interacting with someone in a relationship of trust. Step 5 cannot be worked alone at all. Trust in at least one other human being is necessary for getting well.

∗∗∗

There are also other ways, in addition to sponsorship, to carry the recovery message. Service work in 12-Step programs is another way to give something back. Helping to set up the meeting, sharing in the responsibilities that keep the group going — all these activities are performed by volunteers. These Service jobs are rotated among members. Aside from a few simple guidelines, any member who is willing is welcome to serve the fellowship.

In communities where the 12-Step programs are very active, an office may be staffed to do the clerical work, answer the phone, write letters or keep regular hours for a fellowship bookstore. Tradition states that, although we may hire workers to do these necessary jobs, no one is ever paid to share their story with a newcomer. When it comes to reaching out to newcomers, this 12-Step work is done by volunteers.

Some individuals feel comfortable speaking anonymously at open meetings or in front of civic groups. Sharing our personal story in the community can be an enriching experience. Agreeing to staff a 12-Step phone line for a few hours a week is another opportunity to share in the spirit of anonymous giving back to the program. Simply volunteering to drop off meeting lists and pamphlets at public health agencies is another quiet way that gratitude and goodwill can get translated into action.

12-Step programs try to emphasize anonymity at the level of press, radio, TV, film or in situations where what is said is likely to be reported. In sticking to this anonymity principle, vying for leadership among 12-Step program members is minimized. Professional therapists and others in the public eye who wish to carry the message by sharing their own recovery story sometimes aren't sure if they can do this without breaking this Tradition. One way is to talk about self-help without specifying 12-Step fellowships. Another way, often used by professional therapists who are also program members, is to talk about the 12-Step programs from a professional point of view, without indicating that they, themselves, are members.

∗∗∗

In working Step 12, we remind ourselves that little is to be gained — or given — if service or sponsorship activities become a distraction that takes the focus away from personal recovery. After all, we didn't join a 12-Step program to become an expert on how other people ought to do it. As vital as it may be that we give something back, we need to take care to balance Twelfth Step activities, making sure that giving does not become controlling or "playing the big shot."

Our own lives continue to remain the central focus of recovery, no matter how long we've been around. Service activities may be an obvious way to practice the principles in the 12-Steps, but Service isn't an escape from our other responsibilities. We must seek the guidance we need to keep our priorities straight. If our personal lives do not reflect the spiritual principles we practice in recovery, we simply have no recovery to give away.

Distancing or shutting off connections to the past may be a temptation. Sometimes it may be appropriate to put up very concrete limits and boundaries to shield ourselves from abusive situations, at least for a time. However, our issues have to be faced, if only a little at a time. Those who have attempted to deal with a problem by getting rid of it generally find that similar issues arise again and again. Internally, patterns that connect us to disturbing interactions continue to play out until we finally embrace the lesson that is there for us.

Difficult as it may sometimes be to see a path through personal dilemmas — especially those with deep roots in the past — a solution will come if we will focus on living our program one day at a time. Here are some guidelines:

1. We live only today. If something is before us that needs to be done, now is the time to do it. If we are waiting for a better time, we are missing an opportunity.

2. There's only so much we can expect to do today. Someone said, "Doing a big project is like eating an elephant; you can only do it a bite at a time!" When problems or projects tend to become overwhelming, a day at a time (or an hour at a time) can bring the project back to what is manageable.

3. Nothing lasts forever. No matter how troubling a situation may be, remember that this, too, will pass. We are not condemned to endless struggle, pain, or everlasting remorse. Neither can we depend upon having it made forever, no matter how great a present triumph. It has been said that change is the only dependable constant.

4. We can start again. Living one day at a time gives us the great freedom to begin anew, whenever we believe it is advisable to do so. We are not stuck with our patterns of error, however ingrained. We can start a new day right now and let this day make a difference.

If we make an effort to live a day at a time, we are unlikely to lose our way for long, however inclined we are to stray. Achieving lasting freedom from the pain of addictions and codependent patterns is possible. Those who choose to stay with recovery and who try to practice these principles see the benefits in their lives. Sharing the 12-Step message isn't like trying to sell something or convincing others that the 12-Step way of living works. What we share, we share out of our gratitude and from a sense of appreciation for what has freely been given to us. In trying the 12-Step method for recovery, we've personally seen that "It Works If You Work It!" And so, we think, will you.

Exercises

Exercise 1: The Business of Living

Comparing ourselves to others is a common pitfall in recovery. Are we making as much money as someone else? Do we look as good, sound as good as the next person? Should we be doing more Service work or less? If we've been in recovery awhile, shouldn't we be over certain kinds of problems? Here's an exercise to bring the focus back on our own lives:

1. **Where Did You Start?** Write out a brief list of factors describing your personal situation when you began recovery. How old were you? How was your health? (Include such health features as teeth or physical fitness.) Were you employed? Married? A single parent? Were you suffering from a lack of education, prior criminal record, a poverty background?

2. **What Are Your Interests?** What do you personally want out of life? Are you at an age or a stage in your life when you are mostly interested in finding a mate, creating a family of your own? Do you want to travel or study? Is a career or lifework central to you? Are you willing to do what it takes on a daily basis to move toward your goals, whatever they are?

3. **Are You Making Progress?** Based on where you came from and where you want to go, are you satisfied with your progress since getting into recovery? Do you feel you have become sidetracked in some ways? How can you refocus your efforts toward your own real goals? Is there some baggage from the past that you need to discard to make your goals possible?

Exercise 2: Secret Favors

Our program is anonymous for good reasons that have nothing to do with being embarrassed or ashamed to have it known that we are members of a self-help group. There are spiritual principles underlying anonymity. Here are some brief exercises to help point up the benefits of anonymity as a spiritual exercise:

1. Drop a deserved compliment in a suggestion box at work (or at a public agency) to give someone a pat on the back. Don't sign your name.

2. Give some books you've finished reading or some games or puzzles to your local library or to a senior center. Put them in a bag with a note and leave them where they'll be safely received but don't let yourself be seen dropping them off.

3. Secretly put a Christmas tree, wreath, or birthday bouquet at the door of someone who wouldn't otherwise have a holiday.

4. Play a game with yourself. Watch for opportunities to do a secret favor for someone. If you get caught, it doesn't count!

Exercise 3: Pray for Strangers

Charlie B., one of "AA's original 100" members, shared this favorite 12-Step exercise with us.

1.When you are at a meeting, look around the room and remember what one or two of the people look like.

2. The ones you want to remember are people you don't have any relationship with or attraction towards. Perfect strangers are your best bet, but, in any case, stay away from anyone you'd like to pick up or who you think might have something you could use.

3. When you get home, make a picture of them in your mind and pray for them to have all the things you'd like to have yourself.

4. Do this for different people every time you go to a meeting. See what happens.

Questions to Ponder

1. What is a spiritual awakening in your life?
2. Do you feel you carry the message in ways that are honestly you?
3. How is your program of recovery alive in you and in your life?
4. Are there aspects of your life that your program presently misses?

How does your group elect your Trusted Servants? Do you hold elections, with candidates running against each other, or do you use a different method? Before sharing my own preference, let me share with you what I have against running ACA's against each other:

- First off, think of what the word "against" means.
- Second, this kind of competition results in winners . . . but also in losers.

I know this from experience: At the first ACA election of officers, the losers left the group. Since there was only one group in the ACA fellowship at that time, these human beings effectively left ACA — ready or not!

I abstained from that first election in Westwood, California in 1980, for the reasons given above. And I still abstain. I will vote on issues, because I am a member of the group conscience. Sometimes an issue is identified with the person or persons presenting the issue. In this case, I try to make it crystal-clear that my vote is cast on principles, not personalities.

But we are considering election of officers as Trusted Servants. And even servants have personalities, agreed? To replace the personality-contest-type election, may I suggest a method that's proven useful?

When an election is necessary or desirable, call a Business Meeting for the purpose of nominating officers. At the Business Meeting, ask who is willing to serve the group. Then make sure that everyone who is willing gets something to do and some recognition, through self-nomination.

The first time we used this method was at the Federal Building, where we averaged 100 people per meeting. To serve so many ACAs, we came up with a number of positions for Trusted Servants to fill: Secretary, Co-Secretary, Night Chair (4 in number). In all, 15 ACA's got A New Employer — and every office got a back-up Trusted Servant to fill in as needed.

Since you make the rules for this election game, you can have as many Trusted Servants as you want. If three or more people nominate themselves for an office — great! Or even greater, perhaps, titles (and attendant service) can rotate around your whole group.

I hope I've made this point: Within the group, when two people run for an office, there should be two winners. Nobody joined ACA to learn how to be a loser. We already memorized that script.

To those who lost when the Westwood group had competitive elections, I supported their founding a group of their own. Some did. Some of us kids are that resilient. Kids who are not . . . let's make sure we provide as safe place for them to accept and render Service!

—Jack, an ACA Founder, Westwood, CA

My parents weren't alcoholics. In fact, my parents were both pretty ordinary, affectionate people with a nice home and a good income. The family dysfunction, although serious, wasn't obvious in the community.

My brother had an incestuous relationship with me, when I was between the ages of approximately 18 months to 3 years old. He was then a teenager acting as my babysitter. As a result of this abuse, I was an eroticized toddler. This aroused suspicion, which eventually lead to a violent confrontation between my father and brother, culminating with my brother being forced out of the home and into the armed services a few months before his 18th birthday. My father had his first heart attack at this time. Seven years later, my father died of a second heart attack. Although he had come to adopt an appearance of toleration toward my brother after he had gotten out of the service, no emotional reconciliation had ever occurred between them. When my father died, my mother (deep in denial) gave my brother renewed access to me, and he almost immediately began acting out his rage and shame in acts of physical abuse. The actual incest was never treated nor even acknowledged within the family after the initial confrontation. My mother died when I was 18, and my brother also died twelve years later of adult-onset leukemia.

As a teenager and young adult, I did well in school and creative activities, but I was unpredictable and unable to sustain any intimate bonds. When, in my late twenties, I finally tried to create a family for myself, I found I just couldn't do it.

I had to voluntarily give up my two children to adoption, one at a time, before either of them was two years old. I found that I was phobic about handling them, although I didn't know why. I suffered from nightmares which I know now were fragmentary memories of the incest. As it became clear to me finally that I was incapable of functioning as a parent, I lost all confidence in any of my other skills and I withdrew into depression. I had rage attacks and made suicide gestures. I was hospitalized twice. In late 1975, I was diagnosed as a possible early-stage alcoholic and referred to AA. Since that time, I've been continuously active in my own personal recovery.

To become functional, I had to unravel my dysfunctional patterns a little at a time, issue by issue, as I could access them. I did this by admitting that my life had been, for reasons I couldn't put my finger on, unmanageable. It was important to stay honest about my confusion and inability to remember. I had to resist the temptation to try to stuff myself into one or another pigeon hole of addiction. I'm an alcoholic, yes. I'm also a codependent, an addict, a food-abuser — all those things. But my incest and adult child issues are deeper than any substance issues. I had to remain willing to learn more in order to find lasting comfort and contentment. I've needed to be willing to feel in order to heal — not always so easy.

But as I have become increasingly able to be my own loving parent, my inner child has been able to risk giving me back my story, once deeply buried. My personal story has come back as images. I've been able to contact these nonverbal memories as I've learned to use visualization and other, less verbal, personal inventorying tools. These techniques go beyond simply working with words and the memories that are remembered as words.

I had very few words at three when I was sexually involved with my brother. What I remembered of those experiences was recorded as memories of smells, feelings of being touched in certain ways, and as pictures and sound/image memories. As my inner child feels secure enough, she allows me to experience what she has suppressed for all of these years — much of it searingly painful, terrified, bewildered and grossly overstimulating for a child. She also lets me feel her need and her grief at the losses she suffered before she was capable of understanding what was happening or why. Reclaiming these suppressed memories and feelings has given me back my identity, bit by bit.

I continue to work the Steps to connect with my inner spiritual lifeforce, and to give my violated inner child the resources she needs to be empowered to live today—not as a victim, but as a free and happy woman with a woman's courage and whole heart. Part of working the Steps is being active in 12-Step Service work, too. I had to live my beliefs and learn to communicate my truth. For me, this meant facing and living through fear and authority problems. Service has also given me a way to offer amends to my own children, when and if they reach out for recovery some day. Whether they do or not is not something I want to manipulate. They have their own inner sources of guidance and paths of growth that are their own to follow. But I do find inner peace in doing my part to make sure that recovery from the abandonment they suffered is there for them, too, if they want it. Healing is an option now, even in my family, and that makes me very deeply grateful.

—Kathleen W., Humboldt ACA Intergroup

In 12-Step programs there are many tasks, without financial compensation, which are necessary to perpetuate the program. These 12-Step tasks include Service work such as arriving early to open the meeting place, setting up chairs, making coffee, talking to newcomers, or leading a 1st-Step group. Other tasks include giving leads, reproducing meeting literature for beginners or from Intergroup, purchasing books, or serving as treasurer, to collect 7th-Tradition donations and pay the rent, serving as group chairman, or Intergroup representative.

Many find reasons not to serve their group, citing fear and discomfort as their reasons. But fear and discomfort are integral parts of life and of recovery. They cannot be avoided. And 12-Step work offers opportunities which far outweigh any discomfort.

Some may feel, "Why should I do Service work? I've been serving people all my life!" The truth is, much of the serving we have done in the past may really have been enabling — and enabling is a job which is always undermined by the person we wish to help. In recovery however, we can do genuine Service work — the kind of work which results in actively facilitating others' recovery and our own.

12-Step Service work is one of the most powerful recovery tools we possess. Many of us tend to suffer an isolation more global than merely sitting home on an occasional Saturday night. Our isolation is caused by not knowing how to relate to others, how to love them and ourselves. Performing Service work requires the interaction with others which we deeply need. Working on Service projects gives us a chance to see that others' characteristics and fears are very much like our own. This interaction helps heal our self-centered image, developed in the painful isolation of a dysfunctional past.

Service work provides us with a safe atmosphere for trying out new behaviors. In Service work, we can't be docked, sued, or fired for falling short of expectations. We learn to adopt positive qualities, such as dependability and efficiency, in a slow, natural way — not as a response to fear of punishment. Only 12-Step Service work allows us the freedom to develop at our own pace, and to meet our own needs along with those of others. By sharing in a group goal, we experience relief from painful isolation.

In the protected environment of 12th-Step work, such characteristics as an authoritarian outlook, addiction to excitement and poor or over-developed sense of responsibility are moderated. We feel a sense of accomplishment and togetherness that is not dependent on meeting excessive demands, or living up to grandiose fantasies.

Service work is an effective recovery tool, but it is also a great risk. Like all risks, Service is frightening. The greater the benefit, the greater its threat to old, sick patterns of behavior. We must continually use faith to push past these old patterns, and the fear that habit hides behind. To shrink from risk is to shun recovery.

Action is as essential for our program as is Spirituality. Someone has to conduct the meeting, make the coffee, collect the donations, reach out to the fearful newcomer. Those who make sure they are this someone by doing Service work reap the benefits — and insure the survival of our program. Reluctance to serve the program is common in recovery. The norm for many is to wait for someone else to perform the services needed. A common excuse is often, "I'm in too much pain — coming is burdensome enough."

By taking the initiative to perform Service work, we hand the best opportunity for recovery over to someone else. When we leave it to others to do the meeting's 12th-Step work, we may just as well leave it to others to do our sharing for us, or let someone else to work the Steps for us, make our phone calls or do our praying for us.

What did we see at our very first meeting? Someone chaired that meeting. Someone paid the rent and made sure our meeting was listed in the intergroup directory. Someone set up chairs, made coffee, and cleaned up afterwards, too — probably several someones. If these someones had our self-centered, fearful attitude of leaving Service to others, the meeting would not have been there for us to begin our recovery. The hard truth is that leaving Service work to others is a codependent approach to our own recovery and our own selves. Working a program lacking in Service is the hard way to attempt recovery. In our program, it is suggested we work all 12 Steps — andService is half of the 12th Step!

Life as a non-recovering Adult Child and Codependent is such a wretched experience, it necessitates our making recovery our #1 concern in life. Commitment to recovery requires pushing past the fear of new risks in the pursuit of healthy new goals.

Without the Service half of Step 12, the other 11-1/2 Steps will not be available to others who still suffer — or to us when we need it. Committing ourselves to recovery requires taking action before we quite understand how it will transform our feelings. This commitment to replace fear with faith is the solemn promise we make to ourselves in recovery. In the end, healthy self-love is the truest motivation for 12th-Step Service work.

—Peter G., Chicago, IL

APPENDIX ONE

The Recovery Wheels

> *"Creation gave us instincts for a purpose. Without them we wouldn't be complete human beings...these desires — for the sex relation, for material and emotional security and for companionship — are perfectly necessary and right, and surely God-given. Yet these instincts, so necessary for our existence, often far exceed their proper functions. Powerfully, blindly, many times subtly, they drive us, dominate us, and insist upon ruling our lives...When that happens, our great natural assets, the instincts, have turned into physical and mental liabilities."*
>
> —*12 Steps And 12 Traditions*, 1953, Bill W., A.A. World Service, Inc.

We are each born with some very powerful drives and desires. We aren't passive about whether or not we get fed, stay warm or are kept safe. We reach out for attention, affection. If we don't get enough of what we want, we make a fuss. Healthy infants are characteristically, innocently, demanding. We reach out to the world we have entered naked and helpless to provide for ourselves, communicating our most basic needs.

This demanding side of ourselves is an important part of being human. It is instinct that prompts us to reach out for exactly what we must have if we are to thrive and grow. As individuals, and as a species, we instinctively make a fuss for all of the right survival and social reasons.

But we don't go on endlessly naked and helpless, not if we are even moderately well cared for. As we mature, certain developments take place that make it possible for many basic needs to be satisfied with less of a fuss. We become able to get ourselves a bite to eat instead of having to scream out our hunger. We learn to take care of our own elimination and hygiene. Improved communication skills make it possible for us to feel loved and approved of, even when we aren't being physically held. As we become strong, we can go on without immediate satisfaction of many of our impulses. Putting off, or even missing, a meal isn't life-threatening for a teenager, although it could be for a newborn.

We don't outgrow our instinctive needs, as we develop. We simply evolve appropriate new ways to satisfy them. Gradually, too, we begin to be able to recognize the needs that others have as well. Needs which have been latent within us, such as the need for sexual relating, emerge as our bodies become physically mature. From dependency, we move toward interdependency. Finally, as parents, we become responsible for the care of new infants. The cycle turns again.

∗∗∗

One of AA's early supporters, Dr. William Silkworth, M.D., called alcoholism an allergic reaction to alcohol that set up a craving in people who were sensitive to it. This allergy was said to be coupled with a mental obsession to go on drinking, although to do so sets up a progressive inner conflict with a person's natural drive for self-preservation.

Why would anyone keep doing something that obviously was hurting them? In some ways, alcoholics acted like demanding little infants in grown-up bodies. But not like *healthy* infants. Alcoholics demanded what was, in fact, poison for their systems. Worse yet, having gotten clean for a few days or weeks, they usually couldn't resist the impulse to start drinking again. Lack of resistance to impulse is another trait of very small children.

AA's co-founders, Bill W., Dr. Bob and other early AAs pondered these questions. They, after all, were admitted alcoholics. Addictive patterns, once activated, they knew from their own experiences, had a life of their own. If they didn't take the first destructive act (drink), they wouldn't set off the self-destructive pattern (for alcoholics, an overwhelming physical craving, once started, to keep drinking). But in order to stay out of the old behavior (and not to take the first drink), they had to change their whole approach to living. If they couldn't do that, the mental obsession would creep back (because of stress or letting down their guard) to tempt them to try the old behavior again. The 12-Step process is a response to this cycle of allergy-coupled-with-obsession.

In AA's *12-Steps and 12-Traditions*, published several years after AA was started, Bill W. expanded the materials on the Steps to explore the question of instincts in conflict in more detail. He saw that even non-addicts had to reconcile the same powerful drives that become so obviously skewed in active alcoholism.

Recent research tends to support this point of view. We know now, for instance, that needs for emotional security seem to be anchored in the mammalian level of our brains, while certain self-preservation instincts are resident at even deeper areas within the brain. Our brains appear to contain a hierarchy of drives, each of which has a contribution to make to our lives as whole beings. Denial of these needs always produces a painful sense of inner turmoil and dis-unity. Ideas and beliefs that create a sense of shame about these needs produce inner conflict. Unresolved, such conflicts can prompt us to act out self-destructively. Instead of repressing our biologically rooted drives, we need to seek healthy ways to satisfy them without unduly imposing on others.

Maturity, balance, a sense of inner security—these he saw were the goals of sane living, whether addicted or not. The instincts that Bill W. discusses in the AA 12 x 12— survival, gratification, commitment and identity[1]—are the basis for the Recovery Wheels on the following pages.

Since few of us grow up in ideal circumstances, most of us have areas of immaturity, blind spots of reaction to life and to those around us. If we learned to deny some of our inner drives or to sacrifice ourselves to the demands of others, we may remain stuck in an immature stage of unsatisfied need ourselves. If we don't do this work, the stuck places in ourselves usually become more troublesome. Arrested development issues are not neutral; neglected, they tend to create within us dis-unity that manifests in our lives. We may not be able to be interdependent with other adults, or we may handle parenting responsibilities inconsistently. We may also become addicts ourselves, or compulsive in some other way.

We can, however, go back and fill these needs for ourselves. This is what is meant by re-parenting the Inner Child within us. Although Bill W. did not use this language (which is very recent), the principles of reparenting are implicit in the 12-Step programs.

The repetitious reading that occurs at 12-Step meetings induces relaxation, allowing images and feelings from deep within to gradually return. Writing, drawing or verbalizing slogans and affirmations also help. Peace of mind is attainable, if we are willing to work for it.

The Recovery Wheels

The Recovery Wheels are made up of several characteristics commonly linked with addictive and codependent behaviors. On the Victim Wheel, dysfunctional characteristics are grouped with the instinctive drives that underlie them, as motives. They are also arranged across from each other, in linked pairs of opposites. When one end of a spoke of paired dysfunctional behaviors is stimulated, we tend to instinctively react with the opposite behavior. For example, if we are challenged by ridicule, we are likely to feel the need to justify who we are. If we are threatened, we may seek to appease. Each of these behaviors is out of balance — each is insecure and to a greater or lesser extent, destructive. No matter who starts it, we remain victims so long as we play our parts in this dysfunctional dance.

The circular (mandala) arrangement of spokes is designed as an aid to take the focus off of the other guy, and their faults or weakness, and to bring it back to ourselves, and what we can do to change our own patterns.

In addition, the Freedom Wheel offers positive alternative behaviors and attitudes that can become a substitute for any victim role. If we are challenged with ridicule, we can choose to respond by disclosing how we are feeling. We can own our power to deal with threats appropriately, if we feel intimidated. If standing up to the threat is not realistic, we get help or leave. When we encounter what feels like pressure to play the victim, we can reparent ourselves by choosing to operate from the Freedom Wheel, instead.

Getting used to operating from the Freedom Wheel, instead of from Victim Roles, takes practice. To make the best use of these devices, photocopy or trace the Wheels and put them up where they are easy to see. The Wheels often bring insight into motives and behaviors — your own and other people's. They're more likely to be used if they are posted on the refrigerator than if they're in a book.

Victim Roles Wheel

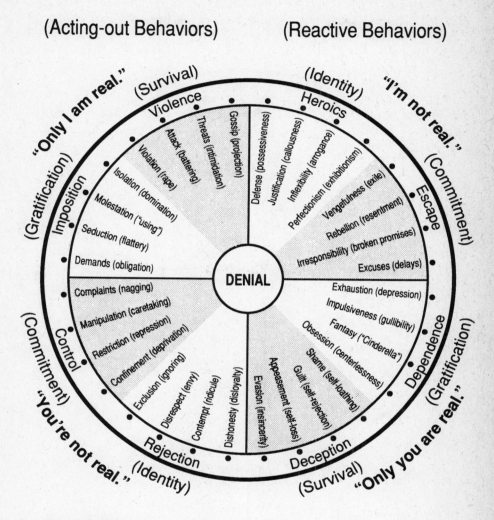

© 1987, 1990 EUREKA! Publishing

153

Freedom Wheel

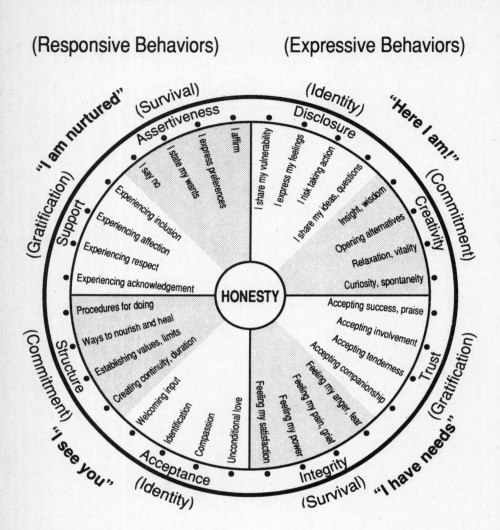

You don't have to wait for anyone in order to begin making progress. Try using the Wheels on issues or problems as they come up in life. Use the Victim Roles Wheel to examine problem areas in your family, personal, or business relationships. Whatever irritating behaviors you are encountering in others, look across the wheel to see what spoke is on the other end of it. Are you slipping into that role, yourself?

Then, on the Freedom Wheel, locate the affirmation concepts to replace your victim patterns with healthy ones.

Using the Recovery Wheels with the Steps

1. Use the Victim Roles Wheel to identify or to inventory your personal issues (Steps 1, 4, 10). Notice where you fit in terms of the four categories of basic needs. Which of the drives tends to dominate you? Which areas prompt strong feeling reactions or judgments?

2. Inventory yourself using the spokes within the Victim Roles Wheel. Are there ways you manipulate yourself, kid yourself, or scare yourself? Do you tell yourself you are a victim?

3. After you have inventoried yourself on the Victim Roles Wheel, discuss your inventory with a trusted individual (Step 5), considering the affirmation concepts on the Freedom Wheel that correspond to the problems you identified. Does using the affirmation concepts to replace the victim habits make sense to you? Do you find you have to stretch your point of view to see how some of them apply?

4. The Freedom Wheel can help bring light into blind spots where there seems to be a lack of choice, or a limited number of mutually unattractive alternatives in working Steps 6 and 7. Do you find yourself faced with letting go of some outdated behaviors from the Victim Roles Wheel? With consciously embracing a more desirable attitude from the Freedom Wheel?

5. Use the Recovery Wheels in connection with any of the 12 Steps to get the focus off the other and back upon yourself. In Steps 8 and 9, examine the family patterns you recognize from the Victim Roles Wheel and notice how they are still being acted out. Are you infected with some of these old scripts? Are your present-day relationships being infected, too? Are there fresh options you can introduce (by living them, yourself) from the Freedom Wheel to bring healing and new hope to your relationships?

6. Create an affirmation for yourself based on whatever spokes you seem stuck on, using the corresponding spokes on the Freedom Wheel. Use your affirmations in your practice of Steps 2 and 3 to expand and deepen your connection with a power greater (or within) yourself, and in Step 11.

7. Experiment. Utilize any spoke on the Freedom Wheel as an affirmation for meditation and prayer to aid in extending your horizons. Build Step 11 meditation into your daily routine. Stick with it for a month. Use one or two spokes as the basis for affirmations toward a goal and see what happens in your life.

Creating with Affirmations: Replacing "Inner Tapes"

Affirmations are positive statements—usually brief—grounded and built from concepts we understand and believe to be true. Repeating a simple, direct affirmation counteracts anxiety, fear of failure or of rejection, and helps keep goals and boundaries in focus.

Affirmations may be used in prayer and meditation. They are unifiers, with the power to open channels in the heart and mind. Most people who utilize affirmations notice an improvement in their personal outlook, and objective changes in their lives.

Try this inner tapes exercise:

1. Look over the Victim Wheel, spoke by spoke. Listen to any inner tapes (self-talk messages) that you hear, and note any false, compulsive or fear-based messages you are presently giving to yourself. Write the spoke phrase down.

2. Look up the counterpart spoke on the Freedom Wheel and write down that affirmation concept next to the Victim Wheel phrase. Write a personal truth in your own words based on your understanding of this affirmation concept.

3. If you have trouble getting a clear understanding of the affirmation concept, talk to a trusted person (such as a sponsor) to exchange views.

4. Say your personal affirmation to yourself out loud to replace your old tape. Saying it (or singing it or shouting it) while exercising or while walking briskly down a beach is even better. Writing it fifty or a hundred times is another good way to anchor this healthy self-message and replace the bad tape. It's a good practice to keep at it with an affirmation for two weeks or more.

Dysfunctional Family Myths

A myth is a story or legend that is passed along which may or may not be based on verifiable facts or events. Most dysfunctional families pass along dysfunctional myths about our basic needs, how you have to live or what you have to expect in life.

Family-held myths presenting false, limited views of what is possible or desirable in life can be both powerful and terrifying. Since everyone in the family hears the myth and sees it acted out, the dysfunctional myth may appear to be true—and life, therefore, pretty hopeless or limited as a result.

Look over the Victim Roles Wheel, this time looking for Victim patterns your family internalized as family myth. Look at what your family believed about satisfying the basic needs—Survival, Commitment, Gratification and Identity. Here are some examples:

A "Look Good" Family: The problems in the family are hidden from the community and the family may enjoy status. People don't end up in brawls at holiday dinners (or those who do become family exiles). It's not O.K. to display (or even to admit having) feelings that don't support the family's self-image. Failure to keep up the family's public image results in scorn, exclusion, ridicule. Drinking and drug use may include throwing big parties or providing the drugs. Various big shots, including community leaders, media stars, and drug dealers, may be motivated by the family myth, "We are better!" The Victim Roles played out tend to be Heroics versus Rejection.

A "Soap Opera" Family: The family is on a constant roller coaster of shifting relationships and emotional benders. Threats of sexual transgressions, jealousy, or other emotional tests create cycles of crisis and uproar between family members. Feuds with outsiders tend to pull family members together. Emotional abuses, including overt and covert incest, are common experiences. Drinking or using drugs to counterbalance the blues is common. Family members may feel very loyal to each other and often want to protect each other — but can't. The family myth is, "We can't help ourselves!" Victim roles in "Soap Opera" families center in Dependence versus Imposition.

A "Not There" Family: The family home may look like an untidy rooming house with stuff stacked everywhere, or it may be as neat and orderly as a hospital operating room, but the atmosphere is not relaxed. Family members live separate lives, preoccupied with goals that are not shared (and may often be actively concealed) from each other. Everyone defends his/her turf and rights. Unpredictability, uproar, broken promises and pleas or demands for change may be the usual level of interaction — or, all meaningful interaction may have ceased. Family members feel abandoned, misunderstood. They may often complain and seek comfort from outsiders. Substances are abused to fuel or medicate the family members. The family myth is, "It's too much for us." Control and Escape are the usual Victim Role ruts.

The "Crime & Punishment" Family: Living in fear of punishment characterizes families dominated by force. Under stated or unstated family rules, dominators are like wrathful gods without restrictions. They may violate physical and emotional boundaries of others to enforce rules they themselves have established. Family members are made to involuntarily serve them, to fetch and carry upon demand. All relationships are seen as based on force and held together by threat, where fights are either won or lost, not negotiated or resolved. Family members may either seek out or become bullies in the community. Alcohol or drug use precipitates violence. The family myth is "We're no good," and the Victim Roles are Violence and Deception.

---

[1]Bill W. called the instinctive drives by slightly different names, which have been modified for clarity: The drive for survival he called physical security; for commitment, emotional security; for gratification, sexual drive; and for identity, social standing.

APPENDIX TWO

Issues in Recovery Inventories

This section includes several special focus inventories. The issues selected have been included because they are serious but not always easy to identify. We have included these quizzes to help expand the adult child and codependent's approach to the Steps, starting with Step 1. Some of them, such as work addiction and overachiever patterns, are often socially encouraged. Others may be buried or masked by painful walls of fear, rage, or denial. Although separate self-help groups exist in some communities for these issues, they are also very appropriate topics for discussion in adult children groups. (See the Chart, "Addictive / Compulsive Disorders", in Chapter 1, for an illustration of the range of addictive, compulsive and codependent patterns.) In some communities, ACA has many special focus meetings as well as open discussion groups. Formats are included in Appendix III and many additional special focus formats may be obtained through the ACA Resource Library, listed in Appendix III under National Contacts.

Although it is an adult child/codependent issue, eating disorder inventories are not included in this book. Special focus inventories created specifically for eating/ dieting are available through several sources. Janet Greeson, Ph.D., provides an excellent 12-Step-oriented approach to eating disorders in her book *It's Not What's You're Eating, It's What's Eating You*, (1990, Pocket Books), including a self-quiz, "Are You A Food Addict?" Overeaters Anonymous also provides a free self-inventory pamphlet, as do separate support groups for anorexia and bulimia.

Literally dozens of special focus self-help 12-Step fellowships have sprung into existence over the past few years. Many of these groups have lists of characteristics to help prospective members identify addictive patterns. Alcoholics Anonymous, Narcotics Anonymous, Cocaine Anonymous, Gamblers Anonymous, Debtors Anonymous, Adult Children Anonymous, CoDependents Anonymous, Al-Anon, Overeaters Anonymous, Marijuana Anonymous, Prostitutes Anonymous, and many other 12-Step fellowships provide free self-inventory pamphlets upon request. There are several different 12-Step programs that deal with incest, molestation, sexual addictions, and abuse. Religious issues, including special formats for Christians, Jews, and Pagans in recovery, and formats for secular "non-supernatural" approaches and for dealing with some religious practices as addictions in their own right are also available. 12-Step programs are listed by name in the white pages of the telephone book in many communities.

Regional and national service offices for these and other 12-Step fellowships can also be located through state and national self-help clearing houses. These non-profit organizations keep up-to-date lists of all kinds of self-help groups and resources.

Addresses for clearing houses are found in Appendix III under National Contacts. In most communities, resource lists may be found through the mental or public health offices, too. These public agencies will usually provide referrals to professional help and therapy, as well as to self-help groups.

Domestic Violence Survivor Inventory

Behaviors

1. Have there been times or circumstances in your life when you habitually (automatically) focused on calming or appeasing those whom you saw as having power over you? As having power over others?

2. Were you trained to take on responsibility for the feelings, especially the belligerence, suspicion or other hostile feelings, of authority figures? Were you encouraged to think it was probably your fault if they became angry? Violent?

3. Were you assaulted, shouted at, held up to scorn, deprived of things, confined or forced to do certain things during a period in your life? Did you accept this punishment as deserved, at the time? Did you resist? Flee?

4. Have you attempted to live up to standards that include the words always or never? ("Never let yourself be angry," or, "Always be calm, kind")

5. Have you become isolated in a relationship with a person you see as controlling or demanding? Is this a pattern in your life?

6. Are you a harsh critic of your own performance? Do you see yourself as a failure if you aren't 100% perfect? Has it seemed that your best just isn't good enough?

7. Have you justified not pursuing your goals because of the risk of an angry reaction from someone? Have you preferred to guess rather than to risk asking questions of authority figures? As a result, have you lost opportunities, rights, or sacrificed your needs? Have you misread situations?

8. What unacceptable family rules, such as forms of punishment, tend to crop up in your own behavior, either as self-messages or as messages toward family members (children)?

Feelings

1. Have you felt so threatened by some authority figure that you feared for your personal safety or survival? For the safety of others in your care?

2. Have you noticed that you have sometimes buried your own angry or fearful feelings toward authority figures? Have you lost touch with your own feelings in your attempts to soothe others? Have you experienced feeling frozen or paralyzed under certain circumstances?

3. Have you felt hopeless to help yourself in life? Do you feel trapped in a world dominated by other people's anger? Condemned to pain, loss, loneliness?

4. Does any open expression of anger, such as loud, forceful talk, sudden movements and gestures, frighten or anger you? Does it turn you off to the person acting angry? Inspire your contempt? Your rage?

5. Do you expect the open expression of anger by anyone, yourself included, to lead to the termination of the relationship involved? Do you have a no-angry-acting rule for friendships? Jobs? Lovers? Marriage partners? Have you acted on this expectation (fear) and enforced this rule on yourself and others?

6. Do you often feel sorry for some of those closest to you? Have you risked exposing yourself, or those in your care, to potential abuse out of pity for someone?

7. Have you allowed those you live with, or work with, to become, in effect, your

gods or your demons? Have you felt controlled? Overwhelmed? Blotted out as a separate person?

Affirmation/Meditation

Imagine yourself, and those you love, in a place of complete safety, free of all threats. Feel how it feels to be safe. Imagine what new options become open to you in a world free of threats. Let yourself see yourself living out these options. Let yourself feel how it feels to experience these opportunities.

Incest/Molestation Survivor Inventory

Incidents of incest and molestation which may have occurred in childhood are often lost to conscious memory. Sometimes, only vague images remain, fragmentary glimpses or feelings which may flash into consciousness under certain kinds of stress.

Incest may also have been covert, a result of inappropriate emotional bonding with a parent figure who encouraged a child to fill emotional needs more appropriately filled by a mate.

Here are some questions which are designed to explore behaviors and attitudes in adult living which may be especially stressful to incest/molestation victims. Note your feeling responses to these questions, and encourage any visual imagery that comes up for you. Be sure to give yourself all the support you need, including professional and spiritual support. It is possible to recover from these injuries. Strong feelings of grief, rage, and shame are not uncommon; they gradually subside as healing integration takes place within us.

Behaviors

1. Do you have difficulty establishing or maintaining personal boundaries? Are you unclear on your rights to privacy, to self-expression, to having your personal space, or to feeling secure in your body?

2. Do you experience problems defining boundaries in the area of personal property rights? Do you have frequent or prolonged disputes with others about these questions?

3. Do you see personal and property boundary issues as your responsibility to resolve? Or do you see yourself as passive, acted upon by others?

4. Have you experienced difficulty seeing or imagining yourself as an effective, practical self-friend in your own behalf when it comes to defining or defending your limits?

5. What ideas or images do you have that get in the way of your being your own best friend? Are there religious, ethical, or romantic ideals you hold which are in conflict with maintaining clear personal boundaries?

6. Are you inclined to believe that complete honesty requires that nothing be held back in communication? Do you tend to swing between extremes of "no talk" or "spill all" in communication?

7. Do you check with people to make sure they are open to being hugged or touched before you touch them? Do you respect other people's property rights and ask before using their things? Do you return things you borrowed?

8. Were your boundaries respected in your family of origin? Were they canceled, violated? Did you experience isolation or punishment when you said no?

Feelings

1. What sorts of interaction with others feel safe to you? What situations prompt you to relax, be at ease?

2. Do issues which involve money, property rights or social standing prompt strong or lasting anxieties, suspicions, or dread of consequences?

3. Do you feel you are dominated by people who have the power to deprive you of emotional or material security? Are you ashamed of these feelings?

4. Do you find that you become suddenly sexually attracted, or sexually intimidated, by interest shown in you from certain physical "types" (or job descriptions, social roles) of persons?

5. Do you feel compelled to act upon these sorts of sexual impulses, without necessarily checking out what is intended by the other person?

6. Do you have a concept of a Higher Power that loves you unconditionally and accepts you with all your feelings, impulses?

7. Do you sense an Inner Child within that feels hopeless, imprisoned, lost or resigned? Do you feel a need for new insight in order to reach this Child?

Affirmation/Meditation

To reach an Inner Child who may have been molested, visualize and allow yourself to feel rosy, warm golden light centered in your heart mixing with your breath. Allow this healing golden light to circulate gently with each breath and heartbeat down into your belly and sexual organs. Blend this golden light with the stronger colors you may be experiencing there. Breathing deeply and slowly, allow the darker colors to be released and replaced with this clear, rosy golden light. Let this released energy move up into the throat as golden speech, becoming pale blue with vivid, colorful designs as all of your being is expressed, creatively, free of denial or imposition. Feel free to direct this energy flow with your hands, in dance or in any form of creative self-expression. Welcome your Child back into the safe, pure temple of your body.

Incest/Molestation Taboo Violators Inventory

Those who have been molested or battered as children are more at risk than others for becoming molesters themselves. Molestation is a violent crime, not a sexual act. When personal boundaries have become blurred to the extent that incest and molest activities have become a part of an individual's sexual response or behavior, professional help is essential for a full recovery. With help, however, healing is possible.

Blackouts (losses of memory) are not unusual either for victims or perpetrators. Here are some additional questions to explore this taboo topic:

Behaviors

1. Are you aware of having initiated a sexual contact with a parent, sibling or other relative? Have you engaged in any kind of sexual activities or sexplay with a child?

2. Have you used emotional pressures, threats, bribes, promises, force, or guilt to get someone to go along with satisfying your sexual desires or fantasies?

3. Have you created a false picture of reality to cover your tracks, protect your reputation, or discredit a person with whom you've had inappropriate relations?

4. Have you been forced, pressured, or talked into sexual activities yourself? Into behaviors against your will or conscience?

5. Have you had some experiences in life that have influenced you to think that people may often use each other? Take advantage of each other's weaknesses?

6. Are you sometimes conscious of serious conflicts between your inner values (beliefs) and what you do?

7. Have you confided a sexual secret or fantasy in someone who then betrayed your trust? Has someone used confidential information to pressure or exploit you?

8. In your family of origin, was your space or person violated by an authority figure? Were you left unprotected by others who you might reasonably have expected to defend or protect you? Were you in a role of being the special one, emotionally depended upon by a parent?

Feelings

1. Do you hate some aspects of yourself? Do you have fears that you may be a bad person? That you may be unforgivable?

2. Do you feel unable to control some of your impulses and desires? Have you sometimes acted without thinking? What feelings take over?

3. Do you feel trapped by guilty secrets of your past? Do you dread possible exposure? Possible punishment? Do you have nightmares? Lose sleep?

4. Are there periods or episodes of your past that are blacked out? Are there hazy or sketchy incidents involving sex or violence in your memory? What feelings come up for you when you try to reclaim these memories?

5. Do you have persistent feelings of resentment, grief, or fear toward someone or toward women or men as a group?

6. Have you felt ashamed to express affection or tender feelings toward others? Have you felt shame for having these feelings?

7. Was your childhood concept of a Higher Power vengeful? Do you still feel you may now be unworthy of God's love, mercy or forgiveness? Is the idea of reaching out to your Higher Power for help alien to you? Are you angry at God?

Affirmation/Meditation

Imagine a concept of God that can forgive you for everything you've ever done in your life, with no exceptions whatsoever. Imagine this concept of God in detail. Draw a picture of a merciful God who can and will forgive you and save you from all punishment and pain — or gather some objects into an arrangement that gives you a sense of such healing. Put this image or arrangement somewhere you can see it every day without being disturbed by anyone or anything. Imagine yourself feeling completely healed of shame and guilt. Give yourself a week or two to open up to this new concept and then admit one of your secrets to this concept of God. It can be a very small secret. See what happens.

Sex Addiction Inventory

Behaviors

1. Do you see yourself as engaging in a kind of game, socially, when it comes to sexuality? Are there rules to be followed or flaunted that you and your co-participants are more or less familiar with when it comes to the chase, for example? Is there an element you see as some form of scoring points?

2. Do you believe that finding the right person is a matter of getting lucky? Are there certain flags that instantly attract you or turn you off? Have you behaved on impulse in choosing a partner?

3. How much of your self-regard or sense of personal value do you find is dependent upon the sexuality feedback that comes to you from others?

4. Do you lose focus in other areas of your life as a result of your sexuality? Do responsibilities get neglected or avoided? Goals postponed? Do you rapidly seem to merge into the personality and lifestyle, perhaps even the household, of a lover?

5. Do you find that you have inner conflict, with your sexuality on one side and most of the rest of your values on the other? Do you feel that your sexuality can make you act the fool? Succumb to flattery? Be used?

6. Are there sexual behaviors you initiate which are degrading to, painful for or against the will of another? Are there sexual behaviors you engage in which involve incest, molestation, obscene phone calls? Are you willing to admit these and accept professional help?

7. Do you say no to behaviors you don't wish to be a party to, without hesitation? With difficulty? In non-sexual situations or other areas of your life, is it easier or harder to say no?

8. What memories from childhood or teenage years come up when you scan the questions above? Were you ridiculed? Treated callously or insensitively? Were your rights to your body or to your privacy violated?

Feelings

1. Is your sexuality often separated from other feelings, such as tenderness, respect? Are you emotionally detached? Emotionally unavailable?

2. Do you become sexually involved with people whom you actually don't like, perhaps really dislike? Do you find that you become contemptuous of your lover? Do you feel justified in rejecting him/her? Hurting him/her?

3. Does being desired by another seem to give you power or value you don't otherwise sense in yourself? Do you fear you'll be found out as not worthy of love? Are you very jealous of any and all potential competitors?

4. Do you feel that a lover has control over some or all aspects of your life? Do you fear rejection in situations where you may want to assert yourself, express an opinion, or make a decision?

5. Are you ashamed of your sexual feelings? Do you feel disgusted with yourself or with your partner for having a sexual appetite? Are you ashamed of having tender feelings? Do you fear being criticized or ridiculed for these needs or feelings?

6. Do you have vengeful feelings you release through your sexuality? Were there

childhood incidents you may have partially blotted out, where you were the victim of sexual abuses? Are there some acting-out elements in your adult sexuality that may require professional attention?

7. In your personal recovery, are you beginning to accept yourself as a human being with healthy sexual needs and desires, free of self-rejection? Are feelings of caring, devotion and friendliness aspects of human sexuality you find yourself willing to embrace?

Affirmation/Meditation

As a recovering codependent in this area of personal sexuality, explore experiencing yourself as a complete sexual being. Ask your Higher Power to guide and support you in restoring your deep, heart-centered spiritual identity. Breathe in joy and self-acceptance with each breath you take. Accept the perfect lover within, and feel this unconditional love fill up your heart to overflowing!

Power Addictions Inventory

Behaviors

1. Does your security or confidence stem from others seeing you as being especially dominant, desirable, fascinating or funny?

2. Are there some forms of feedback you seek to avoid? Do you engage in impression management most of the time?

3. Have you wanted specific forms of recognition as proof that your projected image is acknowledged? Do you demand praise? Money? Status? Do you want others to do more to acknowledge your power?

4. Do you find ways to reward your followers or punish your detractors? Are there behaviors in others you feel justified in trying to control? To get them to do or stop doing?

5. Do intimate relationships tend to drain you? Do you attract people who always want you to entertain them? Make their decisions? Who are self-rejecting?

6. Have you experienced frequently being let down by those who made you promises? Have you done it to them before they could do it to you?

7. Do you doubt the reliability of others, when it comes to the basics — food, shelter, safety? Do you live in a community where you may be robbed or attacked, or where you find it impossible to make enough money? Do you live beyond your means?

8. Did you experience violation of your body, personal space or property in your family of origin? Did you learn to conceal your feelings to keep from being taken advantage of or used?

Feelings

1. What feelings do you experience while you are in the act of performing or competing for attention? How do you feel toward those who make up your audience?

2. What sorts of gratification do your receive from being applauded or praised? Excitement? Satisfaction? Are there feelings you don't have to feel when you perform?

3. Are you unwilling to acknowledge or express some of your feelings toward others for fear the feelings may be too much? (Too angry? Too needy? Too tender?)

4. Do you fear you'll be let down or abandoned if you give others the opportunity to act freely? Are you afraid you'll be fired? Attacked? Unpleasantly surprised?

5. Do you feel compelled to behave a certain way when you feel your basic needs may be threatened? When feeling insecure, what images come up for you?

6. As a child growing up, were you given messages to blame yourself for wrongs done you by others? Did someone call you stupid? Were your things taken or broken? Were you tricked?

7. Was your love for a parent figure not received or returned? Have you felt as though there might be something inadequate or flawed about your ability to love?

Affirmation/Meditation

In reparenting yourself today, imagine yourself as the rightful owner of a beautiful castle, bright and glistening upon a high, high hill. Your walls are hung with tapestries so rich and beautiful just looking at them fills your heart with joy. While someone quietly plays music, the smells of a delicious feast being prepared for you tugs your attention. Those who love you laugh and talk softly around you. This is all yours to keep and to enjoy. In this atmosphere of perfect security, examine all of your feelings as they occur. Allow yourself to say no or yes without worry about consequences. Relax and let love in. Your inner space is your castle and you are welcome here.

Work Addiction Inventory

Behaviors

1. Has your work (career) become an escape from other areas of your life? Is it nearly all you do or think about?

2. Do you feel manipulated in your behavior or in your thinking in other areas of your life? Do you avoid these by going to work?

3. Are there personal relationships which you justify neglecting for, or otherwise sacrifice, to your work?

4. Do you hold beliefs that place work (or career) highest on your list? What are the top three or four priorities in your life?

5. Do you see your own worth as a function of how you are seen by your bosses or peers in the workplace? Do you value yourself in terms of your earnings? Your position in your field?

6. Do you believe your family or friends tend to value you or each other in terms of earnings or assets?

7. Can you identify a pattern of being imposed upon, undervalued or not acknowledged by others on the job?

8. In your family of origin, were your parents generally on a treadmill most or all of the time? Was there no end to work, chores, or other forms of striving in your household? Were demands put upon you to join in? Were you called lazy or other names to goad you into work?

Feelings

1. Do you enjoy a feeling of losing yourself in your work activities or in thinking? Are you so hooked you don't want to stop and go home? Can't wait to get back? Spend more and more time working/thinking?

2. Have you noticed that stress prompts you to react by going to work? Has work become more of an answer?

3. Do you have feelings of resentment toward those who seek to interfere with your work activities? Are you inclined to be indifferent to or unaware of their feelings? Do you take people for granted?

4. What do you fear you may lose or fail to get if you consider reevaluating, rearranging, or changing your personal priorities? How realistic are your fears? Do other feelings come up?

5. Do you find yourself feeling less reassured of your personal worth from the feedback of bosses or others in the workplace? Do you require increasingly greater jolts of feedback—money, status—to feel O.K.?

6. Do you find you have buried feelings of loneliness, hopelessness or depression? Do you feel you can never do enough to be O.K., praised, loved?

7. Are there feelings of anger you have suppressed at one or both of your parents?

Affirmation/Meditation

As the recovering work addict parent of a possibly timid Inner Child, experiment with ways of introducing this Child to a Higher Power who has enough power to give your Child enough love, money and praise without fail or delay and without too much work. Imagine a Higher Power who wants your Child to have fun and laughter every day in life! Make a deal with your Inner Child to spend some time having fun each and every day— and then, keep that promise.

Overachiever Inventory

Behaviors

1. Have you experienced becoming obsessed with achieving goals or maintaining standards you have set up for yourself? In what areas? (Education? Business? Supermom? Fitness?)

2. Do you have values or ideas about the world which tend to tie achievement to being loved? To being worthy? Deserving? To not losing out?

3. What are your expectations or fantasies regarding feedback in response to your achievements? How much of this takes place only in your head?

4. Do you have thoughts or expectations that your achievements will actually change or modify who you are? What do you anticipate being added? Eliminated?

5. What indirect feedback or responses do you anticipate? Do you have a vision or ideal of being among people who behave differently from your present companions or social circle? Who cares for you more?

6. Are you often disappointed in the behaviors or performance of others? Do you find you must leave people behind in life?

7. Have you developed a personal strategy for avoiding becoming the object of gossip or for deflecting personal attacks? Do people envy you? Do you find it hard to let down your guard?

8. Were you rewarded as a child with affection or approval chiefly for your achievements? Did you receive messages that you needed to win, or to improve yourself or your performance to be loved?

Feelings

1. What feelings do you have while you are actively engaged in your achievement activities? Are there feelings you eliminate or shut out as a part of engaging in this activity?

2. Are there real or fantasy figures whose love, admiration or fellowship you desire as a result of your achievements? Are there those you fear you may lose if you do not achieve?

3. Are you afraid to admit, or do you become defensive regarding, your need for love? Do you fear that all love may be conditional? Do you feel secure in the loyalty of your friends? Your mate?

4. Have you felt used and discarded by those you have loved? Have you felt that many of your personal relationships have been one-way streets, where you give, and others take?

5. Do you tend to have internal dialogues in which you make sacrifices to your goals, standards or achievements, while enduring feelings of loneliness?

6. Are you frightened or made anxious by delays, lapses of communication or departures from routine? Do you have childhood memories of being let down or lied to?

7. Was your childhood concept of a Higher Power judgmental? Was your Higher Power the sort that sends a flood for a tiny mistake? How conditional was God's love? How available?

Affirmation/Meditation

As an exercise in reparenting your Inner Child, imagine your Child in the arms of a loving, cheerful Higher Power. This Higher Power is willing to toss and swing you up in gleeful play. Laughter and fun surround you, and you are free to laugh without restraint. Your world is full of fun-loving people who accept you and enjoy your company. You are on a grassy playing field in the sun with lots of friends doing interesting activities. Carry this image with you and keep it in your heart to contact as you move through your daily life. You deserve to be loved and accepted every day of your life.

Codependent "Managers" Inventory

Behaviors

1. Are you preoccupied with controlling others? Is much of your time and attention focused on overseeing the activities of others?

2. Do you hold the opinion that there are spiritual, ethical, social or business basics which are important for everyone to live by?

3. Do you get your sense of security from authority? Do you act according to the rules and stick by them no matter what?

4. Do you think you are justified in using compulsion in dealings with others? Do you have a system worked out for handling resistance from others? Do you believe circumstances justify intimidating others? Who? When?

5. Are there forces in the world (moral weakness, emotional sickness) that you see yourself combatting? Do you see these forces as evil? As potentially overpowering?

6. In your world view, does survival depend on keeping control? Resisting the control of others? Is it an us versus them world?

7. Do you attract people who depend upon your control or decision making? Are you surrounded by followers?

8. As a child, were you the acting parent of a parent or of siblings? Did these responsibilities interfere with studies or school activities? Recreation or play? Self-care?

Feelings

1. Do you have a feeling that something awful might happen or things might not work out if you were to relax your vigilance? Have awful things happened which haunt your memories?

2. Do you feel safe only among those who constantly reassure you by actions and words that they share your same beliefs, ethics, or business theories? Does critical feedback make you angry?

3. Have you experienced feeling fearful, exposed, or powerless in situations where the rules were suspended, violated or ignored?

4. Is there behavior, including body language, tone of voice, or personality types you feel threaten your control? Do you feel justified in rejecting such people?

5. Do you feel it necessary to get everything under control before you can relax? Are you inclined to become hyper-vigilant (very aware of how others may be reacting to you or to each other)?

6. Does your Higher Power test you? Do you feel there is a competition between the God of your understanding and the forces of evil?

7. Do you trust your Higher Power with the care of your life under all circumstances, including when you make a mistake?

Affirmation/Meditation

Consider reparenting your Inner Child by providing a system of beliefs that are compatible with good health, which encourage honesty and creative efforts, and which support self-respect. Build trust with your Inner Child by actively living by these values yourself, a day at a time. Consider ceasing to worry about whether anyone else does!

Phone Addicts Inventory

Behaviors

1. Are many of your personal relationships based more or less exclusively in telephone contact? Have telephone relationships replaced some or most other forms of contact with other people?

2. Do you regularly give hours a day to talk relationships? If a talk connection terminates, do you quickly fill the vacuum by adding a new contact or talking longer to an old one?

3. Are there behaviors you do while you are talking on the phone that you wouldn't want people to see? Do you overeat, drink, smoke or neglect your appearance? Is your house a mess?

4. Are the behaviors of third parties the focus of your phone conversations? Do you share a sense of helplessness or hopelessness with your phone contacts? Do you tend to validate each other's resentments? Exchange "ain't it awfuls?"

5. Has analyzing replaced utilizing? What constructive action, if any, results from the support you give and receive through your phone contacts?

6. Do you accept the role of advice giver in your contacts? Does your self-worth depend on being seen as having answers? Do others try out your ideas, rather than your living them yourself?

7. Do you have memories of being censured or punished for expressing your feelings as a child? Were you told you hurt others' feelings when you tried to stand up for yourself? Was being loved conditional on second-guessing someone else?

8. Reflecting over your past experiences in times of conflict, have you felt resigned? Have you settled for second best? Do you get your aggressions out in gossip? Fantasy?

Feelings

1. Do your phone relationships tend to be limited to the expression of only a few related emotions, such as feelings of frustration, hopelessness, depression, or resentment? Do you talk about the same issues or patterns with person after person?

2. Is there a particular person in your life whom you miss or hate? Do you talk about this person over and over again? Is this person unresponsive, absent? Does it somehow feel safer to remain emotionally bonded to someone who is unavailable?

3. Do you hope someone outside of yourself will come along who will be able to solve your problems or give you step-by-step instructions to solve them? Do you wish to be rescued?

4. Do you feel most real when you are talking about someone else's problems? Do you feel powerful through the neediness of others for your advice or approval?

5. Do you let yourself spend time and attention on your talk relationships so that you neglect responsibilities you have to yourself, family? Do you feel like running away or hiding from some tasks or people in your life?

6. How do you feel about yourself, physically? Do you feel uncomfortable about some aspect of your appearance? Is your energy and vitality at a comfortable level? Are you in pain?

7. Are you afraid of attack or rejection as a potential outcome if you express anger or state limits, preferences, or goals in face-to-face communication? Do you feel vulnerable, weak?

Affirmation/Meditation

As an exercise in reparenting, imagine your adult self going back into your childhood as a warrior on a powerful, spirited horse. See yourself equipped to handle any sort of emergency or trouble. You can take modern weapons, if you like — rocket launchers, submarines — anything necessary to be in control of any situation you may find. Look for your Inner Child in the incidents of your childhood. Find the places where your child needed the extra help of a warrior. Go there to give your child exactly the support your Child wants. Make a commitment to protect your Child, no matter what. If you need more help, bring in whatever is needed for your Child to be safe. Commit yourself to a program of taking action. Add in-person relating to your phone relationships. How about getting together to just have fun, and letting your Inner Children take your warriors on a walk?

APPENDIX THREE

Meeting Formats, Handouts and National Contacts

Permission has been granted to copy the following Meeting Formats and Handouts for 12-Step groups.

Adult Children Meeting Format

The Secretary passes the Problem, Solution, Steps and Traditions to various people for reading during the meeting. Meeting begins at _____. The Secretary starts:

Hello, my name is _____ and welcome to the _____ Meeting of ACA. We meet to share our experience growing up in dysfunctional homes and the strength and hope we have found in recovery. By practicing the 12-Steps, by focusing on the Solution and by accepting a Higher Power of our own understanding, we find freedom from compulsive patterns we learned in our families. We learn to identify the Problem and learn to live in the Solution, One Day at a Time.

Will you join me please, in the Serenity Prayer. "God, grant me serenity to accept the things I cannot change, courage to change the things I can, and wisdom to know the difference."

I've asked _____ to read The Problem. *The Problem is read.*
I've asked _____ to read The Solution. *The Solution is read.*
I've asked _____ to read The 12 Steps. *The 12 Steps are read.*
I've asked _____ to read The 12 Traditions. *The 12 Traditions are read.*

Are there any announcements? *(Read announcements.)* Are there any newcomers? *(Lead applause and welcome newcomers.)* We ask you this to welcome you, not to embarrass you. Once you have made it through these doors you do not have to feel as though you are the only one who has had the experiences, pain, feelings, depression, fears or problems that brought you here. We welcome you and invite you to keep coming back.

This program is not easy, but if you can handle what comes up at six meetings in a row, you will start to come out of Denial. In becoming free from Denial, we and our lives can finally begin to change.

Many of us could not recognize or accept that certain characteristics of our attitude or behavior in the present are the result of our childhood experience as a co-victim in a dysfunctional family system. We behave as Adult Children, often without realization. By attending six meetings in a row at the beginning, and attending regularly after that, we are coming to know and love our real selves. The pattern can change. Now let's go around the room and introduce ourselves by first name. I'm _____. *Each member introduces him/her-self.*

(If there is a Speaker, s/he shares for approximately 10 minutes on some topic, such as a Step or personal story.) The Secretary resumes: This part of the meeting is for open sharing. What you hear at this meeting, leave at this meeting. It is not for gossip or public disclosure. Please respect the privacy of what is shared. Also, we are learning to practice self-discipline in sharing the opportunity to speak. We ask that you try to keep your sharing down to three to five minutes so that as many people as possible will have a chance. Who would like to begin? *Begin calling on people for sharing, continuing until 5 minutes before the end of the meeting.*

It is time for the Seventh Tradition, which states the we are self-supporting through our own donations. Newcomers are asked not to give. *Now the meeting is turned over to the Secretary.*

Thank you for joining us, and please keep coming back. If you needed to share and there was not time, please speak to someone after the meeting. The telephone is our lifeline between meetings. If someone said something that has special meaning in your Recovery, please ask for their phone number. Let's close with the Serenity Prayer. "God, grant me serenity to accept the things I cannot change, courage to change the things I can, and wisdom to know the difference." *The meeting is closed.*

Alternative Meeting Formats

The above is a sample meeting format. Groups may alter this format, or create their own, to suit their needs. Some other types of formats are:

1. **Small groups.** After the speaker presents the topic, the group breaks into small groups (perhaps by counting off), where there is time for individual discussion. Discussion might be about the presentation or about individual issues.

2. **Writing meetings.** Each member of the meeting writes for twenty minutes or so on a given topic or on one of the Steps as it relates their recovery. Afterwards what has been written is shared with the group and read aloud.

3. **Subgroup meetings.** After opening the meeting together as a large group, the meeting divides into discussion groups small enough to allow everyone a chance to share. The smaller groups re-join at a certain time to end the meeting together.

4. **Speaker/Panel meetings.** The Leader shares for 10 minutes, then a Speaker shares for 20-30 minutes, followed by open sharing OR three Speakers form a panel, one serves as Leader and shares for 10-15 minutes, then the other two share for 10-15 minutes each and the rest of the meeting is used for open sharing.

5. **Step Study groups.** These groups emphasize the Twelve Steps as the topic of presentations and discussions, whereas other groups permit more variety in their focus. The emphasis is a matter of group preference. In some book or tape discussion groups, by group decision, crosstalk may be allowed to encourage the exchange of ideas. When the "no crosstalk" rules are modified, it is a good idea to make this known at the beginning of the meeting so that those participating will not be confused or surprised by the meeting's format. All ACA groups do have in common reliance upon the 12 Steps and 12 Traditions as the basis of personal recovery and group operation.

Step Study Meeting Format

The Secretary passes the Problem, Solution, Steps and Traditions to various people for reading during the meeting. Meeting begins at _____. The Secretary:

Hello, my name is _____ and welcome to the _____ ACA Step Study Meeting. We meet to share our experience, strength and hope with each other. By practicing the 12-Steps and accepting a Higher Power of our own under-standing, we find freedom from addictive and codependent patterns in our lives. We learn to identify the Problem and to live in the Solution, One Day at a Time.

Will you join me please, in the Serenity Prayer. "God, grant me serenity to accept the things I cannot change, courage to change the things I can, and wisdom to know the difference."

I've asked _____ to read The Problem. *The Problem is read.*
I've asked _____ to read The Solution. *The Solution is read.*
I've asked _____ to read The 12 Steps. *The 12 Steps are read.*
I've asked _____ to read one of the 12 Traditions. *A Tradition is read.*

Are there any announcements? *(Read announcements.)*

Now let's go around the room and introduce ourselves by first name. I'm _____. *Each member introduces him/herself.*

This meeting is a Step Study meeting; tonight our subject is Step_____. Shall we begin the reading? *(The Step text is read by the group or the Step Exercises are read.)*

The Secretary resumes: This part of the meeting is for open sharing. We also welcome your "Show and Tell" poems, pictures, songs or other creative work that you want to share in this safe setting with the group. Remember, what you hear at this meeting is not for gossip or public disclosure. Please respect the privacy of what is shared. Also, we practice self-discipline in sharing by taking turns having the opportu-nity to speak. We ask that you try to keep your sharing down to three to five minutes each time you speak so that everyone will have a chance. Who would like to begin?

Closing (at the end of the meeting period): It is time now for the Seventh Tradition, which states the we are self-supporting through our own donations. Thank you for joining us, and please keep coming back. This group has commitment to supporting each member in working through all of the 12 Steps, but we are reminded that we need only share what feels safe to share at group-level. Each of us is free to develop our own sharing boundaries. If you find some things too painful or too personal to share at group-level, please take the initiative to develop a sponsorship relationship with an individual you trust to work with one-on-one. Remember to keep coming back and let the understanding, love and peace of the program grow within you one day at a time. Now, let's close with the Serenity Prayer. "God, grant me serenity to accept the things I cannot change, courage to change the things I can, and wisdom to know the difference." *The meeting is closed.*

Talking Circle

The traditional "Talking Circle" is a very old way of bringing native people of all ages together in a quiet, respectful manner for the purposes of teaching, listening, learning, and sharing. When approached in the proper way, the circle can be a very powerful means of touching, or of bringing some degree of healing to, the mind, the heart, the body, or the spirit. One could call it a very effective form of native group-therapy.

The circle leader, teacher or facilitator begins by passing around sweetgrass, cedar, or sage, so that the participants may "smudge" themselves. We have been taught by our ancestors that these sacred herbs have a purifying effect upon our total being. As the smoke from the herbs surrounds us, we are better able to connect on many levels with the others within the circle. We also become more in touch with ourselves and with what we are about to experience.

The group leader (or a volunteer) will then open the circle with a prayer. The circle is now in the hands of Great Spirit, Grandfather, God, or whatever one chooses to call that Higher Power. The leader might next have the people shake hands to acknowledge each other. It is a good thing to do, especially if this is a new circle of people.

The group leader then begins to "talk to the people" without interruption, talking to no one person, but to all who are present. All are expected to listen respectfully until the speaker is finished. All who sit within the circle will have an opportunity to express themselves if they choose or they may simply listen, but all who speak will be given the same respect—they will be listened to.

The group leader and most likely others within the circle, may bring eagle feathers or stones or other sacred objects which are passed around the circle and shared. We believe these sacred things to be helpers in furthering our connections to Spirit and to our Higher Selves. They help us listen; they aid in our learning.

Within this sacred circle we are encouraged to speak not only from the mind but from the heart. We are free to share our innermost feelings if we choose. Regardless of whether one brings a traditional teaching or a personal problem to the circle, all persons are valued, respected and listened to. There is an Indian belief of right time, right place, right people, hearing right things. We rely on that belief within the circle.

When all have spoken, anyone may request that this be a "closed circle," that all that has been said and the identities of the participants be kept confidential. If no one requests a closed circle, all may freely share what they have learned.

The circle is closed with prayer. So — in this old way we have come together again to teach, to learn, to touch each other's spirit. We do this so that we may find strength to live in these two worlds: that our people may live.

Shared at the Seattle NANACOA Gathering, 1990, by the Phoenix Indian Center, Inc. 1337 No. 1st St., Phoenix, AZ 85004.

Differences That Make A Difference

Dominant Society Values	Traditional Native American Values
Self (take care of #1)	Group (take care of people)
Prepare for tomorrow	Today is a good day!
Time (use every minute)	Right time/Right place
Youth (rich, young, beautiful)	Age (knowledge, wisdom)
Compete!	Cooperate
Be aggressive	Be patient
Speak up!	Listen (and you'll learn)
Take and Save	Give and Share
Conquer nature	Live in harmony with all
Skeptical/Logical	Great Mystery/Intuitive
Ego/Self-attention	Humility
Religion (a PART of life)	A spiritual life

I MUST
BECOME AWARE
OF THESE
CONFLICTING VALUES
OR
I CAN BECOME
CONFUSED
ANGRY
FRUSTRATED

UNBALANCED
Mentally
Physically
Spiritually

For New ACA Members

Welcome to ACA! We are adult daughters and sons of alcoholic or dysfunctional families. We meet to share our experience, strength and hope in living a program of recovery and growth. The core of our program is the 12 Steps and 12 Traditions, which guide us on a path of physical, emotional and spiritual healing. We also recognize that we have many characteristics in common. These are summarized in the "ACA Problem and Solution" and other literature. ACA is your program and this meeting is yours. The fellowship is composed of all of us and we are all here for our own benefit. Like any important experience, what you get out of this program depends upon what you put into it — risking is part of growing. We are not here to take your pain away, but we are here to help you grow through it. Best wishes!

***

Each ACA group is self-supporting, and relies on voluntary contributions from us to pay the rent and other expenses. We periodically appoint members to perform various group tasks. These members are our "trusted servants," responsible to the group. We try, through service, to give back some of what we have received as part of our Recovery, but not to repeat our old patterns by giving too much.

We suggest that you, as a newcomer, attend at least six meetings before you decide whether the group is right for you. It often takes at least six weeks to start understanding and feeling how it works. You may find yourself getting physical symptoms: dozing off, getting dizzy, feeling sick, sad or headachy. All are typical. Recovery is no day on the beach. Remember, you have the right to "pass" and say nothing as well as the right to share. You also have the right to ask for, or to not accept, feedback to what you have said. This is not a therapy group. You are responsible for taking care of yourself. Take what you like, and leave the rest!

Most meetings discourage "crosstalk." Each person is allowed to share freely and without editorial comments, one-liners, or interruption. This helps create a safe place to share. Crosstalk often may violate the safety of the meeting by re-creating the family experience of not being heard, or of being ridiculed, criticized or belittled. In some Step or book-study meetings, the "no crosstalk" policy is suspended and direct interaction is encouraged, but when this is the case, these alternative guidelines are stated at the beginning of each meeting.

We avoid giving advice. In 12-Step programs, we share the story of our own disease and our recovery. We give support, by listening, encouraging and validating others. We learn to focus on our own thoughts, feelings, and behaviors, rather than on others, by making "I" statements. Speak up at meetings, even if only to say your name. By sharing, you provide others an opportunity to identify with you and welcome you. Please do respect the needs of others for time, however. If you wish to talk at length about some issue, ask the other group members first. Stick to your issue and avoid going off on tangents.

Above all, remember that everything said in the group should stay there. Our progress depends on building trust between us. Gossip about each other is completely unacceptable. Anonymity is an essential part of our group. What is said and who says it are not to be discussed with others.

ACA's Twelve Steps[1]

1. We admitted we were powerless over the effects of family dysfunction and our lives had become unmanageable.

2. Came to believe that a power greater than ourselves could restore us to sanity.

3. Made a decision to turn our will and our life over to the care of God *as we understand God.*

4. Made a fearless and thorough moral inventory of ourselves.

5. Admitted to God, to ourselves and to another human being the exact nature of our wrongs.

6. Became entirely willing to have God remove all these defects of character.

7. Humbly asked God to remove our short-comings.

8. Made a list of all persons we had harmed and became willing to make amends to them all.

9. Made direct amends to such people wherever possible, except when to do so would injure them or others.

10. Continue to take personal inventory and when we are wrong, promptly admit it.

11. Seek through prayer and meditation to improve our conscious contact with God *as we understand God,* praying only for knowledge of God's will for us and power to carry that out.

12. Having had a spiritual awakening as the result of these Steps, we try to carry this message to others and to practice these principles in all our affairs.

[1]Alcoholics Anonymous' original 12 Steps are as follows:
1. We admitted we were powerless over alcohol—that our lives had become unmanageable.
2. Came to believe that a Power greater than ourselves could restore us to sanity.
3. Made a decision to turn our will and our lives over to the care of God *as we understood Him.*
4. Made a searching and fearless moral inventory of ourselves.
5. Admitted to God, to ourselves and to another human being the exact nature of our wrongs.
6. Were entirely ready to have God remove all these defects of character.
7. Humbly asked Him to remove our shortcomings.
8. Made a list of all those we had harmed and became willing to make amends to them all.
9. Made direct amends to such people wherever possible, except when to do so would injure them or others.
10. Continued to take personal inventory and when we were wrong promptly admitted it.
11. Sought through prayer and meditation to improve our conscious contact with God *as we understood Him,* praying only for knowledge of His will for us and the power to carry that out.
12. Having had a spiritual awakening as the result of these steps, we tried to carry this message to alcoholics and to practice these principles in all our affairs.

ACA's 12 Traditions[2]

1. Our common welfare should come first; personal recovery depends on unity.

2. For our group purpose there is but one authority—a loving God as expressed through our group conscience. Our leaders are but trusted servants; they do not govern.

3. The only requirement for membership in ACA is identification of a compulsive pattern arising from personal experiences in a dysfunctional family system.

4. Each ACA group should remain autonomous except in matters affecting other groups or ACA as a whole.

5. ACA groups have but one primary purpose: to carry its message to adult children of alcoholics and other dysfunctional families-of-origin who may still suffer.

6. ACA ought never endorse, finance or lend our name to any related facility or outside enterprise, lest problems of money, property and prestige divert us from our primary spiritual aim.

7. ACA ought to remain fully self-supporting, declining outside contributions.

8. ACA Twelfth Step work should remain forever non-professional, but our service centers may employ special workers.

9. ACA, as such, ought never be organized, but we may create Service Boards or committees directly responsible to those they serve.

10. ACA has no opinion on outside issues, hence our name ought never be drawn into public controversy.

11. Our public relations policy is based on attraction rather than promotion; we need always maintain personal anonymity at the level of press, radio, TV and films.

12. Anonymity is the spiritual foundation of all our Traditions, ever reminding us to place principles before personalities.

[2]The original 12 Traditions, from Alcoholics Anonymous:

1. Our common welfare should come first; personal recovery depends on AA unity.

2. For our group purpose there is but one ultimate authority—a loving God as He may express Himself through our group conscience. Our leaders are but trusted servants; they do not govern.

3. The only requirement for AA membership is a desire to stop drinking.

4. Each AA group should be autonomous except in matters affecting other groups or AA as a whole.

5. Each AA group has but one primary purpose—to carry its message to the alcoholic who still suffers.

6. An AA group ought never endorse, finance or lend the AA name to any related facility or outside enterprise, lest problems of money, property and prestige divert us from our primary purpose.

7. AA ought to remain fully self-supporting, declining outside contributions.

8. Alcoholics Anonymous should remain forever nonprofessional, but our service centers may employ special workers.

9. AA, as such, ought never be organized, but we may create Service Boards or committees directly responsible to those they serve.

10. Alcoholics Anonymous has no opinion on outside issues, hence our name ought never be drawn into public controversy.

11. Our public relations policy is based on attraction rather than promotion; we need always maintain personal anonymity at the level of press, radio and films.

12. Anonymity is the spiritual foundation of all our Traditions, ever reminding us to place principles before personalities.

The Problem (ACA)

Many of us find that we have several characteristics in common as a result of being brought up in alcoholic or dysfunctional households.

We had come to feel isolated, uneasy with other people — especially authority figures. To protect ourselves, we become people pleasers, even though we lose our own identities in the process. We mistake any personal criticism as a threat.

We either become alcoholics ourselves or marry them or both. Failing that, we found another compulsive personality, such as a workaholic, to fulfill our sick need for abandonment.

We tend to live life from the standpoint of victims. Having an over-developed sense of responsibility, we prefer to be concerned with others rather than ourselves. We somehow get guilt feelings when we stand up for ourselves rather than giving in to others. Thus, we become reactors, rather than actors, letting others take the initiative.

We are dependent personalities—terrified of abandonment—willing to do almost anything to hold onto a relationship in order not to be abandoned emotionally. Yet, we keep creating insecure relationships, because they match our childhood relationship with alcoholic parents.

These symptoms which are characteristic of those who grew up in dyfunctional family systems persist in us even if we were never addicted to alcohol or drugs. We learned to deny some of our feelings as children and to keep them buried as adults. As a consequence of this conditioning, we confuse love with pity and tend to love those we can rescue. Even more self-defeating, we become addicted to excitement in all our affairs, preferring constant upset to workable relationships.

This is a description, not an indictment.

The Solution (ACA)

The Solution is to become your own loving parent.

By attending these meetings on a regular basis, you will come to see dysfunctional family patterns such as alcoholism and sexual abuse for what they are: a disease that infected you as a child and continues to affect you in the present. You will learn to accept yourself and your parents as co-victims of the family disorder and, by keeping the focus on yourself, you will free yourself of the shame and blame from the past. You will become an adult who is imprisoned no longer by childhood reactions. You will recover the child within you, learning to love yourself and to supply your own parenting.

The healing begins as we risk moving out of isolation. Feelings and buried memories gradually return. In releasing a burden of unexpressed grief, we become free of the past. We reparent ourselves with gentleness, humor, love and respect. We grow into people who live life on life's terms in the present.

We use the Steps. We use the meetings, the slogans and the telephone. We share our experience, strength and hope with each other. This work enables us to heal our own defects one day at a time. We become willing to release our biological parents from responsibility for our actions today, and thus we are free to make healthy decisions as actors, not reactors. We progress from hurting to healing to helping. We awaken to a sense of wholeness we never knew was possible. We see that our actual parent is a Higher Power that gave us life. If God gave us a dysfunctional family system, God also gave us a program of recovery.

We do not do this alone. Look around you and you will see others who know how you feel. We will love and encourage you no matter what. We want you to accept us as brothers and sisters just as we already accept you.

This is a spiritual program based on action coming from love. We have found that as the love grows inside us, we see beautiful changes in all our relationships, especially with God, ourselves and our families.

The List of Characteristics (ACA)

Adult Children seem to have several characteristics in common as a result of having been brought up in an alcoholic or dysfunctional family system. If you identify with some of these characteristics and want to change, the ACA program is available.

- We become isolated and afraid of people and authority figures.
- We become approval seekers and lose our identity in the process.
- We are frightened by angry people and any personal criticism.
- We either become alcoholics, marry them, or both, or find another compulsive personality to fulfill our sick abandonment needs.
- We live life from the standpoint of victims and are attracted by that weakness in our love, friendship and career relationships.
- We have an overdeveloped sense of responsibility and it is easier for us to be concerned with others rather than ourselves; this enables us not to look too closely at our faults or responsibility to ourselves.
- We get guilt feelings when we stand up for ourselves instead of giving in to others.
- We are addicted to excitement.
- We confuse love with pity and tend to "love" those we can rescue.
- We have stuffed our feelings from our traumatic childhoods and have lost the ability to feel or express our feelings because it hurts so much. This includes our good feelings such as joy and happiness. Our being out of touch with our feelings is one of our basic denials.
- We judge ourselves harshly and have a very low sense of self-esteem.
- We are dependent personalities who are terrified of abandonment and will do anything to hold onto a relationship in order not to experience painful abandonment feelings which are associated with having grown up living with sick people who were never there for us.
- Alcoholism is a family disease and we became para-alcoholics and took on the characteristics of that disease even though we did not pick up the drink.
- We are reactors rather than actors.
- We guess at what normal is.
- We have difficulty following a project through from beginning to end.

- We have difficulty having fun.
- We have difficulty with intimate relationships.
- We take ourselves very seriously.
- We over-react to changes over which we have no control.
- We usually feel different from other people.
- We are extremely loyal even in the face of evidence that the loyalty is undeserved.
- We tend to lock ourselves into a course of action without giving serious consideration to alternative behaviors or possible consequences. This impulsivity leads to confusion, self-loathing and loss of control of our environment. As a result, we spend more energy cleaning up the mess than we would have spent had the alternatives and consequences been examined in the first place.
- We tend to look for immediate rather than deferred gratification.
- We generally over-react out of fear.
- We are either super responsible or super irresponsible.

Who's An Adult Child?

Who is an "adult child"? The answer is found in examination of family backgrounds, the most important determining factor in who is an "adult child" and who is not. Each of us begins life as a vulnerable child, dependent upon our parents. If our parents are healthy and secure individuals with good parenting skills, then we will have a good chance of emerging into adulthood as secure, happy individuals. But if our parents were individuals who suffered from compulsive or addictive patterns, their messages and behaviors to us were likely to be inconsistent, confusing or even damaging. Perhaps they lavished us with love and attention one day and then ignored or rejected us the next. Being unable to cope themselves, such parents may have expected us to take on adult responsibilities well in advance of adulthood, or to care for, protect or make decisions for them and other family members. We usually felt woefully inadequate and confused under such pressures. Instead of being encouraged to be children, gradually maturing to welcome adult challenges, we may have reached adulthood with little understanding of the maturing process. With such a confusing history, we may have little confidence in our ability to handle life. We may reexperience feelings of being overwhelmed, helpless or resentful under the ordinary stresses of adult life. We are "adult children": we have the bodies of adults, the responsibilities, drives and goals of adults, but the unprocessed emotions of small, dependent children.

Adult Children's Bill of Rights

You Have A Right To:

- Put yourself first.
- Make mistakes.
- Accept all your feelings as valid.
- Your opinions and convictions.
- Change your mind or behavior.
- Protest unfair treatment.
- Negotiate for change.
- Express yourself.
- Ask for help or emotional support.
- Ignore advice.
- Say "no."
- Be alone, even if others prefer your company.
- Not take responsibility for another's problem.

It Is Not Your Responsibility To:

- Give what you can't or don't wish to give.
- Sacrifice your integrity to any cause or person.
- Drain yourself in caring for others.
- Put up with unfair treatment.
- Conform to unreasonable demands.
- Be perfect.
- Follow the crowd.
- Feel guilty for your inner desires.
- Bear the burden of another's misbehavior.
- Meekly let life pass you by.
- Be anyone but exactly who you are.

Am I Getting Well or Having a Relapse?

Feeling uncertain, disoriented, agitated, unprotected, distraught and just plain stumped can be very good for spiritual recovery! Adult Children often feel this way, especially when making progress in coming out of denial. One of the most painful—and important—experiences in recovery entails the shock of coming face to face with the maddening, overpowering feelings and memories we have buried within ourselves, as protective masks dissolve and fall away. Certainly it is painful to see how our lives have been beyond our control, in violation of what seems fair or right. As we experience afresh the feelings of panic and the sense of deprivation which compelled us as children to adapt to the family dysfunction, getting in touch with our long-forbidden needs can feel like a major threat in itself.

We often tend to blame ourselves for the existence of our pain and uncertainty: If we "just try hard enough" or "have the right attitude," shouldn't that make everything all right? We may be inclined to pick ourselves apart, in recovery, imposing upon ourselves the cruel, impossible demand that every move now be a clear step forward. We may be inclined to be intolerant of ourselves and others, allowing for no further error or uncertainty, giving ourselves little room to make mistakes, experiment and learn. Feelings of guilt and shame may convince us that every little thing we catch ourselves saying, doing and thinking is diseased and hateful. The roots of our pain and confusion run deep!

Recovery, as our perceptions open up to past and present reality, brings up hurt — but we find ourselves changing in ways that were unthinkable before. The distorted self-image which we formed in the past begins to be challenged and refuted, gradually, a day at a time. Whether we welcome it or not, we begin to surprise ourselves, spontaneously refusing to conform to what others may say we "should" need or feel. After a while, we do become more comfortable with our re-discovered integrity, although our emotional landscape may remain in glorious disarray. We realize that we need not go through these experiences alone! It takes courage to reach out, and we may be tempted to slide back into our hurt and shame. But, if we will pick up the phone or come to a meeting and share the truth inside ourselves, however painful or grieving that may be, we find help and we do get better.

Recovery may not always be comfortable or feel controllable, but it is real and it's ours to keep and to share for life. Keep coming back! You are no longer alone.

What Do You Mean, "Spiritual"?

Spirituality, simply stated, can be defined as that state or quality of being, in which life and reality are no longer conceived or experienced as just physical or in the material realm. Instead, via the illumination of the heart and/or intuition, we begin to recognize or feel there are intangible principles that give shape, meaning, value or purpose to the universe and to life. We begin to see evidence of an essential interdependence of all things—a life force, the essence of which we do not fully comprehend, that gives rise to the harmony and dynamic balance of the universe. We slowly begin to see that we are connected to our Higher Power, to others and to ourselves by way of this powerful life force. We discover that we are no longer alone.

Spirituality is experienced; it is not dogmas or creeds or moral codes. Instead, it is a quality that infuses life. It moves us in our quest for wholeness. This spirituality avails us of a life force energy that can rebuild our damaged lives, no matter how severely we may have been hurt or neglected in growing up in a dysfunctional family system.

It is this same life force that has somehow held us together even under the most adverse conditions and that brought us to this moment, this opportunity to heal. This life force provides us with healing powers through which we gently put our lives back together; through cultivating this spiritual power, we come to feel centered within ourselves.

Spirituality is available to all. We need to avail ourselves of the guidance and healing power that it offers. It has protected many of us from total destruction without our conscious cooperation. In recovery, this life force needs our cooperation if we are to realize its full healing and integrative powers.

Spirituality gives shape and direction to our lives. It fosters ideals, positive change, and self-discovery. In the spiritual realm, we begin to see that we are inherently good, and that a Higher Power nurtures and guides our lives.

Spirituality provides answers to the perplexing questions of our origins, our purpose, or destinies. Spirituality gives meaning and direction to our lives. For the purposes of adult children specifically, spirituality provides a gentle way of healing to our inner child's past, and of releasing our child's burden of guilt, shame, anger or the shock of abandonment s/he experienced.

—Mark L., Hartford, Connecticut.

Meeting Format for ACA-Teens

Hello and Welcome to the _____meeting of ACA-Teens. My name is _____and I am a teen from a dysfunctional family. Would you please help me open this meeting with a moment of silence, followed by the Serenity Prayer?

"God, grant me the serenity to accept the things I cannot change, courage to change the things I can, and wisdom to know the difference.

Group sharing policy: In this meeting, we want to feel safe to say what we think and feel, so in our discussion groups or while we're listening to anyone who is speaking, we do not interrupt or make comments about other people's statements. In this meeting we speak about our own experiences, thoughts and feelings; we listen without comment to what others say, because it is true for them. We work toward taking more responsibility in our own lives, rather than giving advice to others.

I've asked _____to read the Problem.
I've asked _____to read the Solution.
I've asked _____to read the 12 Steps.

In keeping with our practice of one Tradition per week, I've asked _____ to read the Tradition of his/her choice.

Are there any announcements? *(Reads them.)* Is there anyone here attending your first, second, or third ACA-Teen meeting? If so, please tell us your first name so that we can get to know you. We welcome you to ACA-Teen. We will now go around the room and share our names; my name is _____.

Explain the phone list. This list is just for private ACA-Teen use, in case we need to talk with someone, have a problem or need a ride to a meeting. Newcomers are welcome to take one. We have a hot-line phone list for anyone needing phone numbers of different Crisis Centers, including help with sexual abuse or battering in the home. Professional help is available.

Our 7th Tradition reminds us that we are self-supporting through our own contributions. We ask that you donate as you can. Donations are used for meeting expenses, literature, and general ACA expenses. Newcomers are not asked to contribute at your first meeting.

Like all Twelve Step programs, ACA-Teen is an anonymous fellowship. Everything that is said here in the group meeting, and member to member, must be held in confidence. Only in this way can we feel free to say what is in our minds and hearts. This is how we help one another in ACA-Teen. The opinions expressed here are strictly those of the person who gave them. Take what you like and leave the rest. And please remember, "What you see here and what is said here, when you leave here, let it stay here."

Introduce the speaker, if one is present, or introduce a topic or a particular problem for the group to discuss. If a book is being studied, let the group know which book is being read and how many pages will be read during this meeting. After the material is read or the speaker has spoken, each individual is free to share, either relating to the speaker's topic, the material read, or whatever else you wish to share. Please limit the time you speak so everyone will have a chance to share. *(If the group is more than 10, it is suggested that the group break up into smaller groups by counting off so everyone can share).*

I would like to thank everyone for sharing. For the Newcomer, we want to welcome you again and remind you to stay after the meeting so we can give you a Newcomers Packet and answer any questions you may have.

ACA is a fellowship of individuals who share their experience, strength and hope with each other. Our common goal is to recover from the mental, physical, emotional and spiritual effects of having been raised in a dysfunctional family system.

The only requirement for membership is a desire to come to terms with the dysfunction which has existed in our families and to overcome the effects in our lives today. ACA-Teen is a spiritual program, not a religious one, and does not endorse any specific faith. Our primary purpose is to recover from the effects of family dysfunction and to help other ACA-teens to experience personal recovery, serenity and joyful living.

Let us join hands and close the meeting with the Serenity Prayer (or the group's choice). Keep coming back, it works!

ACA-Teen Affirmations

- Today I love and accept myself.
- Today I accept my feelings.
- Today I share all my feelings appropriately.
- Today I am allowed to make mistakes.
- Today I like who I am.
- Today I accept who I am.
- Today I am enough.
- Today I accept who you are.
- Today I will not criticize myself or others.
- Today I let others be.
- Today I ask my Higher Power for help and protection.
- Today I am honest with myself and others.
- Today I forgive myself.
- Today I treat myself with care and gentleness.
- Today I ask my Higher Power for strength and guidance.
- Today I live without blaming myself or you.
- Today I have the right to protect my thoughts, my feelings and my body.
- Today I can say "no" without guilt.
- Today I can say "yes" without shame.
- Today I am the wanted child of a Loving Parent.

Starting ACA-Teen Recovery Meetings

What Constitutes An ACA-Teen Group?

An ACA-Teen group is composed of two or more individuals, ages 11 through 19, whose purpose in meeting is a desire to recover from the effects of growing up in a dysfunctional family system. The group applies the principles of the 12 Steps and 12 Traditions, as adopted for our purpose from Alcoholics Anonymous, and uses other ACA literature, such as the "Problem and Solution." Each group is autonomous, so matters of choosing literature, tapes or the precise wording of the format are a matter for group decision.

What Is A "Closed" ACA-Teen Group?

A closed group is for a specific segment of the population. An ACA-Teen group is, by definition, closed, and only those ACAs who are between the ages of 11 and 19, or adults who act as Teen Meeting Hosts, may attend these meetings. This is to give teens a chance to share without the possible intimidation of dealing with adults. Teen ACAs may, of course, also attend "open" ACA meetings.

What About Adults Attending ACA-Teen Meetings?

Adults who are interested in becoming ACA-Teen Hosts can attend an ACA-Teen meeting only if they are invited to do so by the group in question. Usually, the interested adult lets the current Host know of their interest and the Host asks the group to take a group conscience a week in advance. Some ACA-Teen groups may choose to make one meeting a month "open" to adults who are interested in becoming Teen Hosts. In no case, however, should the parent or relative of a teen-member seek to attend that person's meeting or to become its Host.

How Do We Let People Know About Our Meeting?

A notice in school counseling offices, or in a local paper stating that the ACA-Teen group is available is a good way to get the word out. A flyer can give more details, such as explaining anonymity and the "closed" age group, along with some basic ideas about ACA and the 12 Steps. It's a good idea to state that sexual and physical abuse in the home is not O.K., and that professional help is available, although ACA is not a professional agency.

How Is ACA-Teen Funded?

ACA's 7th Tradition states that each group is fully self-supporting, and declines outside contributions. Because school-age teens (and adults who are in hospitals and institutions) often do not have dependable incomes, ACA groups (or Intergroups) often act as Hosts to these meetings, and pay for the rent, literature and incidental expenses of these groups. Usually, a can with "ACA-Teen Groups Contributions" written on it is passed at the meetings, or placed on the literature table. These funds are periodically turned over to the ACA-Teen Hosts Committee or Hospital & Institutions Committee. Teen groups can be self-supporting if the members have jobs or allowances that make this possible.

What Are The Qualifications Of An ACA-Teen Host?

- ACA-Teen Hosts are "active" in their own Adult Child recovery. It is suggested they attend at least one ACA meeting a week, and be familiar with sponsorship.
- ACA-Teen Hosts need to have a commitment to applying all 12 Steps to the challenges of living life on life's terms.
- Hosts should have at least one year of ACA recovery and not be related to (or the teacher, counselor, employer of) any ACA Teen in the group.
- ACA-Teen Hosts are not there to pity, care take of, "fix" or manipulate teens. They are there to provide a healthy role model and reliable support for teens.
- ACA-Teen Hosts don't provide therapy, crisis counseling or professional services, but will supply the teens with hot-line numbers to contact appropriate professionals.
- An ACA-Teen Host must be of legal age as an adult for their individual state.
- ACA-Teen Hosts are but trusted servants, they do not govern. They are there to share their experience, strength and hope. All group decisions are made by group conscience.
- It is suggested that ACA-Teen meetings have two Hosts, if possible, one male and one female, who are not a couple.
- Hosts need to be good active listeners, patient, and let their Higher Power work through the group.

The Purpose Of An ACA-Teen Meeting

The primary purpose of an ACA-Teen meeting is to provide a safe, quiet, and supportive atmosphere of acceptance for young people to have the opportunity to validate themselves and what they are feeling. Many young people are being raised in dysfunctional families where they have taken on the feelings, attitudes, and behaviors of others. It may be difficult for teens to express themselves, especially at first. In time, and with the support of the group, even the most withdrawn teenager may begin to trust and to share. Acceptance is an expression of love and emotional support. The group acts as a mirror of validation in which young people may begin to learn to trust, and express their perceptions and feelings. Teens, like everyone else, want to be HEARD. Listening quietly is a powerful gesture of support and acceptance.

ACA-Teen groups practice the 12 Steps and 12 Traditions as adapted for our purpose from Alcoholics Anonymous. The Steps and Traditions provide hope-filled choices for dealing with painful problems stemming from unhealthy family relationships and dysfunctional family behavior patterns and attitudes. These principals, along with the support of the group, become vital in providing teens with a roadmap to a new way of life. These Steps and Traditions introduce teens to a loving and nurturing Higher Power, which will enable them to learn to trust and have faith in themselves and in the choices they are guided to make. The support of the group is imperative during the recovery process. Teens experience a lot of peer pressure to participate in unhealthy ways of escaping from their problems. Added to the pressures at home, sticking with healthy choices can be difficult. Recovering teens need other recovering teens!

Program Contact Information

Self-Help Clearinghouses

Because there are now so many different 12-Step organizations, we have included the clearinghouses that keep up-to-date lists of these programs and how to contact them. There is no charge for the referral services offered by self-help clearinghouses. These non-profit organizations provide referrals to national and regional self-help programs, not all of which are 12-Step programs. When you call or write, be sure to specify 12-Step program information unless you are also interested in other group formats. Most 12-Step programs will be listed, some with regional contacts in several cities and countries. In the United States, some 12-Step programs have their own national (800) phone numbers. Community contact information for some 12-Step programs is also usually available in local phone books.

United States and Canada
National and Regional Self-Help

National Self-Help Clearinghouse
(212) 642-2944
Graduate School Center of the City University of New York
Room 620, 25 W. 43rd St., New York, NY 10036
Provides national and regional contacts, formats and models for starting groups. Publishes *Social Policy*, a quarterly magazine dealing with issues of empowerment strategies for individuals and their communities.

American Self-Help Clearinghouse
(800) FOR-MASH (Mutual Aid Self Help) (New Jersey only)
(201) 625-7101, (201) 625-9053 TDD
St. Clares-Riverside Medical Center, Denville, NJ 07834
Provides national and international contacts, models for self-help groups. Publishes *Self-Help Sourcebook*, $10/postpaid. This reference contains 600 resources, models for groups, and many toll-free numbers.

For Native American Common Concerns:
National Association of Native American Children of Alcoholics
(NANACOA)
(206) 322-5601
P.O. Box 18736, Seattle, WA 98118
Provides international network, newsletter and supportive educational materials which are respectful of native American traditional values. Holds an annual conference gathering on reclaiming health.

California Self-Help Center
(800) 222-LINK (California only)
(213) 825-1799
UCLA Campus, 2349 Franz Hall, 405 Hilgard Ave., Los Angeles, CA 90024-1563
Provides statewide (California) self-help contacts which are listed by county. Publishers *Self-Helper*, a quarterly newsletter for support group information. A catalogue of print, audio and visual materials for starting groups is available. Also offers referrals to trainings and community resources through Regional Self-Help Centers serving six districts throughout the state.

Canadian Council on Social Development
Consell Canadien de Development Social
(613) 728-1865
P.O. Box 3505, Station C, Ottawa, Ontario, Canada, K1Y 4G1
Provides referrals to self-help and to regional self-help centers throughout Canada. Training and audio-visual aids.

Connecticut Self-Help/Mutual Support Network
(203) 789-7645
19 Howe St., New Haven, CT 06511

Illinois Self-Help Center
(312) 328-0470
1600 Dodge Ave., Suite S-122, Evanston, IL 60201
Provides regional and national self-help contacts, referrals, research information.
Alternate resource: ACA Resource Library (National)
(312) 525-2171
C/o 4009 N. Damen Ave., Chicago, IL 60618
Provides ACA literature, formats, service materials, international contacts.

Iowa Self-Help Clearinghouse
(800) 383-4777 (Iowa only)
(515) 576-5870
33 No. 12th St., Ft. Dodge, IA 50501

Michigan Self-Help Clearinghouse
(800) 752-5858 (Michigan only)
(517) 484-7373
109 W. Michigan Ave., Suite 900, Lansing, MI 48933

Minnesota First Call For Help
(612) 224-1133
166 E. 4th St., Suite 310, St. Paul, MN 55101

Nebraska Self-Help Information Services
(402) 476-9668
1601 Euclid Ave., Lincoln, NB 68502

New Jersey Self-Help Clearinghouse
(See American Self-Help Clearinghouse, above)

North Carolina Supportworks
(704) 331-9500
1012 Kings Dr., Suite 923, Charlotte, NC 28283

Northwest Regional Self-Help Clearinghouse
(503) 222-5555
718 W. Burnside St., Portland, OR 97209

Texas Self-Help Clearinghouse
(512) 454-3706
8401 Shoal Creek Blvd., Austin, TX 78758-7544

Self-Help Clearinghouse of Greater Washington D.C.
(Washington D.C., Virginia, Maryland)
(703) 941-LINK
7630 Little River Turnpike, Suite 206, Annandale, VA 22003

International Self-Help Clearinghouses

International Information Centre on Self-Help
30-891-4019
E. Van Evenstraat 2 C, B-3000 Leuven, Belgium

The Collective of Self-Help Groups
(03) 650-1455/1488
247-251 Flinders Ln., Melbourne, 3000, Australia

Servicestelle Für Selbsthilfegruppen
222-66-14405
Schottenring 1-24/3/31, A-1010, Vienna, Austria

Social Radgivning og Bistand
31-31-71-97
Sortedam Dosseringen 3, st. th., 2200 Kobenhavn N., Denmark

National Self-Help Support Centre
01-636-4066
26 Bedford Sq., London, WC1B 3HU, England

Nationale Kontakt von Selbsthilfegruppen (NAKOS)
30-891-4019
Albrecht-Achilles-Straebe 65, D-1000 Berlin (W) 3, Germany

National Self-Help Clearinghouse
661231 (telephone)
J.D.C. Hill, Jerusalem, Israel, 91034

Paco-Project Rijksuniversiteit Limburg Medische Faculteit
043-888-504
Beeldsnijdersdreef 101, NL-6200 MD Maastricht, Netherlands

Programme "Cronicat," Facultad de Medicina (Despacho 15)
93-256-3612
Hospital de San Pablo, Padre Claret 167, E-Barcelona 08026, Spain

Distriktlakare
961-11230
Villavagan 14, S-9390 Arjeplog, Sweden

Team Selbsthilfe Zurich
01-252-3036
Witfriedstrabe 7, CH-8032 Zurich, Switzerland

College of Nursing, University of Zagreb
(050) 28-666
Mlinarska 38, Y-41000 Zagreb, Yugoslavia

ADDITIONAL READING

12-Step References and History

Alcoholics Anonymous (AA's Big Book), A.A. World Service, Inc., 1938.
12 Steps and 12 Traditions, A. A. World Service, Inc., 1952.
Alcoholics Anonymous Comes of Age, A. A. World Service, Inc., 1957.
ACA Group & Service Guide, ACA, GSN AdHoc Committee, 1990.
         Box 6672, Eureka, CA 95502 ($10 postpaid, permission to reprint.)

Kurtz, E.,
AA, The Story, Harper/Hazelden. 1979, 1988.

Pittman, B.,
AA, The Way It Began, Glen Abbey Books, 1988.
Stepping Stones To Recovery, Glen Abbey Books, 1988.

12-Step & Meditation Books

Easy Does It (daily mediations), Lakeside/Glen Abbey Press, 1990.
Body, Mind, Spirit (daily meditations), Parkside, 1990.
Growing Through The Pain, Parkside, 1989.
Al-Anon's 12 Steps & 12 Traditions, Al-Anon Family Groups, Inc., 1981.
Sparks of Sound, (Reflections from 12-Step Meetings), CompCare, 1991.
The 12 Steps: A Way Out, Recovery Publications, 1987.

L., Elisabeth,
12 Steps for Overeaters, Harper & Row, 1988.

O., Jack,
Dealing with Depression in 12-Step Recovery, Glen Abbey Books, 1990.

V., Rachel,
Family Secrets: Life Stories of ACoAs, Harper & Row, 1987.

W., Kathleen,
Healing A Broken Heart, 12 Steps for Adult Children, Health Communications, Inc., 1988.

W., Kathleen, & E., Jewell,
With Gentleness, Humor & Love, Health Communications, Inc., 1989.

Cultivating Spiritual Development

Addington, J., C.,
Drawing the Larger Circle, Devorss & Sons, 1989.

Beck, P., Walters, A.,
The Sacred: Ways of Knowledge, Sources of Life, Northland Publishing, 1990.

Bly, R.,
The Kabir Book (poems), Beacon Press, 1977.

Booth, L.,
Meditations for Compulsive People, Health Communications, Inc., 1987.
Breaking the Chains (Religious Addiction), Emmaus Publications, 1990.

Bowden, J., Gravitz. H.,
Genesis, Health Communications, Inc., 1987.

Cady, D.,
Journey to Serenity (affirmations journal), The Crossing Press, 1990.

Cameron, A.,
Daughters of Copper Women, Press Gang Publishers, 1981.

Coggins, K.,
Alternative Pathways To Healing, Health Communications, Inc., 1990.

Cohen, A.,
The Dragon Doesn't Live Here Anymore, New Leaf Books, 1983.

Davis, B.,
The Magical Child Within You, Celestial Arts, 1986.

Fishel, R.,
Time For Joy (daily meditations), Health Communications, Inc., 1988.
Healing Energy: The Power of Recovery, Health Communications, Inc., 1991.

Four Winds Project,
The Sacred Tree, University of Lethbridge, Alberta T1K 3M4, Canada, 1984.

Fox, E.,
The Golden Key, Devorss & Co., 1931.

Gawain, S.,
Living In The Light, New World Library, 1986.
Creative Visualization, Bantam New Age, 1982.

Golan, T.,
The Lazy Man's Guide To Enlightenment, Bantam, 1980.

Hay, L.,
You Can Heal Your Life, Hay House, Inc., 1983.

Hull-Mast, N., Coleman, S.,
Our Best Days (Daily Meditation For Young Adults), Parkside, 1989.

Izard, J.W.,
Mandala Coloring Pad (coloring book), Doubleday & Co., 1988.

Kritsberg, W.,
Gifts For Personal Growth & Recovery, Health Communications, Inc., 1987.

Lerner, R.,
Daily Affirmations, Health Communications, Inc., 1987.

Mariechild, D.,
Mother Wit, The Crossing Press, 1986.

McMurray, M.,
Illuminations, The Healing Image, Wingbow Press, 1983.

Neu, R.,
Dreams and Dream Groups, The Crossing Press, 1989.

Orr, L., Ray, S.,
Rebirthing in the New Age, Celestial Arts, 1977.

Peck, M. S.,
The Road Less Traveled, Simon & Schuster, 1978.

Prather, H.,
A Book of Games, Spiritual Play, Doubleday & Co., 1985.

Price, J.R.,
With Wings As Eagles, Quantus Books, 1983.

Rickman, D.,
Northwest Coast Indians (coloring book), Dover Press, 1989.

Stein, D.,
Casting The Circle, A Woman's Book of Ritual, The Crossing Press, 1990.

Summers, K.,
Circle of Health, The Crossing Press, 1991.

Understanding The Issues

Ackerman, R.,
Children Of Alcoholics, Health Communications, Inc., 1983.

Bass, E., Davis, L.,
The Courage To Heal, Harper & Row, 1988.

Black, C.,
It Will Never Happen To Me!, M.A.C. Publishing, Inc., 1981.

Bolen, J. S.,
The Tao Of Psychology, Harper & Row, 1979.

Bradshaw, J.,
Bradshaw On The Family, Health Communications, Inc., 1988.

Carnes, P.,
Out of the Shadows, CompCare, 1987.

Cermak, T.,
Diagnosing and Treating Codependence, Johnson Institute Books, 1986.
A Primer On Adult Children Of Alcoholics, Health Communications, Inc., 1985.

Clarke, J.I.,
Self-Esteem: A Family Affair, Harper & Row, 1988.
Growing Up Again, Hazelden, 1988.

Covitz, J.,
Emotional Child Abuse: The Family Curse, Sigo Press, 1986.

Fort, J.,
The Addicted Society, Grove Press, 1988.

Friel, J.& L.,
Adult Children: Secrets of Dysfunctional Families, Health Communications, Inc., 1988.
Being Functional: A Guide To What's Normal, Health Communications, Inc., 1990.

Johnson, V. E.,
I'll Quit Tomorrow, Harper & Row, 1980.

Jung, C. G.,
Essays on a Science of Mythology, Bollingen, Princeton University, (Kerenyi).

Kasl, C.,
Women, Sex and Addiction, Harper & Row, 1989.

Milam, J., Ketchum, K.
Under The Influence, Madrona Publishers, 1981.

Miller, A.,
The Drama of the Gifted Child, Farrar, Strauss, Giroux, 1981.
Thou Shalt Not Be Aware: Society's Betrayal of the Child, Farrar, Strauss, Giroux, 1984.
Banished Knowledge: Facing Childhood Injuries, Doubleday, 1990.

Norwood, R.,
Women Who Love Too Much, Jeremy P. Tarcher, 1985.

Samuels, M., Samuels, N.,
Seeing with the Mind's Eye, Random House, 1975.

Sanford, L.,
The Silent Children, McGraw/Hill, 1988.

Satir, V.,
Conjoint Family Therapy, Science and Behavior Books, 1967.
Peoplemaking, Science And Behavior Books, 1972.

Scales, C. G.,
Potato Chips for Breakfast, Bantam Books, 1986.

Schaef, A. W.,
Co-Dependence: Misunderstood, Mistreated, Harper & Row, 1986.

Sheehy, G.,
Passages: Predictable Crises in Adult Life, E.P. Dutton, 1974.

Subby, R.,
Lost In The Shuffle, Health Communications, Inc., 1987.

Viorst, J.,
Necessary Losses, Simon & Schuster, 1986.

Wegscheider, S.,
Another Chance: Hope For The Alcoholic Family, Science and Behavior Books, 1981.

Weil, A.,
Natural Health, Natural Medicine, Houghton Mifflin, 1990.

Whitfield, C.,
Healing the Child Within, Health Communications, Inc., 1987.
A Gift To Myself, Health Communications, Inc., 1989.

Wholey, D.,
The Courage To Change, Houghton, Mifflin, 1984.

Woititz, J.,
Adult Children of Alcoholics, Health Communications, Inc., 1983.

Therapy, Self-Study

Achterberg, J.,
Imagry in Healing, Shambala, 1985.

Beattie, M.,
Codependent No More, Harper/Hazelden, 1988.

Braheny, M., Halpernin, D.,
Mind, Body, Spirit: Connecting With Your Creative Self, Health Communications, Inc., 1989.

Bratton, M.,
A Guide To Family Intervention, Health Communications, Inc., 1987.

Burns, D. D.,
Feeling Good: The New Mood Therapy, William Morrow, 1980.

Fox, A., Fox, B.,
Immune For Life, Prima Publishing/St. Martin's Press, 1989.

Gorski, T.,
Staying Sober: A Guide to Relapse Prevention, Herald House/Independence Press, 1989.
Understanding the 12-Steps, Prentice Hall/Parkside, 1991.

Greeson, J.,
It's Not What You're Eating, It's What's Eating You, Pocket Books, 1990.

Grinder, J., Bandler, R.,
Tranceformations: Frogs Into Princes, Real People Press, 1981.

Kellerman, J.,
Alcoholism: A Merry-Go-Round Called Denial, Hazelden, 1980.

Kellogg, T., Harrison, M.,
Finding Balance: 12 Priorities for Interdependence, HCI., 1991.

Larsen,
Stage II Recovery: Life Beyond Addiction, Harper & Row, 1985.

Lazarus, A.,
In The Mind's Eye, Rawson Associates Publishing, 1977.

Lerner, H. G.,
The Dance Of Anger, Harper & Row, 1986.

Levin, P.,
Becoming The Way We Are, Health Communications, Inc., 1974, 1988.

McKee, M.,
Thirty-Two Elephant Reminders (healthy rules), Health Communications, Inc., 1988.

Mellody, P.,
Breaking Free: A Recovery Workbook (codependency), Dell, 1990.

Middleton-Moz, J.,
Children of Trauma, Health Communications, Inc., 1989.

Miller, J.,
Addictive Relationships: Reclaiming Your Boundaries, Health Communications, Inc., 1989.

Moe, J., Pohlman, D.,
Kid's Power: Healing Games for Children, Health Communications, Inc., 1989.

O'Gorman, P., Oliver-Diaz, P.,
12 Steps to Self-Parenting ACoAs, Health Communications, Inc., 1988.

Ostrander, S., Schroeder, L.,
Superlearning, Dell, 1979.

Smith, A.
Grandchildren of Alcoholics, Health Communications, Inc., 1988.

Stokes, G., Whiteside, D.,
Basic One Brain Integrative Therapy, Three In One Concepts, Inc., 1986.